THE SMART GUIDE TO

The Perfect Job Interview

BY DAVID HOLMES

SECOND EDITION

The Smart Guide To The Perfect Job Interview - Second Edition

Published by

Smart Guide Publications, Inc.
2517 Deer Chase Drive
Norman, OK 73071
www.smartguidepublications.com

For information, address: Smart Guide Publications, Inc. 2517 Deer Creek Drive, Norman, OK 73071

International Standard Book Number: 978-1-937636-65-4

Library of Congress Catalog Card Number:
11 12 13 14 15   10 9 8 7 6 5 4 3 2 1

Printed in the United States of America

Cover design: Lorna Llewellyn
Copy Editor: Ruth Strother
Back cover design: Joel Friedlander, Eric Gelb, Deon Seifert
Back cover copy: Eric Gelb, Deon Seifert
Illustrations: Lorna Llewellyn
Production: Zoë Lonergan
Indexer: Cory Emberson
V.P./Business Manager: Cathy Barker

TABLE OF CONTENTS

16 Preparation: Time is and is not on Your Side 173

17 Practice: Want to Fly a Chair? 185

20 Execution: Relationship Management as a Second Differentiator 227

21 Execution: Sales Skills as a Third Differentiator 239

PART ONE

On The Road To The Perfect Job Interview

CHAPTER 1

Anatomy of the Job Interview

> ### In This Chapter
>
> ➤ What is an interview?
>
> ➤ Key points about interviews
>
> ➤ What does a perfect job interview look like?
>
> ➤ What a perfect job interview is and what it is not
>
> ➤ Getting an interview

In this chapter, you will discover what an interview is and what it is not. You'll learn what the key features of an interview are and what is meant by *the perfect job interview*. We'll agree on a set of rules for getting the most out of this book, and then, of course, discover what it takes to succeed. Finally, you have to get an interview before it can be perfect, so let's keep first things first, or said otherwise, let's keep the horse out in front of the cart where he belongs!

The Interview

Let's start with the first building block. Exactly what is an interview? Some reading this book may have considerable job search experience, while others may have little or none. We can start on a level playing field by understanding that a job interview is simply a conversation that occurs between someone wanting a job and another person who could choose or recommend that person for a job.

Interview Vocab

A job interview is a meeting staged in various formats by a hiring firm or person to compare the abilities, personality, and relevant experience of a prospective employee over other candidates relative to the job requirements.

Interviews can be structured and formal, or they can be void of formalized structure and appear almost casual. It usually depends upon the whims of the interviewing company or its representative, or upon common practice and convention in a specific industry. Like alien space creatures, interviews are conducted in a variety of mutated, hybrid forms:

➤ Over the phone

➤ In person

➤ By videoconference or over the Internet

➤ By one person or many

➤ With one candidate or many

➤ In an office or in the field

➤ During a party, during a ball game, or during any other venue

➤ As an initial screening tool or as a one-chance meeting

➤ Short and sweet, or days-long affairs

➤ One in a succession

➤ Technical or nontechnical

➤ Formal or casual

➤ Information-only or job-giving

➤ Conclusive or not

➤ Any combination of the above

The point is that there is no single structure, form, or venue that describes the interview. It comes in all shapes and sizes. However, probably the most prevalent form is still the one-on-one discussion in an office setting. You will learn about the most common types of interviews in a later chapter as well as different coping strategies for various types of interviewers. But for now, simply understand that preparing for an interview requires information about its type and its content.

Main Purpose Behind Interviews

Simply stated, an organization is looking to fill a vacant position with a competent person. That position has certain requirements in terms of experience, education, personality, and physicality. The organization interviews candidates to determine who has the requisite attributes to fit specific needs. Since the organization's search is a needs-based endeavor, candidates must learn what those needs are and show the organization they can fulfill them. Simple, right?

Most of the time, you will determine those primary needs from a job placement announcement or from a friend or professional job placement service. But there are usually secondary needs that cause the firm to announce a job vacancy. They are often caused by some of the following:

Key Topic

The interview should not be a one-way, one-sided conversation but should be a mutual dialogue between a candidate and a representative from a hiring company. That's not to say that one-way conversations don't occur, but the idea is for the candidate to learn about the company as well as for the company to evaluate the candidate. As a candidate, you should pay close attention later as we discuss how to steer conversations the way you want them to go. You should not allow an interview to degenerate into a one-way "love fest" where the interviewer is infatuated with his or her voice. If that happens, you can't get your message out.

> ➤ Issues with a previous or incumbent employee
> ➤ New strategic direction of the firm
> ➤ New managers
> ➤ Introduction of new technologies or products
> ➤ Changes in behavior of competitors
> ➤ Employee workload or productivity issues
> ➤ Growth

Most likely there are others. You should determine what needs are really driving the firm to hire a new person. Remember, the firm's primary and secondary needs are those that you must satisfy if you want an employment offer. Someone knows the answer—discreetly find that person and ask the question.

Your Life is an Open Book—or is It?

If you are looking for a job, then certainly you will go through at least one interview to get it. Even if you are looking to enter college, law school, or some other professional program, or if you're trying to secure a teaching position (there is a long list of other examples), you may well have to sit in front of someone who wants to learn about you. So get ready for questions about your background, experiences, personality, education, shoe size (just kidding!), and other information the firm believes is relevant to the job.

There are rules concerning what can and cannot be asked during an interview, which is covered later in Chapter 26, but sagacious (a fancy interview word for nosy) interviewers can dig deep and get to issues obliquely to find out whether you are a good fit or not.

Remember, it is your choice to answer a question—you can always refuse. But if you decline, you may run the risk of not getting the job. If you don't get the job, you will probably never know if your refusal to answer a question is what hurt you—you may suspect, but the reason given for not choosing you for the job may be general and appear unrelated. For example, you may hear that you are not a good fit for the company's needs. America could reduce its budget deficit if candidates contributed a dime every time they were subjected to that little ruse.

Interview Insights

Be careful of the "odd" question that doesn't seem to have anything to do with the job. For example, an interviewer may ask about your favorite sports figure, then follow up with a question about that person's key attributes you admire. The hidden motive might be to get you to speak about the impressions you have about any rogue behavior exhibited by the athlete. Remember that everything you say should support the reason you are in the interview, and that is to get a job.

You don't have to answer inappropriate questions—don't sacrifice your principles or values for a job. Be forewarned, however, of the consequences if you refuse to answer a question. We'll cover more about how to answer these types of questions without really answering—later in Chapter 25.

Interview Intimidation Syndrome

Some people are intimidated by interviews and believe interviews are to be feared. Some job seekers have heard interviews are like:

➤ Prisoner of war interrogations

➤ Psychic games with a magician

➤ The Spanish Inquisition

➤ A frontal lobotomy with Dr. Jekyll

➤ Dinner with The Godfather and his baseball bat

➤ A criminal investigation with Eliot Ness of the FBI

That's you screaming, "Please say it's not true!" isn't it? Ok, you can relax. While interviews can feel invasive and intimidating, the interviewers are really glad you are talking to them. Remember, they have a need to fill and they are hoping you are the person they are looking for. If you can solve their problem, then as the old song goes, "Oh, Happy Day"! You just need to be sure you, not the person behind or in front of you, are the one who's making them happy. That is what this book is all about.

A Word about Expectations

Perhaps one of the biggest impediments to a successful interview is the mismatch in expectations between the candidate and the prospective employer. The interviewer will arrive at the meeting with a set of expectations about the job candidate. Some of those expectations were determined by the person's job application, history, or other information collected by the organization's human resources unit. Recall that they are looking to satisfy a set of requirements and they need to assess the candidate's ability to fill those needs—and they have a limited amount of time to do it.

You as the job candidate also have a set of expectations. For example, you expect certain benefits, responsibilities, title, compensation, and the like. If your expectations are off base, then you will be in for a rude awakening and will have wasted their time and yours.

More will follow in later chapters, but your expectations about the firm and the prospective employer's pre-interview impressions about you will largely depend upon the nature of the job. For example, educational requirements can define the types of questions asked during an interview. Likewise, if the person being hired is to manage a company, then the interviewer arrives with a set of experience-based preconceptions about the candidate's business judgment or core set of skills.

The bottom line is that you must do your part to ensure that your expectations match the company's, or the interview will be less than perfect from the start.

It's All about Content

As with the format, the actual substance discussed during an interview can be wide ranging. Other than the pesky legal restrictions alluded to earlier, there are few topics that can't be discussed. Is it possible to prepare for such an open-ended exercise, for a meeting that could cover almost anything? The answer is yes and depends partly on the specifics of the job and partly with you. In other words, can you demand enough of yourself to prepare adequately for such a defining event as an interview?

Consider the following question: Do you want to do just well enough to get the job, or do you want to perform at such a high level that you knock the cover off the ball? Either way, you must hone your presentation skills and refine your personal story to meet your objectives and those of the hiring firm. If you want a high-octane interview experience, you need to understand what knocking the ball out of the park by achieving the perfect job interview actually means.

Pizza and the Job Interview

In short, a perfect job interview is like pizza. Everyone appears to have an opinion about what constitutes really great pizza. Some like thin crust, some prefer deep pan varieties, and others don't care as long as it doesn't have anchovies. The best test of a pizza's quality is whether there is a slice left at the end of the party. If you are left staring at an empty pizza box, you could say it measured up to perfection. It is hard to contradict the evidence: pizza eaters were left wanting more.

And that is how you want the prospective hiring firm to feel about you. You want them to salivate over the idea of hiring you.

The Perfect Interview: What It Is and What It Is Not

This book is not your standard how-to interviewing manual. It's about helping you craft the best possible interview to get the results exemplified by that empty pizza box. This book is written for those who are serious about getting a great job and want advice from someone other than another person with a counseling background or a personnel specialist from a human relations (HR) department.

The store shelves are filled with such standard recipes, and you already know the perfect job interview is not about shopworn ideas. Rather, the perfect job interview is the final product of a process, a system based upon a businessperson's perspective, applied with a keen understanding that the long-run health of an enterprise is based upon selecting and hiring people who can get the job done and improve the profit line of the business. It's that simple.

As a rule, interview candidates want to learn from someone who has run a business, hired, managed, and (unfortunately) fired people. I'm a former line business leader and manager, and I offer practical insights you won't find in other sources because I've developed and applied my insights to enhance my own career.

Interview Vocab

Interview Sidebar: A line business leader or manager is usually the highest-ranking person in the unit and is tasked with the responsibility and accountability for growing revenues and controlling costs in a business unit of an organization. The business unit is usually where the firm meets the customer, products are sold, and costs are incurred. Hiring and managing people, while optimizing capital and other resources, within a strategic context is a principal duty. A key measure of success for the business manager is growing profits.

Whether you are graduating from high school or college, are an experienced executive or someone in mid-career, these tips, techniques, and strategies will apply equally well. The content and intensity during an interview may vary, but the approach offered here to increase the number and quality of your interviews is germane to any person in any career field.

High-Definition Performance

It is true that interview performance means everything in the hard business of getting a job offer. And peak performance during the interview, regardless of type or nature, should be the quality standard that drives your preparation.

Simply stated, you need solutions that will impress hiring managers. If you religiously take the advice offered in the following pages, then you can achieve the level of performance you need—just like so many others before you have done.

While performance means everything, the end result is the real measure of success when considering employment interviews. Be forewarned that getting the job you want can be a daunting task filled with challenges. In the coming pages, the initial task is to define exactly who you are, what you really offer a hiring firm, and whether you have the discipline to possibly redefine yourself. Can you do that?

Again, at the end of the job acquisition process, the primary question to be answered is this: Did you or did you not get the job you wanted?

But I Was the Right One for the Job!

By now you are probably shouting, "Performance is everything? But I was the right one for the job and I didn't get it!" You may be right. On occasion, life intervenes and there are qualifiers and inexplicable disappointments, but if you are steadfast your time will come. Your responsibility is to ensure that you didn't lose the opportunity because you failed to do all you could to be ready.

It is possible to have a perfect interview, perform at a high level, and still not get the job. For example, someone's cousin sits on the board of directors and the interview process is for show, with the selection having been determined beforehand. Sorry about that, but life happens. Or the interviewer doesn't have hiring authority and is overruled by someone else who does. Or perhaps the interviewer "didn't have a clue."

As you go through the book, assume candidate selection is not predetermined. If you have a perfect interview once, you most likely will have one again—and then land a different job that perhaps is even better for you in the long run. You may have encountered these types of situations. You may be frustrated and discouraged. Keep trying—your day will come.

Interview Insights

Mr. X interviewed for a very prestigious position as Chief Executive Officer (CEO) of a private company. Everyone within the firm loved his qualifications, personality, and vision. Everything seemed on track for a great hiring decision. As a matter of formality, the head of the owner-family wanted his wife to visit with the prospective new CEO. That meeting went very well also. Coincidentally, the wife went to a charity event later that evening where her niece was also an attendee. Before the evening was over, the niece's husband had convinced the CEO's wife that he could do the job, and for less money. Although the man was clearly less qualified than Mr. X, two days later, the CEO informed Mr. X that a relative was taking the position. Sometimes the ball bounces in funny ways.

The Answer to Getting the Job You Want

Surprise! The answer to getting the job you want is staring back at you from the mirror each morning. You are the answer. That new job is within your reach, but it takes perseverance and (here comes an important word) planning. And you need to mix the right ingredients in the right proportions—just like that perfect pizza. In the end, you are the one who must provide the commitment and discipline to get to perfection.

Oh, and a pinch of luck helps too. But as the old saw says, you make your own luck. That is why you need to hear the hard truth about what works.

Rules, Rules, and, Alas, More Rules

Here are a few guidelines that should keep you on track as you work your way through this book. First, know that simply reading a book about interviews is not enough. An interview is a mental and physical activity, and any preparatory work should also require your active participation. In order to get the most out of this book, you should:

➤ Be open to learning new techniques

➤ Be introspective

➤ Be diligent and accomplish the suggested exercises and practice the techniques

➤ Be receptive to criticism

➤ Be disciplined

➤ Be willing to concoct a plan

➤ Be faithful to the conduct of your work

This book is full of tidbits about what interview candidates did well and where they fell short. Your success is dependent upon how vigorously you assimilate the lessons and how diligently you strive for perfection. Remember: open, introspective, diligent, receptive, disciplined, willing, and faithful. These are the attributes of a winner—that's you, right? Good luck!

CHAPTER 2

A Prelude to Getting the Job You Want

> ## In This Chapter
>
> ➤ Recognize the need
> ➤ Make an investment
> ➤ Learning methods

In this chapter you will discover what an interview is and what it is not. You'll learn what the key features of an interview are and what is meant by *the perfect job interview*. We'll agree on a set of rules for getting the most out of this book, and then, of course, discover what it takes to succeed. Finally, you have to get an interview before it can be perfect, so let's keep first things first, or said otherwise, let's keep the horse out in front of the cart where he belongs!

This chapter focuses on a need most interview candidates share: help getting the job they want. The chapter also introduces the major tools you will use as you proceed through the program.

Darwin and the Competition

Charles Darwin (1809–1882), author of *On the Origin of Species*, was an English naturalist who championed a theory about the origin and sustainability of species via natural selection. In the late nineteenth and early twentieth centuries, coincident with the rise of industrial capitalism, a number of prominent philosophers, novelists, and intellectuals attempted to extend natural selection to social evolution by positing theories known by the term *social Darwinism*.

At times, searching for a job can seem like a case study in natural selection, where survival of the fittest best describes the outcome of the interview process. Theory aside, despite times of economic distress and other person-specific issues, some people manage to get great jobs under the most competitive conditions. You need to be one of those people.

Interview Vocab

Natural selection is a major tenet of evolutionary biology and a cornerstone of the theories of Charles Darwin as set forth in *On the Origin of the Species*. It is often described by the term "survival of the fittest" as an essential element in the theory of adaptive selection. Identifiable heritable traits are passed along in a presumed non-random process that affords longevity to affected species. Propagation of the species is a natural outcome according to his theory. Many parts of Darwin's work remain controversial to this day.

Work While You Search

A wise boss once said, "The best job is the one you've got." He didn't mean you couldn't upgrade and change jobs. On the contrary, he meant that a great current job is one that affords you the opportunity to perform at a high level and showcase your talents, and in so doing, it becomes so much easier to get the next great job. The bottom line is that if you have a job now, then use it as a platform to perform well. The situation changes for the worse if you are out of work as you must explain why you left your current firm and what you are up to now. So, keep the job you've got until you secure the next one.

Interview Insights

If you are out of work and looking for a job, then consider self-employment as a consultant, student, or part-time teacher. Unemployment creates time gaps in your resume the day you leave your current firm and these periods have to be explained during an interview. The point is: do not be idle for long.

In some industries, if a boss finds out you are looking for another job, you could be in jeopardy. Contrary to what some say, avoidance is the best policy. Don't take time away from your current employer to interview for another job—some would say it's unethical and you might get caught! Use your lunch periods, vacation days, personal days, and off hours instead. In this way you won't compromise your integrity and lie to your boss about your whereabouts when on the company payroll.

So, while continuous employment seems to come easily for some, many of you must contend with a job environment and social culture seemingly more accurately described by Mr. Darwin than by St. Francis. As economic conditions grow harsher, so does the level of competition for those jobs. In order to compete, you have to start at the beginning by asking yourself if you want a job or if you want to start a new career; if you want a position that truly inspires you and for which you are the best qualified or if you are willing to settle for less.

Teaching Methods

The methods in this book can energize your prospects. They can help ensure that you will do more than just be one of Darwin's survivors. The methods work because the process and the tools make common sense and come from a variety of professions. It is all about how people act, react, and perform.

The sole entrance requirement to this "school" is to perform at your very best in front of an interviewer and not to settle for less. The people who benefit the most from the techniques in this book are those who dedicate themselves to a dose of hardcore discipline and have a goal in mind.

If you are willing to work hard, perhaps change opinions about yourself, and challenge your assumptions, you can achieve your targets. The only real question is if you want it badly enough to try something new.

Seminars and Tools

Participants in seminars that teach the methods of the *Smart Guide to the Perfect Job Interview* make a commitment—a commitment that takes them from a mere job to the start or enhancement of a special career. The seminars utilize leading-edge pedagogical tools (the word *teaching* works too, but fancier words sound cool!). Some of the tools are:

> ➤ Models to provide structure to your job acquisition planning

> ➤ Preparation methods to ensure you know what you need to know

> ➤ Practice techniques to hone your ability to perform at high-level peak performance

> ➤ Execution tricks to stand apart from the competition and pull off the perfect job interview and to close the deal

Mock Interviews and Other Methods

Throughout the book, you will utilize practice sessions called mock interviews. These sessions are usually three-person simulated interviews revolving around preplanned scenarios. Participants include a candidate, an observer who offers feedback, and a simulated interviewer. Don't underestimate the powerful impact these simulated interviews can have upon your eventual success. As you will learn, mock interviews are only as good as the quality of the role-playing enacted by the participants. A number of practice scenarios are offered in Appendix B.

Interview Vocab

A few terms are associated with mock interviews, starting with the term *mock interview*, itself.

A mock interview is a simulated job interview involving a candidate and a volunteer interviewer, perhaps from a company or other interested party, and a trusted agent or independent observer who gives feedback to the candidate.

A trusted agent is a person familiar with your goals and has knowledge of your industry, who offers candid, accurate feedback on your performance during a mock interview. A trusted agent should be used multiple times to record your progress.

A candidate is a person who is eligible for a job and is enduring the trials of the interview process.

Closing a deal is a term of art used to describe the process of concluding a sale; in this case, securing an offer of employment.

Other methods used in *The Smart Guide to the Perfect Job Interview* are:

➤ Case studies: business stories that test your analytical and communications abilities. Your trusted agent and a fellow candidate conduct a simulated interview followed by a presentation of what was discovered during the case. The interviewer and observer should offer insights gained about your performance. Case studies are applicable to anyone who will need to show analytical skills in an interview—and that is just about everyone.

➤ Team exercises: These are scenarios acted out by a group of people who are also practicing for interviews. Participating in team exercises will keep you from feeling isolated and can replicate some of the dynamics and synergies found in a group setting. You should plan on sharing concerns, progress reports, and techniques with this group, and meet on a regular basis.

➤ Personal assessments: self-evaluation exercises to determine your strengths and weaknesses. You will also ask your trusted agents to evaluate your leadership potential. The goal is to rate your abilities and investigate enhancement areas. These assessments form the bedrock of your capacity to create the perfect job interview.

➤ Research methods: a set of research sources you develop that includes notification channels and implementation techniques that will help you deliver information effectively during your interview. Research sources may include reading lists, data sources, checklists, timetables, and schedules.

➤ Tips to close the deal: instruction on how to close a deal, which is an often neglected but crucial skill. These tips can be used to secure the job you want and can also be used on the job.

➤ Enhancements: knowledge that can separate you from a pack of rivals and turn a good interview into a great one. You receive instruction on new client acquisition, client relationship management skills, negotiation skills, and how to implement inspired leadership as a new hire or an old hand. Some reading this text may have those skills already while others may not. In each case, however, a dose of new ideas never hurts the patient. We all need it from time to time.

Now it's time to hang on for the ride, spread your wings, learn to fly. Examine yourself, your career, and your goals. Engage! Get the job you want. But first, let's set the stage by considering the somewhat unusual question in the next chapter.

Interview Insights

Many top graduate schools of business, banks, and consulting firms use case studies as a venue for evaluating students'/candidates' ability to dissect companies across financial, organizational, marketing, human capital, strategic, IT, and other dimensions. Even if your interviewer does not present a case study, you can offer your own to show how you would analyze a difficult situation.

CHAPTER 3

How Fast is Your Jet?

In This Chapter

➤ What is your story?

➤ What are the traps of interview success?

➤ How good are you relative to competitors?

This chapter discusses the issues you may face in the process of acquiring a new job. And, importantly, coming to grips with tough questions concerning your chances to actually win the position you want. It also introduces common mistakes made by interview candidates.

How Fast is Your Jet?

That unusual question about performance is a colorful way of getting to the heart of an important matter: just how competitive are you? Are you as good as you believe you are relative to others who are also trying to get the job you want? If you were a jet fighter pilot, can you fly as fast as the bad guys fly? Are there gaps in your training or experience that will overwhelm your other positive attributes? Do you feel you have insurmountable barriers in front of you? Some people feel the obstacle isn't a hurdle (remember that term for later!), but more like a pole vault. How do you determine just how high the hurdle is, beat the odds, overcome objections, and land the job you want?

Assess Your Key Talents

You may have heard the old maxim that we all have "baggage." You may have a sense of how much that suitcase weighs, but have you ever done a personal inventory to determine just how heavy it really is? In the interview context, "baggage" describes all of the areas where you come up short relative to someone else. It could be a lack of experience, personality, connections, and/or a host of other negatives.

Get a legal pad and at the top write down the name of the job (and the firm) you want. If you don't know, then write The Perfect Job for Me. Now, list all your key talents—those you believe you have and those that others say you have. Then list your negatives, or areas that need to be improved. Those are skills that you sense are not your strong points or that others say you just don't have.

As you go about your business during the day, I want you to reflect on that list—a lot. Ask yourself if you really are strong at a key talent you've written down. Can you really accomplish that type of work that well? What did a criticism about that trait in your last performance appraisal from a supervisor really mean? Be honest with yourself.

After undertaking this serious inventory of your key talents and the threats to your success, ask yourself a few more questions. Do you need to educate and rejuvenate yourself? If you were a different person and stumbled across the key talents list or your own résumé, would you be impressed? Where are the gaps in your background?

Finally, put the key talents list aside (we will use it later) and ask yourself, "Do I know people who can help me appraise my chances? Do I know people who can position me for success?"

What Are the Traps of Interview Success?

Understanding the obstacles to your success is more than just listing a set of problems. The results you desire spring from the disciplined art of defining solutions and from practicing the mechanics of their implementation.

A number of themes have emerged after my experiences with hundreds of interview candidates. The demands of operating a business have created specific job requirements, and the number of candidates ready to meet those requirements is surprisingly lower than you might think. Practice sessions I've led with hundreds of candidates have verified that many people are just not well prepared for their job interviews.

Interview Insights

Interviews with hundreds of diverse candidates from the finest MBA programs, fast-track and experienced executives, ex-military, and many others from a mix of industries often reveal some surprising results. Across the board, interviewers find gaps in preparation and planning by interview candidates. This creates opportunity for those who are ready.

Here are some common mistakes made by candidates:

> ➤ Little knowledge of the firm's current business

> ➤ Confusing career changes and lack of direction

> ➤ Communications issues

> ➤ Language skills (international candidates)

> ➤ Inappropriate dress and lack of simple courtesy

> ➤ Uncertain leadership potential

A candidate who is really well prepared, professional, and articulate stands out like a light in a dark room. Get the idea?

Your Personal Challenge

You can be one of those bright lights in a dark room full of dull competitors. The key is to focus like a laser beam on overcoming any obstacles between you and the job you want.

Don't suffer from delusion; everyone has obstacles obstructing progress toward attaining a desirable job. The first step is to realistically determine just how high the obstacle is.

Interview Insights

Ever notice a hurdler's eyes as he/she stares down the track at the obstacles in front? They are truly focused on clearing the first obstacle ahead and getting off to a clean start without hitting the hurdle. Do you think they know how high they have to jump? You bet. So, now imagine you are in the starting lane staring down the lane at that first hurdle. On the other side is the job you want. The starter's gun is about to explode. Do you know how high your obstacle is?

The Hurdle Can Be High or Low

Whether or not that obstacle (from now on, let's call it the hurdle) is insurmountable is dependent upon a number of personal factors. Many of these impediments are external to you, but others are internal and self-inflicted. These factors are varied and can change depending upon your personal circumstances.

In the next few pages you will learn a method of analyzing how intimidating a hurdle really is. Then you will determine how to jump over it and execute a nearly flawless interview.

Is Your Jet Fast Enough?

Every person comes to a crossroads at some point in life. Some have multiple opportunities to steer their lives in one direction or another. Dramatic twists and turns may be less common to you, but you no doubt have faced challenges and opportunities from time to time that have led to fundamental change in your life. Regardless, all of us must make decisions—or they will be made for us. This choice may inalterably affect the way you and your loved ones live. Market factors influence those decisions and so does the competition for the job you want.

You may have separated from your company through downsizing operations, or you may be thinking of a preemptive move to jump-start your career in a new industry. Whatever your situation, you need to understand your talents, who you are, how to present yourself, and what you may need to do to change.

You need to know how good you are relative to your interview competition, your own hoard of bandits in a dogfight. So, again, ask yourself how fast your personal jet is. Do you really know? How good are you at what you do relative to competitors? How good are they? Perhaps more importantly, how competitive are you relative to what you want to do?

The next few chapters will help you answer those questions. At the end of this book, you should be able to say, "My jet is fast enough."

Chapter Homework

1. Take the key talents list and the answers to the questions above and discuss them with your spouse or significant other—someone who knows you really well and with whom you can be completely honest.

2. Record their reactions and perspectives on your strengths and weaknesses and your ability to articulate answers about both.

CHAPTER 4

The Challenges You Face

> **In This Chapter**
>
> ➤ The basic challenge: train like a boxer
>
> ➤ The macroeconomic environment

In this chapter you will think about the challenges you face and what you need to do to accomplish your goals. You will also think about the overall economy, and how the turbulence of the past few years has affected opportunities for those in the job market. A one-word summation of what is required to steer through the turmoil is *flexibility*.

Train Like a Boxer

If you have looked for a job recently, you know how tough the environment can be. Whether you are an athlete, accountant, musician, teacher, construction supervisor, or banker, you must train for the employment "fight." There is an old maxim, "To win, you must train like you will fight, and you must fight like you trained!" There is a lot of truth there. Pugilists (a dandy's word for *boxers*) and fighter pilots understand this better than most. Some of you may feel as though you already have a bloody nose, or are likely to get one, when you think about finding a potential job and then interviewing. Not to worry—help is on the way.

The Economy and You

Stand by, here comes the first chart! Look at the S-shaped curve in the chart below (figure 4A). First, imagine along the horizontal x axis that we were able to actually measure the degree to which the economy restructures itself. Along the vertical y axis, imagine the number of new job opportunities available to workers. Admittedly a fuzzy notion, the graph nonetheless represents the changing nature of jobs that are available to workers.

The S-curve illustrates that in the early days of economic distress, unemployment goes up, and economic numbers wane. A period of uncertainty follows and the labor markets come under pressure. For many, that is where we are now. As private and public capital start to influence labor and production, the economy starts to recover in new ways, and explosive growth happens—usually in niches. After a period of time, rationality emerges and more protracted, sustainable patterns of growth supplant earlier abnormal growth periods. More than likely, just as the new economy stumbled quickly, the new economy will also recover more quickly than the numbers and experts understand. Such turmoil is troubling, but it also creates opportunity.

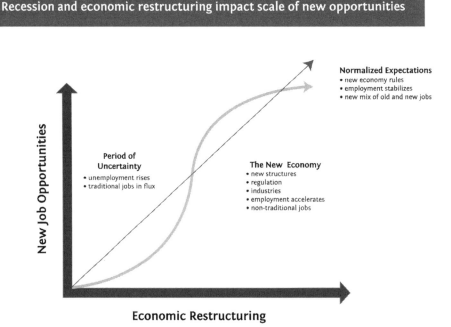

Figure 4A Source: Cavender Park Consulting, LLC

Consider the following example of economic restructuring:

Partly due to the introduction of the personal computer, more and more people enjoyed tremendous increases in productivity on the job. The rapidity of technological change astounded even the most astute observers. We had gone to the moon on a slide rule (a bit of hyperbole), and less than twenty years later we enjoyed the benefits of the microchip embedded in our desktop computers. Aided by the miniaturization of circuit boards, PC users could do work at their desktop that previously took large stacks of computer punch cards to accomplish. An entire industry of keypunch operators was put out of business.

These moves enhanced computing power and vastly shortened processing times; thereby producing even more startling increases in productivity per worker. The economy even saw enormous spillover benefits in leisure-based industries as a result.

Times Are A-Changin´

Times of economic restructuring require flexible thinking and innovation. You may have to retool your weapons arsenal. That may mean going back to school, taking a course or two, redefining your overall goals, or changing your lifestyle. There is no sugar coating the economic distress you may be facing. However, you do have many positives in your favor. Your family, friends, and experiences all should help calibrate your sights. If you want to stay in your current industry, you may need to learn or relearn skills that have been dormant for some time. If you want to move up, then you will be in a dogfight.

Interview Insights

It's a big, big world out there. We now live in a global economy where natural disasters, new consumer products, terror incidents, elections, and other phenomena cross over traditional national borders and affect everyone in almost real time. In many respects, the global economy is indeed "new". A key question for policymakers will be: do traditional models of comparative advantage and international trade and finance still work?

Countries that were "emerging" just a few years ago are well along in restructuring into "mature" economies where growth rates rival or exceed many industrialized nations. New skills, especially language and cultural ones, will be needed by workers willing to compete for global jobs. These demands and many more will stress the economic system for decades to come and will make interviewing across borders a commonplace reality.

During the late 1990s and early 2000s, pundits crowed about the latest new gadgets, and technology innovation was the new paradigm. Many people did not realize the dramatic effects such progress would have upon individual consumers and employees. Outsourcing functions and people became a business strategy and even found its way into the common public vernacular. It took time, however, until revolutionary innovation and change was fully assimilated into the economy.

In the meantime, markets have become more globally integrated and emerging countries seem more fully developed than their name implies. And all of this has had an impact on the employee and also upon those who are looking for work.

Full Employment Economy

What does a full employment economy mean? This is the rate of acceptable unemployment where all those wanting and able to work can do so. Naturally, some do not meet this criterion, and so a natural unemployment rate of around 4 percent is considered acceptable in the United States, and Congress is committed to it by law. A percentage of workers are always between jobs as differences in supply and demand in the labor markets cause some unemployment. Some of you fit that category.

As of the first edition of this book, the unemployment rate was an abnormally high 9.2% in the US. Now as of the second edition in mid summer 2014, the unemployment rate appears to have decreased to 6.1%.

The word "appears" is important because this number has become a lightning rod of political dissension in the country. Why? Because the calculation depends upon how you count an unemployed person. From the BLS website: "the basic concepts involved in identifying the employed and unemployed are quite simple". Really? According to the government, they are:

> ➤ People with jobs are counted as employed

> ➤ People who are jobless, looking for jobs, and available for work are counted as unemployed

> ➤ People who are neither employed nor unemployed are not in the labor force

Interview Vocab

The Volatility Index, or VIX as it is known, is a measure of variation in the broad stock markets. It is sometimes used as a forward-looking indicator of investor fear. Developed by the Chicago Board Options Exchange in 1993, it is a gauge of market sentiment for the next 30 days based upon implied volatility, or the volatility computed from econometric models, of the prices of various "put" and "call" options (instruments bought and sold by and to investors for the right but not the obligation to purchase or sell an underlying security associated with the option). Initially more narrowly defined, it is now computed for the S&P 500 stock index of 500 large companies. A reading over 30 generally signifies a higher degree of investor trepidation about investment prospects.

But what about those so discouraged they have given up looking for work and are no longer counted in the labor force? Should someone who is so discouraged about finding work, but wants to, not be counted in the basic unemployment formula? Yet, the oft-quoted base unemployment rate does not count this person. As the Bureau of Labor Statistics (BLS) footnotes highlight (see next ViewVocab), when counting these workers and others who are "marginally employed" in jobs less attractive than should be the case, the number balloons to an alarming 12.1% at this writing in July 2014. Isn't that an important number? So who is counted as discouraged? The BLS says:

> ➤ They believe no job is available to them in their line of work or area

> ➤ They had previously been unable to find work

> ➤ They lack the necessary schooling, training, skills, or experience

> ➤ Employers think they are too young or too old, or they face some other type of discrimination

Sound like anyone you know?

Statistics can tell many stories, so another number that is often used to round out the labor picture is the labor participation rate, a number perhaps less easily manipulated, as a measure of economic/labor strength. It is the labor participation percentage of civilian non-institutional (not in school, prison, or the military) workers.

At this point, it stands at 62.8%. That number needs to be higher for sustained economic growth. It has declined markedly in the past six years and is back to levels not seen since the mid-70's in the US. Even the lower unemployment base rate of 6.1% is too high. Some econ-political pundits are trying to argue that these numbers reflect the "new normal" for America, due to demographic factors and an aging population. Still, economic policy must account for these conditions and for your sake as a job candidate, these figures need improvement and cannot remain stagnant.

The Economy is a Beast

The 2007–2009 turmoil offers evidence that no one completely understands this new economic beast. Econometric models seem to be off more than before, pundits are outlandishly mistaken, and volatility in stock, bond, and commodity markets continues to be the word of the decade, if not the century. How many people in the country knew what the volatility index (VIX) of market variation was before the turmoil around the mortgage markets in 2008–2009? More know about it now.

At this point the analysis is as good as any—no one can predict the unpredictable. But the American market model of economic capitalism will most likely reemerge as the powerhouse it has been since World War II and act as an engine of global growth but more productively and efficiently. That is if we can get the government to address the national debt and curtail its runaway spending. Most likely the U.S. economy and the private sector will eventually provide its customary, saving answer: rational growth solves lots of ills.

Interview Insights

One man says, "Hey Joe, which horse is your pick in the 3rd at Santa Anita?"

Joe says, "The same one I liked last week."

The first man says, "What? How come?"

Joe says, "Paddy, I figure he was so far outta' the runnin' then, he's still on the track somewhere with a head start!"

In an interview, take any advantage you can muster, just like Joe did.

A key question for you during this period of uncertainty is can you define yourself in ways that make you competitive in this new era? If the answer is a question mark, then you need a disciplined model, an approach that will help you understand what you have to do and how to promote yourself in front of a firm; in other words, how to sell yourself to an interviewer.

Broad Themes for This Year and Beyond

A number of industries are undergoing fundamental change. Even if you do not have experience in these industries, the spillover effect may have ramifications for the industry you target in your job search. Because of the financial crisis that developed in 2007–2009 many industries are restructuring as increased regulation and congressional initiatives are creating new oversight regimes. All businesses need capital and the financial crisis understandably enveloped many seemingly unrelated industries in its vortex. The industries listed below are in the midst of confronting new and old challenges and most likely will be for the medium term. A few of the major issues and opportunities facing companies in these fields are shown:

➤ Energy: In the United States, independence from foreign sources, and the availability/practicality of alternative energy

➤ Banking and financial services: Consolidation, new global risk protocols, asset exposure, reestablishing trust

➤ Health care: In the United States, universal coverage, cost, mandates, government intervention, aging demographics, and potential physician shortages

➤ Consulting and accounting: Workouts and bankruptcies, healthcare advice, business forensics, disclosure, and regulation

➤ Infrastructure: Reconstruction projects and urban development, the green movement, traffic congestion, water resources

➤ Education: Competition; privatization; teacher accountability; federal standards versus local/state control; need for scientists, engineers, and mathematicians

➤ Not-for-profit: Micro-finance, funding sources, new operating models.

Interview Insights

In business, the concept of a "going concern" is crucial to the long-run success for both the employer and the employee. Can the firm survive? Will it make enough money to pay employees, invest in new equipment, produce and market its products, and accomplish a hundred other things essential to the effective running of an enterprise? If it does not make enough money, then eventually it will go out of business.

In order to come to grips with these challenges you will need to:

➤ Define your goals

➤ Assess and upgrade your talents

➤ Develop your plans—are you willing to change careers?

➤ Practice storytelling

➤ Execute flawlessly

➤ Learn hard lessons

➤ Match goals and expectations to abilities and opportunities

The Only Certainty is Uncertainty

In tough economic times, firms hire fewer people; in fact, they downsize people left and right. The only certainty in this type of environment is the unsettling nature of job insecurity. Even if you know someone who can get you an interview with a new firm, you will still need to perform well during the interview.

Many of you may hold advanced degrees and have extensive work experience. Still, you will need to impress the interviewer across the interview table—someone who may not possess firsthand knowledge of your sterling record, have your level of education, or appreciate your finer qualities. This is especially true if you are entering a new career field. Controlling your emotions and ego are critical to your success in a new endeavor. If you have been downsized, it is hard to swallow that bitter pill—hang in there. Smart, creative people succeed provided they plan for and accept the changes that are necessary during economic restructuring and uncertainty.

Whatever your circumstance, when in front of an interviewer, you need to answer a number of questions. There are questions interviewers will ask, and those they are just thinking about. Regardless of the first set, an interviewer has one central question particularly in mind. In fact, it is the single most crucial question you must answer in an interview. Answer it well and you may find that other concerns and barriers come tumbling down. Call it the million-dollar question.

Interview Vocab

The million-dollar question, whether you will make money for the company, is what interviewers are thinking about as they stare at you while you are answering a question about something else. The interviewer may or may not ask it overtly but may be thinking, "Can this person help the firm and me make money?" A shadow question is this: If this candidate is in front of a client, will the client buy our product or service?"

And what is the all-important question? It is this: Can this new candidate help the organization or me make money?

It's that simple. Can you help the firm continue to be a profitable organization? It doesn't matter if the "firm" happens to be a not-for-profit (NFP) organization or charity. Can you help it meet its required financial requirements or not?

Changing the Game with the Million-Dollar Question

A big-time gambler in Vegas might say, "A million dollars on 21 red," then roll the dice and hope for the best. You can up your odds for winning the pot in an interview if you control the agenda instead of letting the "house" control it.

Like Mr. Big in Vegas, engaging with an interviewer seems like a roulette game at times. But if you know what is really important to the firm, and, hopefully, the interviewer, then you change the game entirely. The long-term question every firm must answer is this: Can it make enough money to meet its obligations and grow? So in its purest form, interviewers, knowingly or not, are asking themselves the same question as it applies to you—the job candidate.

Depending upon the organization, *money* could mean grant money, donations, etc. A research and development (R&D) manager certainly helps the firm make money by creating a pipeline of potential new products. An information technology professional sells an idea for a software upgrade to increase the firm's productivity, which also helps the firm become more efficient and make money. If you are a twenty-year-old auto mechanic, you'd better believe you help the company make money by doing outstanding repair work and getting repeat business.

Your experience may be from a different industry, and it may be awesome, but you still need to answer the million-dollar question for the new company in the new industry.

The point is that you could be an internal non-sales person, or a teacher, student, banker, government worker, or an astronaut. It doesn't matter. Everyone has a constituency that must be satisfied and everyone must be linked to the fundamental mission of the organization. The million-dollar question is the core of that mission. If someone isn't fulfilling that mission and if management is doing its job properly, it should question having the position on the books.

Answering the Question

Answer the question affirmatively, that you will make money for the company, and barring a hidden agenda, you are on your way toward receiving an employment offer. Therefore, before each interview, when you construct your résumé, when you answer a question, when you practice, when you eat and breathe, you need to ask yourself this question: How can I show interviewers that I can help them make money? Am I a net add or a net drag to the bottom line? Is everything I say or do geared toward providing a positive answer to this question? Can I tie my skills to this ultimate goal of the organization?

In advance of your job search and interview, if an activity you are performing is not connected to those questions, then you should not spend time on it. Get focused.

Interviewing for schools

There is an equivalent million-dollar question pinging around the minds of admissions officers for college or professional schools. In order to allocate a precious seat, the interviewer needs to consider you relative to other applicants. There are many elements to the decision: grades, extracurricular activities, an essay, etc. But I believe all interviewers, in academia, government, or business, are harboring one fundamental question that must be answered well or the interview comes to a full stop in the interviewer's mind.

You need to determine what that question might be. It could be whether the student will meet academic standards for graduation or if the student will contribute to the quality of discussion in a classroom. Or it simply could be whether the student is as well rounded as another candidate.

Unlike business in which making a profit is paramount, the fundamental question in academia varies depending upon the school and admissions office. One university may stress academic achievement, while another may be less rigorous and emphasize the total student experience. One school tests applicants' motivation and commitment to their chosen academic discipline. For them, the million-dollar question is, "Why do you, as a standard bearer for this college, want a (name the major) degree and what do you hope to achieve in life with that knowledge?"

Whatever the hot-button question is for your school, you need to discover it and formulate your answer. Then apply all the techniques presented in this book to highlight your answer during the interview. You have the same basic goal everyone else has, and that is to answer the question well and be memorable while doing it.

Chapter Homework

1. Begin by finding three companies in each of the new opportunity sectors listed earlier, e.g., energy, microfinance, infrastructure, etc. Locate information about products, career opportunities, trends, leadership, regulations, and so on. Begin folders and fill them with materials such as articles, reports, and press releases about the companies

2. How can you help an organization make money? Write down your answer in one detailed paragraph. Leave nothing out, then go back and pare it down to the essential elements.
If you are interviewing for school, create three possible million-dollar questions for your chosen program and compose a one-paragraph answer to each. Keep responses for later use.

CHAPTER 5

Four Components to Crafting the Perfect Interview

In This Chapter

➤ A training model

➤ Preparation

➤ Practice

➤ Execution

➤ Integration

In this chapter you'll discover the foundation of the system that drives all of the content in this book. The dynamic interview training model (DITM) will prepare you for the perfect job interview by guiding your preparation, practice, execution, and integration efforts before, during, and after the interview. Each of the following chapters in the book describes elements of one of the four components of the model.

The Dynamic Interview Training Model

This book is about creating an edge, an edge that will help you beat the competition and secure the position you want. Your guiding hand will be the dynamic interview training model, a four-part model designed to direct your efforts and raise your performance level over time. It starts with your preparatory efforts and extends through actual execution at the job interview. It works because it reinforces knowledge and behaviors based on common sense.

If this were a college course, your professor might talk about a systems model. Okay, so here is a systems model. Figure 1 on the next page depicts the dynamic interview training model.

It is a continuous closed-loop (meaning it goes around and around until it runs into itself again, and then starts over) system of preparation, practice, execution, and follow-up. This loop will help you create and refine your content—the story you will tell at your interviews. This is an easy concept, but it requires discipline. Let's talk about that for a moment.

Figure 1
The Dynamic Interview Training Model (DITM)

Discipline is a Lubricant

Discipline is the grease that makes the interview model's wheels run smoothly. Discipline is also the grit and determination to follow the model. Just as with an exercise program, go through the model even when you don't feel like it. Believe it, because it will make you better. World-class athletes are world class because they have the discipline to train every day—they never break. Their training on an off day may be mental and not physical, but they train, baby, train. And then they execute at game time.

The power behind the DITM is the iterative, cumulative effect of exhaustive preparation and relentless practice. This results in better and better execution each time through the cycle. By integrating lessons you learn in one cycle back into your efforts in a subsequent cycle, you reap the rewards of repetition: flawless execution. In other words, you achieve the perfect job interview.

The activities in the following chapters fit into one of the four steps in the model. Underpinning the DITM is the idea that careful planning, not haphazard thinking, should drive your behavior.

Step 1: Preparation is the Key

Robust preparation is the cornerstone upon which you should build your interview strategy. Chapters 6 through 16 cover this aspect of the DITM. But what exactly does *preparation* mean?

First, you may have very little time to spare in your job search, so make your preparation pointed, specific, and disciplined. There are many books and articles you can read on the mechanics of planning, but the real test of the marketplace is in delivering a first-class product or service consistently over time. And it starts first with thorough preparation.

Most job seekers are, by their nature or the nature of their circumstances, very competitive. The will to succeed and survive is strong. It has been my experience, however, that far too many candidates were unprepared for their interviews and then performed poorly relative to a small number of their peers who were ready for the fight.

So why are so many people unprepared when they hit the interview? It is perhaps because they do not understand the process, are consumed with other concerns (current job, family demands, illness, travel, other interviews), or are unprepared if they are interviewing for an upgrade to their career and haven't interviewed for a higher-level position before. Even seasoned professionals need to remember that with more experience comes a higher level of expectation about performance.

Step 2: Disciplined Practice is Important

Practice makes perfect is sage advice proven over time in many fields such as the performing arts, medical operations, sports, and in interviewing. You must hone your communication skills to articulate your message with clarity. Yet so many people fall short. They are awkward, stilted, nervous, arrogant, self-absorbed, condescending, disinterested, unprepared, and so they underperform. Whether a person is as just described or projects that image, the result is the same. You must practice, practice, and practice even more to present the image that you want while under stress. Major-league pitchers speak of the mechanics of their pitching motion as a way of saying they must practice so many times that their throwing motion becomes second nature during the heated arena of the game.

While, chapters 17 through 18 cover this aspect of the DITM, there are numerous exercises, practice mock interviews (Appendix B), role playing, and discussions of practice techniques sprinkled throughout later chapters as well.

Just as eating chicken soup acts as a remedy for colds, so is mama's sound advice that practice makes perfect. The more you practice the better your execution will be. It is a crucial determinant of a successful interview and the one most missing by many candidates.

Interview Insights

Just as eating chicken soup acts as a remedy for colds, so is mama's sound advice that practice makes perfect. The more you practice the better your execution will be. It is a crucial determinant of a successful interview and the one most missing by many candidates.

Step 3: Superb Execution Wins Ball Games

Anyone can plan, but it is in the execution phase that plans for companies, wars, and people can fail. How then can you execute flawlessly? Executing the perfect interview requires thoughtful exercise of scenarios, and preplanned orchestrations of those scenarios to lead the interview where you want it to go. On game day, all of your practice and preparation must come together with precision and confidence. The model works on the precision aspect; you must develop confidence in your ability to execute. The execution step in DITM runs throughout chapters 19 through 29.

Step 4: Integration and Follow-Up Makes Perfect Pizza

Integration is the act of learning from your mistakes and successes and rolling that information back into your process. Assimilating learning from your first practices and interviews is key to growth and achieving better performance in subsequent interviews. As you follow up on lessons learned, mistakes, omissions, and such, you must capture what went right and what went wrong and fold those lessons back into your preparation and practice session. Do it over and over. That is the iterative process. Think frequent flyer program gone mad.

Of course, there is a hoped-for exit phase from the iteration cycle and that is a job offer—or at least a second interview! But more about that later.

Just Like Aerial Combat

In the intense arena of aerial dogfighting, a fighter pilot's preparation, discipline, and aggressiveness are rewarded with a chance to fight again another day. The same is true in the interview. The perfect interview is as much about mental toughness as it is about knowledge. There are plenty of smart people languishing in dead-end jobs. Those who outperform others have a psychological perspective that is as good as their intellectual one:

➤ Nothing less than victory

➤ Be ready

➤ Engage

➤ There is no second place

➤ Do not accept the minimum

➤ You are known by your last performance

Pithy aphorisms (now that's academic!) sound like they belong on a locker room wall, but they capture a mindset that says I will not accept anything less from myself than excellence. The competition is tough, but so are you! (Oh brother, another one for the locker room.)

Chapter Homework

1. Pick a speech from a famous person. For example, select The Gettysburg Address. Use the DITM model to prepare a verbal presentation of the speech to a friend or family member.

2. Write down the six psychological sayings above on an index card and paste them in a prominent place you will see each day. Memorize them.

Quotable Quotes

"It isn't the mountain ahead that wears you out—it's the grain of sand in your shoe."

—Robert Service, Canadian poet

CHAPTER 6

Preparation: Learning New Lessons

In This Chapter

➤ How to create a perfect interview

➤ The art and the craft

This chapter introduces DITM preparation skills needed to create the perfect job interview experience and fundamental training concepts. There is craftsmanship and artistry in delivering the perfect performance, and the perfect interview must be a superior award-winning performance that is also memorable.

Learning Objectives for the Perfect Interview

To accomplish the perfect job interview, you must adopt four learning objectives:

➤ Develop job-prospecting skills and secure an interview

➤ Prepare and practice systematically to tell a positive and memorable story

➤ Execute excellence in artistry in such a way that you outperform rivals

➤ Finalize the deal so as to secure an offer or next interview

Preparation and Practice

One of the first lessons taught in the military is to prepare and practice the way you are going to fight. In other words, realistic practice techniques supported by superb preparation can mean the difference between accomplishing the mission or not going home at all. For interview candidates that means getting the job you want or going home disappointed.

Interview Vocab

➤ Defining some key terms will ensure that we're all on the same page.

➤ Artistry: Of art or artists; a quality of being done skillfully or tastefully; aesthetically pleasing

➤ Artless: Lacking skill; clumsy; crude; uncultured; not artistic

➤ Craftsmanship: The ability to exhibit a high level of skill with painstaking, technically dexterous work; rises to the level of artistry

➤ Deliverable: A colloquialism indicating what is learned from a specific instructional media; a term for learning outcome, or sometimes an informal description of output received from a learning process. Your deliverable to a hiring firm is a perfect interview.

Most people realize athletes and musicians need practice. But how many times have you, the job candidate, practiced for an interview under game conditions?

Whether trying to secure a job, a slot at college, or a multimillion-dollar business deal, students and executives often dive into the process without practicing what they need to say and how they will say it—and unfortunately it shows. A lost sale or rejection is usually the outcome.

Disciplined preparation and practice go a long way toward perfecting the interview. In the end, what you desire is to stand out in the interviewer's mind in a positive, memorable way—and beat the competition. To do that, you have to practice in the vein of a craftsman or an artist.

The memorable Ignacy Jan Paderewski, a nineteenth- and early twentieth- century Polish piano virtuoso and composer, once said, "If I miss one day of practice, I notice it. If I miss two days, the critics notice it. If I miss three days, the audience notices it." The same holds true for interviewing.

Blowing the Game

Many people in highly respected professions practice the intricacies of their craft. Fighter pilots, actors and musicians, surgeons, police officers, lawyers, trained interrogators, athletes, public speakers, all practice so much that they can perform superbly when under pressure.

Occasionally you might hear a losing pitcher in a baseball game complain that the game was lost because his mechanics weren't right. In other words, his execution was horrible; he wasn't well prepared.

Don't let this happen to you. Don't work hard to get an interview, and then blow it executing the interview itself. For whatever reason, many people leave the mechanics to happenstance, or they wing it based on misplaced self-confidence.

The Seasoned Delivery of a Veteran

In many firms, product knowledge, often complex in nature, is given plenty of development resources. The actual follow-through, however, of explaining or selling those products is often left to the imagination. Less experienced people might see a seasoned veteran walk into a room, wow the customers, and then think they can do that, too. For every seasoned professional, there are scores of others fallen by the wayside that you do not see. Use your head. Few of us are naturals; we need to rehearse to be any good.

Therefore, don't let the actual interview be the first time you describe your ability to accomplish a task associated with the job, discuss leading a team or how to deal with the public, or how to create a grant request. Whatever the job may require, you need to describe it concisely, perform it accurately and efficiently, illustrate it plainly, and always in terms that highlight your abilities.

Full Dress Rehearsal

Don't short change the effectiveness of dressing in your interview attire and practicing your entrance into a room, your opening lines, and your departure. A full dress rehearsal can uncover issues that if left unattended would have surfaced during the actual interview itself. This is especially true if it has been some time since you last went through the interview mill.

Interview Insights

Grandpa was right—practice makes perfect. The interview is your chance to shine, so train like you mean it and you will execute your interview brilliantly in comparison to rivals who just show up and are ill prepared. Every day should include a practice activity. You should practice new ways of phrasing your strengths, speaking your introduction, and asking questions in the right way. Every day. Remember Paderewski's quote.

Becoming Memorable

Most people who interview candidates for positions in their firm have other duties as well. They are busy people. Many times the interviewer has only a few minutes before the interview starts to review the résumé for the first time. Is this ideal? No. But it is reality.

At the end of the day, the interviewer is usually tasked with summarizing his or her impressions of each candidate. Sometimes this occurs hours after the interview is over. If you are the only one applying for the job, then bully for you. For many of you, however, standing in a long line for that dream job is the norm, not the exception. If that is the case, then the poor interviewer has to remember enough to summarize thoughts about each person.

You want the interviewer to recall your superb answers, your insightful questions, your willingness to work hard, etc., etc., etc. When you call for a follow-up, you definitely do not want the interviewer to ask, "Now which one were you?" So you need to be memorable. That may sound as doable as your old coach yelling, "Have fun!" while you run sprints for the umpteenth time.

In an interview, being memorable does not mean you tell a funny joke or stand on a chair screaming, "Give me this job!" Being memorable means that you impressed the interviewer by knowing a lot about the position; the company and its products, markets, and competition; and by stating your reasons for being the right person for the job. Remember this: What you offer a company during an interview must be a shortened version of what it can expect to see from you every day on the job. Read that statement again.

The end result must be that you impressed the interviewer by answering the million-dollar question. Everything you say should support your ability to be profitable with purpose, clarity, and conviction. Your closing statement should be exactly what the interviewer was hoping to hear. That is what makes you memorable. Remember, the firm wants to hire someone. You need to make sure it is you.

Begin right now by thinking about how you can be memorable. Here are some ideas to get you started:

> ➤ Have a new perspective on an old problem
>
> ➤ Have a quick mind that isolates a bottom line issue
>
> ➤ Know more about the company's recent business than the interviewer
>
> ➤ Give correct, concise, interdependent answers
>
> ➤ Prove to be a well-rounded, articulate ambassador for the firm, maybe by being fluent in a second language

➤ Offer a proposed solution that actually might work

➤ Give a perfect closing statement that summarizes who you are, what you want, and what you can do

What If I'm Not What The Company Wants?

If you have a skills mismatch that you simply cannot overcome in the interviewer's mind, don't be relegated to the bin of nameless, forgotten rejects. Make the interviewer think well of you even if you don't get the job offer. Be memorable even in defeat.

Try something like this if it's obvious you lack what the company is looking for: "I may not have the exact [skill set, experience set, etc.] you are looking for, but what I lack, I make up for in diligence, honesty, and a willingness to learn. I am a quick study as evidenced by…" Or another approach might be, "It would be an honor to work with you, and all that I really need is a chance to become a great employee. Don't give up on me, I can do an excellent job for you." Who knows, the company may just take you up on it.

Practice Reality

When military pilots first learn to fly fighter aircraft, a grizzled combat veteran teaches them how to use the aircraft not as an airplane, but as a weapon. Tactics are critically important to a fighter pilot, and practicing those tactics while incorporating real-world contingencies makes the difference between a successful mission and one that is not.

It was said during the Vietnam War that if the U.S. Air Force could simulate the first ten missions of a pilot's tour, then his effectiveness and survival rate in actual combat would go up substantially.

As a response, the Air Force began to simulate those first ten combat missions through a set of realistic (and hazardous) peacetime exercises called Red Flag in the deserts of Nevada. After completing the training, a young pilot going to war for the first time should act as if he were flying on his eleventh mission. Amazingly, the theory worked. Pundits contend that the combat effectiveness of our pilots during the Cold War, the desert wars in the Middle East, and in Afghanistan are cases that prove the value of Red Flag's realistic approach.

Making Blunders

Make your blunders during practice, not during the actual "war" itself. You should absorb flak during mock interviews, not when you are getting shot at for real. Try to simulate interview room conditions, if possible. For example, put a thirty-minute timer in the room to keep you and your practice companion from getting too long-winded.

You will find a number of mock scenarios in Appendix B. Create your own Red Flag, complete with contingencies, pressure points, and the like. For example:

➤ Have someone call into the room, creating a distraction

➤ Put a television on in the background

➤ Have the simulated interviewer randomly interrupt your answers

➤ Tell interviewers to challenge your answers

➤ Give interviewers the questions list in Appendix B

➤ Use a timer to create time pressure

➤ Invite a second or third candidate

➤ Have the interviewer talk too much

Interview Vocab

The Masters of Business Administration (MBA) is a graduate degree that offers instruction in finance, marketing, strategy, operations and production, organizational behavior, accounting, and sometimes other specialties such as agribusiness and entrepreneurship. Many CEOs of major companies possess the degree. Those who possess the MBA from a top-rated school are jet-propelled to the executive suite. Universities often associated with a top program are Harvard, MIT, Stanford, Northwestern, Wharton (University of Pennsylvania).

A Customized Plan Just for You

A number of companies and websites discuss interview skills and offer advice on careers. Some have been around a long time, while others offer the latest fad.

In contrast, the approach in *The Smart Guide to the Perfect Job Interview* is simple—you create an individualized, customized plan. However, your efforts to get the job you want must start now, while reading this book; otherwise, you are wasting time. This program requires you to think about interests, to develop timelines, to react to questions, to practice mannerisms, and to learn a host of other tips and techniques. Start by finding your trusted agents and explaining your version of Red Flag.

Becoming Perfect

To become perfect, you have to learn from your failures. Don't get discouraged. Part of training for perfection focuses on your ability to react to difficult questions and situations where your knowledge and experience may be limited. You find the answers, and then move onward to success.

Don't Dig Deep

Have you heard the expression, "When you are in a hole, stop digging?" I have seen this violated so many times it hurts just to think about it.

Many candidates hate to admit to themselves that they really don't know how to answer a question; they hate to admit this to an interviewer even more. Experienced interviewers get the picture within the first few seconds. The candidate continues to dig and before long, he or she is out of sight several feet below floor level.

If you don't know an answer, confess it and move on. It is better to write a letter afterward, or send an e-mail with the correct answer than to fumble the ball during the interview. Nowhere is this most evident than in problem sets or case studies where the interviewer hands you an issue to study and then resolve.

Selling Yourself

If you don't have selling experience, or you aren't very good at it, then learning to market yourself as a product may be a new skill you will need to learn. You may fail in your first attempts, but that's where DITM comes into play. Part of the selling process is obtaining a prospect to buy your product (you). The next chapter should help you overcome any anxiety you may have.

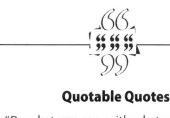

Quotable Quotes

"Do what you can, with what you have, where you are."

—Theodore Roosevelt

Chapter Homework

1. What is it about you or your experience that could make an interviewer think positively about your interview on his or her drive home? Record your thoughts for later use.

2. Use a camcorder or other video device to record your entry into a simulated interview

room. Shake someone's hand, sit, and record your response to the question, "Tell me something interesting about yourself." Review the tape and record ten observations about your taped performance.

 # Preparation: How to Get an Interview

In This Chapter

➤ The job acquisition process

➤ Handling gatekeepers

➤ Six degrees away

➤ Leave no stone unturned

➤ A business development exercise

In this chapter you will learn ways of obtaining an interview by developing a structured, disciplined approach to job acquisition. Other topics include handling gatekeepers and recruiters, conducting searches on the Internet, and treating the whole process like a new business exercise.

Getting a Shot

Perhaps one of the most difficult issues surrounding the interview is actually how to get one. The competition is very tough—in this environment more people are waiting outside interview rooms than in previous years.

The job acquisition process is to some degree a numbers game. The more opportunities (interviews) you have, the greater the odds are that you will get the job you want. Easily said, you think. In this process, your operating mindset should be that you will find opportunities in unlikely places. Ingenuity is called for.

As a job candidate, you need to sell yourself to a company much as a salesperson converts a prospect into a new customer. If you obtain interviews, you show evidence of strong sales skills. Employ those sales talents to build your own network of job contacts, apart from a school or other recruiting channel.

"Leave no stone unturned" in your quest for a job. That means asking friends and family, networking with old colleagues, using various information channels including both old and new media, utilizing informational interviews, attending events, joining charities, and a host of other efforts.

Blindly sending out hundreds of résumés and hoping for the best is a fool's game. You probably have a better chance of hitting it rich in Vegas on ole 21 Red—especially since many larger firms now require résumés to be submitted online—and who knows where those really end up.

So you may be asking, "How do I go about getting an interview?" I hate answers that start with "it depends," but here goes. It depends on whether you are still in school, in a profession and already have a business or social network, or use the services of an employment agency or recruiter.

Key Topic

Combine the rifle shot approach, where you target specific firms or people for job opportunities, with the shotgun approach, where you broadcast messages to larger communities (alumni clubs and such). This maximizes your potential opportunities and increases the odds in your favor.

For Students

Schools usually have a career services center or placement office on campus to help students with their job search. Many schools have an interview season with a recruiting calendar for their graduating students. In some cases, the student merely signs up for an interview with a selected company; in other instances, schools use a lottery or points system.

Some hiring firms use recruiters to prescreen candidates and/or use a book containing résumés of interested students from an entire class. More prestigious firms are booked early, and some will only see specific candidates. How can you stand out?

The career center usually mandates specific formats for a résumé, but differentiating your background is still possible. (See the section on résumés later in this book.) You should work closely with the career service personnel and learn their process. They help a lot of students, so be persistent.

College placement centers vary in quality from highly professional to nearly incompetent (sadly). Most schools have online services, offer résumé writing help, and some give interview advice.

The people who work in these groups should help with career counseling, job search strategies, and discuss the interview calendar with you. They should also actively recruit firms to appear on campus. If your school's center is unhelpful, then you may have to rely upon your own devices to secure a sufficient number of interviews. Regardless of the quality of the center, you should simultaneously conduct searches on your own.

For the Currently Employed

If you are currently employed, your ability to secure an interview is an indication that you know how to conduct a marketing campaign. Yep, conducting a successful marketing campaign is directly tied to the million-dollar question. See how easy it is?

If you are currently employed, then most likely you have existing contacts to help develop leads, make other connections, and secure interviews. You might even use the help of an executive recruiter or headhunter. In some instances, recruiters or hiring firms will reach out to you directly. That is a plus, but you should not bank on it.

Handling Gatekeepers

Interview Vocab

A headhunter is a professional recruiter, a person acting to broker a hiring transaction between a firm and an individual. Not to be confused with certain natives living in the South Pacific known for more bloodthirsty pursuits.

When you first try to set up an interview, there will be people you must deal with in order to secure the meeting. Often called gatekeepers, these people are paid to control access to the firm and to their bosses. They can be snobbish, incompetent, bored, antagonistic, questioning, uncommunicative, unhelpful people. You might as well get used to it. When you do encounter these gatekeepers, remain professional and don't let them get under your skin—you will usually lose.

The upside is there are many gatekeepers who are the exact opposite—they are professionals who know how to represent their firm regardless of the circumstance. Many interviews are secured by working as much with the gatekeeper as by trying to reach the principal.

Try these techniques for getting around or dealing with a gatekeeper:

> ➤ Call the company at 7:30am or 5:30pm. It may well be the principal who answers the phone. Most gatekeepers aren't at work yet or have departed.

> ➤ If you speak to the gatekeeper, be especially courteous. State your reason for calling, and use the name of the person who referred you to the principal. If you have no referral, state how you know of Mr. or Ms. XYZ and what compelled you to call.

> ➤ Be professional, concise, and speak slowly enough to be understood.

> ➤ Make a personal connection by ending a comment with an interrogative. Say something like, *I read an article about Ms. XYZ in* Fortune, *and her remarks were very insightful. Do you work closely with her?*

> ➤ Communicate appreciation.

> ➤ Build rapport—gatekeepers have the keys to the kingdom.

> ➤ Record the gatekeeper's name and write down the date of the call.

> ➤ When calling back, refer to a discussion point you had with the gatekeeper. For example, "When we last spoke two weeks ago, you mentioned the firm was extremely busy. Have things eased a bit for you?"

> ➤ Make known your intention to write an introductory letter. Address it to the principal, but in care of the gatekeeper.

Another technique involves immediacy: How can you be helpful to the gatekeeper? Try something like the following hypothetical conversation:

Caller: "I know you are busy. Does Ms. XYZ have voice mail? I can use that if it is helpful to you."

Gatekeeper: "I am Ms. XYZ's voicemail."

Caller: "That must put an extra burden on you. You work for a terrific firm and I hope to discuss my qualifications and career goals with Ms. XYZ. Please mention my name and number (give it quickly and make sure the spelling and contact info is understood). Is there a better time for me to reach her?"

If you leave a voice mail, then read it from a prepared note card complete with calculated pauses to make it more conversational. Do not exceed one minute in length; thirty seconds is sufficiently long.

Six Degrees Away

Let's discuss the six degrees of separation phenomenon. Part of any job search plan should involve networking in every conceivable circle you can enter. In the process, you will learn that you are usually only six people away, or six degrees of separation, from the person you would really like to meet.

The example below illustrates how the six degrees of separation works:

An executive once wanted a job on Wall Street. He was thousands of miles from New York in a foreign country, and he wasn't in the financial services industry. His wife worked at an accounting firm. Her boss, the partner-in-charge, introduced this executive to the head of the local American Chamber of Commerce. That person introduced him to the chairman of the finance subcommittee, who subsequently invited him to join. Also sitting on the subcommittee was a man who later introduced our executive to the ranking in-country banker for a major U.S. investment bank. A year later, the banker introduced our hero to the CEO who was on a business trip from New York. Soon, our protagonist was hired and off to the races in his dream career. Let's see; that was six people—wow!

Think of it, you may be only six contacts away from the person who could offer you that coveted job—but you must network to make it happen.

Direct networking is only one of at least four major ways to uncover job opportunities, and they all involve connecting with people. The others are attending events, making direct overtures, and utilizing third parties and technology. You may think of other ways, and that's good. Be creative, be professional, and be interactive. Meet people who are "in the mix" by going places they go to and being interested in the ideas, events, products, and charities that interest them. It will pay dividends.

Direct Networking

Networking is a way of leveraging contacts to make other contacts. The number of ways to network is almost limitless. Use your imagination; go where others in your field go, and then meet them. You could even go online using one of the social networking web sites. Contacts to use as sources are:

> ➤ Classmates

> ➤ Firm alumni

> ➤ Professional contacts

> ➤ Social contacts

If you are an introvert, networking might be daunting. If that is the case, first try easier, safer venues and then move to the more challenging ones. Join alumni groups; use social media (LinkedIn, Facebook, Twitter, etc.) and professional organizations germane to your industry. For example, if you're an engineer, join the National Society of Professional Engineers; if you're in business, join the American Management Association; or join any other organizations associated with your interest area.

Most of these associations have offices in most states and are a valuable source of industry information, career opportunities, and most importantly they are a great networking device. Many of them hold conventions. Networking is about talking to people and engaging mutual interests. Someone will know someone who will know someone, etc. The heart of it is the six degrees of separation phenomena discussed above.

Interview Insights

Joining LinkedIn or Facebook are great ways to reconnect with former colleagues and classmates. You may find out that your best friend from high school, whom you lost contact with, is now the CEO of a major company in the career field you wish to enter.

Attending Events

A great way to meet people is at a social or business event. Consider these types of events to meet the people who might be connected to employment opportunities:

➤   Philanthropic fund-raising activities

➤   Analyst meetings or conferences

➤   Societies and clubs

➤   Interest-based affinity groups

Interview Vocab

Networking is the process of meeting people who are connected to other people who are also willing to make introductions. It is simple in concept but hard to implement. It is a necessary tool for most people and instrumental in a job search.

Charity and Philanthropic Events

Most really wealthy people earned their money, they didn't inherited it. And what did they do to earn it? Many of them built companies. Building a private company, or, in some cases, building an industry can be enormously profitable. What do they do then with all that money? Rather than leave most of it to Uncle Sam, many engage in philanthropic endeavors. They fund charitable causes and attend events around those causes. What a great way to meet interesting people—sitting at a table you helped sponsor for an event supporting children's reading programs, for instance. It's good for the charity and potentially good for you.

Likewise, during hypercharged political times, attending a public policy forum is a great venue to meet interesting people. Who attends such events? Wealthy people do. And what do wealthy people do for a living? Many of them run businesses, and these enterprises might just need a person like you.

Wall Street is Good for Something

Wall Street is a primary source of research information about many businesses looking to attract fresh capital from investors. Try to wrangle an invitation to attend an analysts meeting or industry conference, where financial firms host the leaders of public companies to speak about their firms. This is a great way to learn about exciting technologies, new companies, and the movers and shakers in the industry.

Societies, Clubs, and You

Other great networking venues are professional societies and clubs specific to your industry of interest. Examples might be the local CPA society, chambers of commerce, oil and petroleum clubs, speakers bureaus, etc.

Take a course at a local university or a culinary program at a community center or an upscale restaurant equipment company. You just never know where you will meet the person that can part the Red Sea for you and make that new job happen.

Affinity Groups

Interesting people tend to cluster around unusual interest areas such as the ballet and the arts, safaris, fly-fishing, racecars, photography, literary societies, etc. These affinities are more than just hobbies to wealthy people; they are passion-inspired hot buttons.

Many entrepreneurs are type A personalities with energy to burn. Many are athletic and use sports as an outlet for the angst they might feel starting a business. Therefore, think about joining basketball and softball leagues, rowing clubs, marathon and cycling clubs, touring clubs, golf clubs, tennis groups, and squash leagues. Energetic people are most likely doing energetic things away from the court. They run things, they build things, and they hire people.

Direct Contact

There are at least four proven ways of gaining direct access to job opportunities. They are:

➤ Cold-calling

➤ Working at troubled firms

➤ Contacting key executives

➤ Conducting pro bono research projects

Cold-Calling

Most of us have received cold calls and hate them. Many of you may have even made those calls. Can they work in the employment search? Yes they can, if done properly and with a bit of research to back them up. Direct contact through cold-calling is a low-percentage game, but for the not-so-faint-of-heart, it can be rewarding. Usually only between 1 and 3 percent of cold calls are successful, but it only takes one to make your day. Like selling your house in a down market, you only need one buyer!

Here are some common sense rules you can follow when "dialing for dollars" via cold calls:

➤ Reserve time in your day to make calls (according to U.S. law, only between 8am and 9PM at the person's location, unless the location is a business.)

➤ Develop a long list of calling prospects

➤ Be concise in your messaging—even on voicemail

➤ Answer "why should I take this meeting with you?"

➤ Try to get a meeting, not a job

➤ Record date/time and results of the call

➤ Try lower-choice companies first, then your first choice

➤ If you call xxx-xxx-xxx1, and no answers, try -xxx2 etc.

➤ Be pleasant regardless of response

➤ If your recipient is unreceptive, move on to the next prospect

➤ Don't leave more than two messages

➤ Follow up with a short note

➤ Use the methods above to get around gatekeepers

➤ Call early or call late

Remember, federal and state law governs the time periods such calls may be made to people at their home (generally only between 8 am and 9 pm). It makes little sense, though, to cold-call someone at his or her home—the risk is too great that the recipient of your call will be offended by the invasion of privacy. Calls may be made to a place of business at any time.

Who should you call? Should you call the chairman of a Fortune 500 company? That probably won't work, but it has worked for a few. Cold-calling small business owners is a good place to start, and they are often easier to reach. Due to their size, you could have a large impact upon a small business. They may pay less (but not necessarily so) and have fewer benefits than a company like IBM, but you don't have as far to climb to get to the top, either. And the principals are often easier to reach.

Working at Troubled Firms

Pursuing jobs at troubled firms is another consideration when trying to gain access to job opportunities. The lines are generally shorter there than at a firm everyone desires.

Interview Vocab

A cold all is a marketing call made by a firm or individual to an unknown person as an attempt to solicit business, information, or donations. According to the Federal Communications Commission (FCC) and Federal Trade Commission (FTC) guidelines, rules governing cold calling activities to individuals are designed to protect consumers from harassing and unwanted phone calls. You should first check available "do not solicit" lists and any state and national Do Not Call registries. Individuals can register for the national lists via the FTC and FCC and it is a violation to call someone who has placed their name there. If a person asks not to be called again, then you should put their name on your "do not solicit" list. In general, if they are not on the lists, then you can call them. You should be courteous and truthful and identify why you are calling. Check www.FTC.gov for more information on exceptions and other restrictions.

In difficult times, there are a host of firms that are not ready for bankruptcy but are confronting serious problems. Send letters and make phone calls to ask for an interview. Get familiar with the firm's issues and have an idea of how you might help solve them. Should the fortunes of the firm turn around, you can rightly say you were part of something special.

Volunteer Work

Not-for-profit (NFP) organizations usually need volunteers to support their endeavors. Moonlighting, or working for free, is a great way to learn about some terrific groups and also to meet vibrant people who are passionate about their work. If you have needed skills, donating your time can be more valuable than donating money! And, you never know who might walk through the doors of the organization; you may have a chance to meet someone who runs a company.

Pro Bono Research

One way to get noticed and get a foot in the door is to craft a well-researched, well-reasoned article and send it to key executives. The impact is especially strong if your research is better than what they are getting from their own staff.

Conduct your research on a company using the analytical framework offered in chapter 15. Pick one of the firm's products, craft a memo outlining challenges and opportunities versus those of the competition, and send it to an executive at the firm. Try to emulate the memos used in the target company if you can get that information.

Using Third Parties and Technology

There are at least two methods of gaining access to employment opportunities by using a third party, and technology provides a powerful tool as well. They are:

> ➤ Employment agencies
>
> ➤ Executive recruiters
>
> ➤ The Internet

Interview Insights

Employment is obviously a concern for all developed countries. As such, an extensive body of law has emerged as governments have attempted to bolster employment and ensure fair treatment. In the United States, for instance, public employment agencies are regulated both by the state and the federal governments under acts such as the Workforce Investment Act of 1998.

Employment Agencies

Employment agencies are a large category of both public and private entities that are engaged in the business of matching prospective workers with employers. In broad strokes, employment agencies, including those servicing the trades, tend to concentrate on the lower-ranked workforce and on temporary workers. They often provide companies with large-scale staffing solutions. Kelly Services (www.kellyservices.com), and Manpower (www.manpower.com) are two of the larger, better-known firms.

Employment agencies provide a range of staffing and employment counseling services across a broad range of disciplines such as science, healthcare, and finances. If you conduct a random search, you'll see that employment agencies advertise domestic U.S. and international jobs such as marketing project managers, software engineers, senior auditors, junior accountants, administrative assistants, junior financial analysts, business analysts, senior payroll manager, development and quality assurance engineers, and bank manager.

Executive Search Firms

Those interested in procuring a high-level position can call in the services of executive search firms. Sometimes known as headhunters, search consultants, or executive recruiters, executive search firms come in all shapes and sizes. Some are regionally oriented; some are national firms with extensive global reach. And some specialize in particular industries, whereas others are generalists.

Search consultants generally work for hiring firms, but they also retain potential candidates in a pool of candidates for consideration as new job opportunities arise.

Their fee is sometimes paid by the hiring company in the form of a retainer or as a percentage of the new employee's annual compensation. In less common cases, the employee will pay the fee directly. If you work with such a consultant, find out up front how he or she is to be compensated.

Often executive search firms are looking to fill positions from chief executive officer and board positions to senior or managing director/partner levels. In many cases they target niche, highly educated professionals such as physicists, high-end finance professionals, lawyers, physicians, and turnaround specialists.

Interview Insights

Treat meetings with headhunters as you would any interview. They are in the matching business, and your job is to put your best foot forward. Remember, they generally work for a hiring firm and for themselves, not always strictly for you. They may be your advocate, but only as long as you serve the needs of their client firm, unless, of course, you are the one paying the bill.

To learn more about executive search, go to the Association of Executive Search Consultants (AESC) at www.aesc.org.

A search consultant may have relationships with employers and may be hired to harmonize the firm's people strategy and human capital needs with overall business strategy. Depending upon the level of staffing required, a consultant might work with senior management of the firm to establish written job requirements, minimum qualifications, and search parameters.

Be under no illusion, consultants are on the prowl to find candidates that fit the needs of the firm. They generally hear about potential candidates from their own networking and research. If you contact such a consultant out of the blue, you may discover rather quickly that he or she has little time for someone cold-calling them. Here are some hints for working with headhunters:

➤ Be courteous and professional at all times

➤ Keep current on trends and events in your industry

➤ Know what you want to do

➤ Keep your information up to date

➤ Keep them current on your status

➤ Periodically touch base with them

➤ Take an interest in their business and needs

➤ Refer business to them

➤ Be a trusted source of information for them

Aside from those caveats, working with headhunters can be enormously beneficial if the moon and stars align perfectly. They know the job opportunities and the company. They also can be extremely helpful in compensation negotiations once the hiring firm determines you are the person it wants. But keep in mind that they are in business also, so treat them professionally, and do your homework.

Interview Insights

Don't let a day pass without performing a job search activity or some form of practice. In fact, try this awards system on a regular basis:

➤ Research: 1 point

➤ Do exercises in this book: 2 points

➤ Make calls: 3 points

➤ Make an appointment: 4 points

➤ Informational interview: 5 points

➤ Actual interview: 6 points

See if you can get fifteen points by the end of the week. If you don't, then step it up! Research might simply be reviewing an article, and then thinking about how it relates to your skill set.

String days and weeks of this together and you will be amazed at how much better off you are. And you will be better at analyzing cases, presenting facts, discussing your experiences, and securing interviews.

Using the Internet for Job Searches

The Internet is a wonderful, perplexing, and overwhelming phenomenon of modern invention. For job searchers, it can be an undeniable source of information, cost cutting, and exposure. Many of your job searches can be saved on most job-related web sites, and e-mail alerts can be sent to you when certain types of jobs, locations, and titles are posted.

Many sites require an account, and many are also free, but you should make certain prior to signing up. In some cases, basic searches are free, but other services such as résumé help and other assistance are not.

In fact, these days many companies require people to enter web sites to apply for a job. Therefore, get used to posting your résumé and cover letter online. Many hiring firms force applicants to enter their online application process to ensure a legal defense or as a method of standardization but some are sinkholes for résumés. Some organizations' processes are efficient, while others are cumbersome, irritating, and a waste of time. Don't hold your breath for a callback.

The best way to cope with this anonymity is to find a human contact at the target company by using one of the channels described earlier. However, many firms require the online process before someone will even speak with you.

The Internet gives enormous insight into the jobs picture in the economy. It also does what computers do so well: aggregate and disseminate. Realize, of course, that these sites play to a broad audience; many millions of people hit these sites regularly looking for a job that you want.

The Internet facilitates the following job-related activities:

> ➤ Research on specific companies, industries, and people

> ➤ Targeted help with basic résumé and cover letter preparation

> ➤ Networking within your circle of contacts and beyond

> ➤ Contact with companies

The Internet is a perfect example of the power of leverage. Think of it, a little sleight of hand can reach millions of people—and they can reach you. Be forewarned to never divulge personal information unless you know the people, are working on a protected site, and feel comfortable with the site's privacy rules and safeguards.

Keep in mind just as you search for information using Google, so do many companies. If your friends can see your information, so can prospective employers. Remember those rude, crude, and socially unacceptable comments you posted? Think twice, before you write.

Several web companies excel at aggregating information from various sources and creating expanded searches on the Internet with a simple stroke of a keyboard. Some of the large search web sites are Zoo (www.zoo.com), Excite (www.excite.com) and Dogpile (www.dogpile.com).

If you want to know the answer to questions like which are the top political web sites or social networking sites, and other popular questions about web sites, then try www.ebizmba.com, an e-knowledge resource for answering online business questions.

For help with choosing a site that is best for you, try using a ranking service like www.consumersearch.com/job-sites. It ranks employment sites across several criteria, including best search engine, most popular, and best targeting.

Five Popular Job Sites

The list below describes five popular job search web sites and their relevant characteristics. Refer to chapter 15 on research for a longer list of web sites useful to the job searcher.

Based upon statistical measuring services such as Quantcast, some of the more popular sites get on average over 10 million hits and some average over 20 million distinct visits. Ranking sites such as www.ebizMBA.com offer additional insight; simply type "most popular job sites" in the search window.

Monster.com

Monster.com is probably the largest and best-known all-purpose site. Use it to post résumés, search for specific jobs (it has a large database), receive general interview advice, link to other sites, use career tools and skills inventories, and join communities. The site also offers interesting articles on careers and job environments (for working moms, for instance). It offers an advanced search feature, résumé writing resource (for a fee), sample résumés by industry, and company profiles. Monster is a straightforward, expansive site with free basic membership.

Careerbuilder.com

As of this writing, CareerBuilder advertises it has over 1.5 million jobs offered through its database. You can post your résumé (from which you get job recommendations), and search by category, industry, and location. The site also offers members a free résumé review service. You can take a career interests quiz, match jobs with the results, and create an interests profile.

The site allows a prospective employer, for a fee, to search the résumé database along specified criteria. It also includes an international job search function by country.

When you sign onto the site, you get a window showing jobs most recently posted. Sign-on is simple and free.

Indeed.com

Indeed offers a straightforward job board with direct links to hiring firms' application processes. It allows searches for jobs based upon criteria such as salary, industry, and title. You can use its advanced search ability by using key words or phrases. For instance, simply typing in "Los Angeles" in the location window and hitting the search button revealed over 103,000 L.A.-based jobs listed on the site by employers. There were jobs ranging from executive managing director to delivery clerk.

The site offers simple access to other sites along specific criteria such as jobs that pay over $150,000. Some of the linked sites require a fee for their services. You can also search by employer or limit searches to positions offered via a recruiter. It offers free access to job postings.

Simplyhired.com

Simplyhired is an aggregating job-listing site. It is very easy to use, according to many consumers, offering links to helpful external sites plus a large jobs database that includes opportunities from other databases. If you choose, you can exclude specific companies from your searches. You also gain direct access to offering companies' sites.

This web site offers limited direct content concerning ancillary services, such as résumé writing services, and it offers e-mail alerts for jobs that have specific criteria you've set.

A recent search revealed over 350,000 listed jobs by simply typing in "New York" into the location window. A representative sample of listed jobs across the web were database analyst, software engineer, healthcare consultant, financial analyst, print sales managers, research scientist, operations managers, managing directors and many others. Membership is free and easy to establish.

IMDiversity.com

IMDiversity is a site dedicated to minority interests. It offers separate villages, or communities, for underrepresented minorities, such as Asian Americans and women, and includes relevant articles about current events unique to each village. The site also includes a diversity registry to compare prospective employers via a set of diversity criteria. Recently, a search under its global village page revealed a primer about the H-1b visa program.

Interview Insights

If you are not a frequent Internet user, you may be astounded by the power this medium affords. For instance, with the advent of meta search engines, like metacrawler.com, you can ask the most mundane or most complicated questions and receive amazing results. For example, the simple inquiry "best spaghetti sauce recipe" yielded three pages of web sites.

Entering the Blogosphere

For some of you, the term blog sounds like a muddy mess in the Scottish highlands or a creature living under a bridge.

In the Internet world, a blog, officially known as a web log, is a personal news column. It's a chance to post commentary on just about anything. The same caveat applies from above about vulnerability and privacy, but the blog can be an exciting way to get your message out. Your current employer might become aware of your content, so be careful what you write. Think of a blog as personal advertising space for your job search, a place where you can show off your expertise.

You may want to direct your interviewers to your blog so they can see how you think and write. Be careful, though; your writing and thinking skills must be first-rate. Visit www.blog.com for more information on blogs and how to create your own. Other blog-oriented sites useful to researchers and job hunters are:

➤ www.icerocket.com

➤ www.technorati.com

➤ www.twitter.com

Chapter Homework

1. Record the names of four charities in your employment region of interest. Find four associations in your area related to your industry of interest. Find four troubled firms. Find four companies of interest and identify the CEO, then write a practice letter asking for an interview.

2. List all of the people you know well enough to call if necessary. Determine possible connections among people on the list.

PART TWO

The Dynamic Interview

CHAPTER 8

 # Preparation: Learning to Market Yourself

In This Chapter
➤ Marketing as art and craft
➤ The maximum power résumé

Selling is a craft, a skill that is also a form of artistry in the hands of an artisan. In this chapter you learn that there is more to marketing yourself than meets the eye. To be successful and deliver the perfect interview, you have to sell a product—yourself—and there is no way around it. The résumé is your selling brochure.

Selling Skills: the Art and Craft

Many pundits agree that the following are essential elements in the selling process: market the brand properly, frame discussions correctly, and deliver coherent, intelligent solutions to buyers' needs. In interviews, you are the product and you must learn to market your brand, frame the conversation, and present yourself as the solution. Most of the skills to accomplish the three elements are common sense, but they are hard to implement.

Memorize the skills and watch how others apply them. Wherever you go, it seems someone is selling you something. Rate their ability to do so if they were successful. What was it that made you buy the product? Take notes as you shop for clothes, an automobile, a computer. How good were the salespeople at selling? Can you adopt something they did well?

Artistry is nuance, form, and interpretation. There are a lot of technically correct ballet dancers in the world who know the craft. At the highest levels, however, it is the subtle act of compelling the observer to fall in love with what he or she is seeing in the dancer that distinguishes a true artist from a good dancer. Learn how to do that in an interview, and the offers will roll in. Maybe you will even get a standing ovation. Implement these suggestions to achieve artistry:

➤ Listen carefully.

➤ Focus on customer (hiring firm) needs and objectives, and then ask the right questions.

➤ Communicate the value and features of your product (you).

➤ Link your value to the needs of the customer (hiring firm).

➤ React effectively to the customer's (interviewer/hiring firm) objections and issues.

➤ Be objective, empathetic, and not self-centered.

➤ Motivate the customer representative (interviewer) to trust your story and the value offered by the product (you).

➤ Be a solution to their problem .

Falling Short

Many candidates don't appreciate or understand the importance of applying these skills in interview sessions. Think about each skill during your preparation efforts and record the ways you are going to manifest each one. Selling is not rocket science, but it often feels that way. Plenty of people, like the dancer, know the technical craft. You have to know the craft, but you must also show your artistry to stand above your rivals. The interview is a selling exercise: you are the product and the firm is the buyer. Imagine this scenario:

Your competition is waiting to sell a product. Your potential buyer isn't committing to buy from you. Economic conditions stink, and perhaps your product has some disadvantages. You must convince the buyer that he or she needs your product.

Show your artistry by saying the right thing, in just the right way, with emphasis placed on just the right word—you have just the right touch. You understand, you empathize, and you ask, learn, and struggle hard to find solutions. You are convincing. The buyer likes what he or she sees and hears and believes you have his or her best interests at heart. The buyer begins to trust you and is compelled to buy from you—to deal with you, not the competition. Success!

The Résumé—Your Life as a Short Story

Imagine distilling your life onto one or two pages. In essence, that's what a résumé is asking you to do. The résumé is used as a crutch by both interviewers and job candidates. It should be a vehicle through which you discuss how you can help a company. It is a tool, not an end unto itself.

While a résumé is a recapitulation of your history, it should also be a selling tool; one that is forward-looking and offers a translation of your experience into a story that relates to the business of the hiring firm. The résumé should provide a reviewer with a snapshot of your relevance, your ability to contribute. What must stand out is your ability to make it through a trial period or training program, and then be able to contribute to the growth of their business.

Too often job candidates look at the résumé as the center point of the discussion and neglect discussing its relevance to the future. It is history and should be a springboard from which you discuss what you can do for the company. You should think, *This is how I am going to help you, Mr. Interviewer.*

Interview Insights

Many websites and other books describing the latest fad in résumé presentation exist, but in general, choose a style that puts your strengths in their best light. Use the section at the bottom of the résumé to highlight something unique about your background, interests, hobbies, etc. Put a thought-provoking idea in this section. For instance, if you enjoy listening to music, do not just list music as an interest. Try something like, Ella Fitzgerald aficionado. This could provoke an interesting discussion about the relationship of jazz to other fields of endeavor such as math, culture, American history, politics, etc. All sorts of discussion threads could arise. Such connections add flavor to your story.

Creating Content for a Powerful Résumé

There are several ways to organize your résumé for maximum effect. You should pick the type that highlights your positive attributes or is more targeted to a key element of the job or industry you desire. Pick one that accentuates and generates power. Many interviewers peruse the résumé for several minutes, put it aside, and then begin to evaluate your potential. Therefore, you need to present your content in a style that highlights potential—with impact.

For example, let's say the opportunity involves coordinating the training of several groups around the internal rollout of new computer software. Perhaps your previous experience involved retail apparel. Think of experiences implementing a promotional campaign. The connection between the two may seem tenuous, but you should be able to find a thread. For instance, what if the retail promotion required you to go to each store location and train people on the features of a new hooded parka promotion? If so, weave a credible story about the similarities in communicating a message, training and creating buy-in from reluctant employees—and don't forget to include your accountability.

Imagine your effort resulted in an 18 percent increase over previous promotion efforts. You should convey a message saying something like, "Ms. Interviewer, you will see the same sort of increase in productivity if I rolled out your new training program." In other words, link your experience to specific job requirements for the new job and put it on the résumé.

Key Topic

The form of your résumé should support the story. Don't let the impact of the story be diminished by burying it five blocks low on the résumé in its normal time frame. It belongs where it hits with the most impact.

Basic Résumé Types

There are two basic types of résumés, although there are many variations. They are:

➤ Historical or chronological: Events such as education and work history are presented with the most recent date first, descending to the earliest. This type of résumé presents a logical flow and usually points out the most recent indicator of future job performance first—your last job. It could, however, pose a problem if the job you want is most closely tied to a job held earlier in your career.

➤ Function specific: Work areas are presented according to the type of work performed. For instance, work history is presented under neat categories like accounting, public relations, teaching, etc. This type of résumé highlights areas of particular expertise and can closely target your ability to fulfill requirements of the target job. Map your skills and experiences onto those characteristics that are most applicable to the job opportunity. This type of résumé is used less frequently used. It does not stress your most recent work experience and can be viewed suspiciously by interviewers for that reason.

There is nothing wrong with combining both types of résumés, functional and historical, into one. You run the risk of making the résumé too long and perhaps duplicative, but if it serves your purpose, then do so.

Highlight Specific Expertise

Some components of the résumé are readily apparent, such as your GPA from college or graduate schools. Generally, as experience increases the importance of some information such as grades diminish, but leaving them off a résumé could send a negative signal to some interviewers. They might think that you got bad grades if you left them out of your résumé. If your grades were bad and you left them off your résumé, be ready to explain any mitigating circumstances and why academic prowess should not be a primary indicator of performance on the job.

Focus the résumé by highlighting areas where you added economic value in past jobs. For example, you saved $X on an initiative and produced $Y revenue on another. Provide relevant details about the old job that point to an attribute or skill necessary to the new one. A dollar figure is worth ten words of prose.

Most jobs involve people, issues, and opportunities. Wherever possible, quantify evidence of your assertions. If you have industry experience with a major competitor, point to skills that transfer easily and those that are less apparent but still valuable. You should spotlight specific courses, projects, or internships that are directly relevant to the new job.

As mentioned previously, the interviewer you want to impress is busy. It is common for those responsible for businesses, and the person carrying the most weight in the hiring decision, hurry over a résumé in the few minutes prior to an interview. Consequently, they often miss your most significant feature. To avoid this problem, spotlight key abilities and experiences in italics, bold letters, or even yellow highlighter. This is especially true if you possess a unique skill that is relevant to the new job.

Don't be bashful about blowing your horn—as long as you provide evidence that you can do what you say.

Interview Insights

A young woman from a top MBA program once interviewed for a coveted job in New York. She was an ideal candidate in many ways. She had super experience, was well groomed and articulate, driven to succeed, etc. The interviewer noticed on her résumé she listed fluency in Japanese. The interviewer, recently returned from living in Japan, was also fluent. He couldn't resist asking a question in Japanese. She didn't have a clue. She had padded her résumé and admitted she had rolled the dice. She said, "What are the odds that I would run into someone who could speak the language?"

Everything on the résumé must be defensible, and you should have a talking point or two about each item. If the interviewer asks about a specific job, start and finish the answer in a few short, well-prepared sentences. Then ask if he or she would like you to elaborate. Steering a thirty-minute interview into a ten-minute discussion of a project you accomplished six years earlier creates little value. If an interviewer wants to know more detailed information, then he or she ask for it.

The Résumé Grand Canyon

Gaps in your résumé need to be explained, and the explanation needs to support your objectives. It is usually better to preempt questions if they support your overall case. Otherwise, when the interviewer asks, have a ready explanation for periods of absence, unemployment, etc. Storytelling is the key—how you cast the plot. If you took a year off to find yourself, for example, then stress that the period allowed you to focus on other projects and that the time inspired you to compete for the job at hand. Translate your time at a Tibetan mountain retreat into business language useful for the new job. It can be done.

Key Topic

If you are newly unemployed, start working on projects that exercise your skills. Do not become dormant—job hunting is not work experience. That seems self-evident, but many people act as if it qualifies. They work hard at getting a new job, but they don't do enough to enhance their skills while doing so. You should not say, "I have been out of work for two years and have been looking for a job." Instead, be able to say, "I am working on several computer projects, including a developmental program for a local elder care center."

Consider the following job fillers; they are good for the community and provide defensible arguments against inactivity during periods of unemployment. These can stand out on a résumé and make you different from the last person the interviewer saw. They describe a well-rounded and interesting person, not a person desperate for a job.

> ➤ Volunteer at your place of worship or charity

> ➤ Tutor

> ➤ Start your own business, no matter how small

➤ Learn a new language or go back to school

➤ Develop an Internet presence, perhaps as a blogger

➤ Volunteer as a researcher for a professor or an author

➤ Substitute teach or become an instructor at a community center

➤ Become a travel writer

➤ Try community theater

➤ Become involved in politics

➤ Form a musical group and book some gigs (if you are any good)

In other words, become expert at some endeavor—it will come in handy as a discussion topic during your next interview. Put it on your résumé under Personal Interests.

Structure

Whether the résumé is historical or functional, there are a host of styles to choose from. Pick one that is easy to read (don't use a font size requiring a magnifying glass) and supports your primary arguments. Remember, the résumé's purpose is to provide a snapshot of who you are from an employment perspective. It is not an announcement, invitation, or a novel! Look at the tips below and modify the résumé as your circumstances dictate.

Name and Contact Information

Center your name and contact information at the top. Include an e-mail address, cell phone number, or website URL. Be certain that the voice mail greeting on your phone is professional. Make certain you keep the data current.

Summary of Qualifications

Place your summary of qualifications and objectives several lines underneath your contact information. Use specific language about what you can do, but don't go overboard. Avoid innocuous, say-nothing words and statements like, "Executive seeking responsible position with a good firm." Could the interviewer possibly think you are seeking an irresponsible position in a bad firm?

Be definitive about the qualifications you want to highlight. Use bullet points where necessary!

Work History

The work history section of a résumé is often the most important. The following tips will help.

➤ List company name, dates of employment, summarize responsibilities and duties, show major accomplishments (boldface if needed for emphasis), and support those accomplishments with hard data.

➤ Be short-winded.

➤ Use bullets to highlight major points.

➤ Use sentence fragments to save space. Start sentences with active verbs as much as possible. For example, "Saved xxx dollars" or "Developed new process."

➤ Do not start sentences with "I."

➤ Be concise and use quantitative evidence to support your claims. For example, "Generated $400,000 in incremental second quarter revenue via three sales promotions."

➤ Keep the résumé to one to two pages if possible, depending upon experience.

Education

List schools you attended; your major, emphasis areas, or special projects of relevance; your degree or highest level of education attained; any technical schools or courses you've attended. Show your GPA or other distinctions if helpful.

Personal History

List interest areas, hobbies, special awards, civic or volunteer activity, clubs, etc. Be certain to list items that are unique and of real interest. This section is often overlooked. Here you show who you are and what really makes you stand out. Think about any unique talents you have that could stand out to a reviewer, and then tie them to the job during the interview.

Final Thoughts

Let's spend a moment on résumé building. If a résumé is a snapshot of who you are, then you want a résumé that is incredible—to show off an incredible you!

Do not pad a résumé with irrelevant, superficial, or untruthful information. Construct the résumé so that a busy person can get at the important stuff quickly. Put a detail or two on the résumé that is eye-catching. Don't be silly, just thought provoking. You need to come across as a serious, interesting person who has a lot to contribute to the new team.

Interview Insights

The most glaring and destructive mistakes made on résumés are spelling and grammer erors (I did those on purpose). They indicate you might be sloppy and lack attention to detail—especially since the errors are on such a short, important document. Spelling and grammar mistakes stand out like a red hat in a sea of white bonnets (got you looking for errors?).

Although good spell-checking software is the most efficient way to catch errors, you must be careful. It is easy to accept a suggested correction that isn't really correct, and then have the software correct all instances of the malapropism in your résumé without a blink. For example, it's possible that the incorrectly spelled *seel the campaigne* is corrected to *steal the champagne*, which although spelled correctly has a totally different meaning from your intended phrase, *seal the campaign*. Sometimes reading the résumé backwards can help identify errors like these.

Some ways you can enhance your résumé to help you stand above the crowd are:

> ➤ Relate to the future

> ➤ Translate your experience to the position in question

> ➤ Highlight your economic value added

> ➤ Match the needs of the firm

> ➤ Showcase who you are—add something unique

> ➤ Be 100 percent truthful and defensible

> ➤ Be concise without jargon and acronyms

Be careful of these résumé traps:

> ➤ Wordiness

> ➤ Topics irrelevant to the job or the future

> ➤ Use of acronyms

> ➤ Failure to show who you are as a person

> ➤ Spelling and grammar errors

> ➤ Failure to show economic impact of your experience

> ➤ Innocuous, worthless sentences, often called fillers

A Word about Cover Letters

A cover letter does as the name implies: It accompanies the résumé and tries to incite enough interest from the recipient to cause the person to contact you. A sample letter is included in Appendix D, but make sure to compose your own letter with your own words and flair.

Cover letters vary with the situation, but in general they should be concise, targeted, and interesting. They should include a hook that sparks interest and separates you from other applicants. The letter should include:

> ➤ Why you are writing

> ➤ Exact position you are interested in

> ➤ Statement with a hook

> ➤ Why you are different from the pack

> ➤ A request or statement of intention

> ➤ A thank-you for considering the application

In Summary

The power résumé should provide insight into how your experience is relevant to the new job or firm. Write the résumé so that Star Trek's Captain Picard would say, "Make it so!" Write your résumé, especially the work history section, with an eye to the future. Write it with the million-dollar question in mind. It's not the time to be overly humble, so say good things about yourself. But remember everything must be defensible.

Chapter Homework

1. Review your résumé and how it stands up to the advice in this chapter.

2. Pick a consumer product, think about its value to purchasers, and write a one-paragraph pitch to sell the product. Use your recorder to capture how well you can sell a product. Let a friend see the video and make comments.

3. If you're unemployed, review the list of ten activities that were suggested as job fillers and decide on one or two, or come up with two of your own activities. Develop a plan.

CHAPTER 9

Preparation: Interviews Are Scary, Right?

> ## In This Chapter
>
> ➤ What interviewers do
>
> ➤ Types of interviews
>
> ➤ The hurdle

In this chapter you continue your preparatory efforts and learn about different types of interviews, the pitfalls awaiting you, and how to cope with interview apprehension. We will also consider what interviewers look for and how you should handle them. Finally, you analyze whether you can actually attain your goals.

The Games Employers Play

Employers need to know how you will act on the job. If theirs is a pressure-packed work environment, then expect them to simulate stress with a few interview antics.

Distractions of all kinds are used. Firms will employ such techniques to gauge candidates' ability to deal with unusual situations. They may, for instance, seat you next to a television monitor to distract you with background noise.

Some firms will ramp up the pressure through a tag-team interview by rotating different interviewers in and out of the session. Others use group interviews where three or four interview candidates engage with one or more interviewers.

Some firms will send junior human resources (HR) associates to act as screeners for a later round of interviews. Some interviews occur in formal settings. Others can occur over lunch or on a golf course or while walking through a shop floor. In some cases, it may take only one thumbs-down vote to lose the day.

Your reactions, your overall psyche, your ability to handle the ebb and flow of conversation will be judged.

In general, screeners may ask questions that are more behavioral and life-experience based. They are trying to narrow the field from a large number to a manageable number for the hiring team to consider. In some cases, firms may use an associate who has recently graduated from school in this role. Don't be defensive with a younger interviewer. It's all part of the game.

In later rounds of interviews, firms also engage candidates over a meal to determine the ease and social grace with which a candidate can operate.

Stress and the Interview Experience

There is little question the interview is a demanding experience with a lot at stake. It is fraught with personality and loaded with many attributes of the human experience—each with its contra-attribute. Major components of personality-driven core attributes are factors such as ego, social skills, cultural sophistication, presence, appearance, focus, academic knowledge, and experience. Most of those attributes will be played out on both sides of the interview table.

Fear, Sarcasm, and Ridicule

Interviews and some interviewers can be intimidating. First and foremost, remember the hiring firm wants to hire someone; it doesn't conduct interviews just for fun. You just need to make sure that someone is you.

Some of you reading this may be apprehensive about the experience. You have heard war stories about the jerk interviewer or the pressure. If so, then if you try some of the techniques below, I believe you will be able to confront your interviews with much more confidence. So, work to overcome any apprehension and keep your eyes on the target— the job that is out there waiting for you. They can help slow your heart rate, focus your mind, and give you strength before you enter the battle! Try these techniques to overcome apprehension:

➤ Control your breathing—don't hyperventilate. Take a few slow, deep breaths. Let the air fill your lungs, close your eyes, and relax. Hum a quiet tune

➤ Visualize a happy life experience

➤ Visualize an experience where you gave a terrific answer to a question

➤ Recall a major success in your life and let it lift you up—remember the accolades you've received

> ➤ Think of your strengths, your positive attributes

> ➤ Imagine yourself doing great in the new job

> ➤ Be well rested and drink plenty of water

> ➤ Maintain a nutritious, balanced diet

> ➤ If able, maintain an appropriate exercise program

> ➤ Just before the event, listen to up-tempo music

> ➤ Imagine yourself crossing the finish line as the winner in the New York Marathon! Say to yourself, "I am a winner!"

Interview Types

Interviews are not all the same. There are several types of interviews, and their structure is largely dependent upon firm preference, interviewer psychology, nature of the job, channel, and stage. Format varies from individual sessions to group interviews, some with multiple interviewers and candidates. A recent entrant is the online interview conducted either via chat technology or e-mail. Even so, individual, one-versus-one interviews predominate.

Different strategies exist for coping with the different types of interviews, and how you handle each strategy can make or break the interview. Some jobs are heavily team oriented, whereas others require the employee to be entirely self-sufficient. Hence, the type of interview the firm uses could be different for each of those types of jobs. One might employ a panel with multiple candidates, and another might be a sequence of one-on-one discussions.

Interviews generally fall within six basic categories, and the methods taught in *Smart Guide to the Perfect Job Interview* will help you prepare for each. A seventh advanced category is what may be described as a dislocated interview enabled by technology. Some people may claim there are more types, some may claim fewer. The techniques used in one may be similar to those used in others. The seven categories of interviews are:

> ➤ Behavioral: Based upon the idea that past performance indicates future performance

> ➤ Situational: Candidates are given an issue and expected to formulate a response. It is the central task in the interview session

> ➤ Group: One or more interviewers interview one or several candidates

> ➤ Social: Candidates are evaluated over a meal or some other event; this could be formal or informal

➤ Technical: How well you do depends upon your grasp of technical issues and your answers to quantitative, analytical challenges. This could include a psychological screening test

➤ Informational: Meetings to learn more about an industry or company; may or may not be with people from a target firm; not an interview per se

➤ Dislocated interview: May incorporate elements of all six above but are enabled by the Internet, video-conference, standard e-mail, or telephone and are conducted remotely

➤ There are variants and combinations of the seven. For example, a technical interview can certainly occur over dinner with a group of interviewers from the firm. Each of the categories has its own unique characteristics, and it is helpful if you understand the differences

Behavioral

Based upon the idea that past performance indicates future performance, behavioral interviews are probably the most common. These discussions center on your résumé, your experience, work history, interests, etc. The emphasis is usually on your last job: your responsibilities, examples of work performed, effectiveness, and such. The challenge is to link your past with your future. Often candidates spend too much time discussing past projects without connecting their comments to the open job opportunity. You should prepare comments that illustrate how your experience relates to the new job.

Psychology-based screening tests are sometimes used to predict the applicability of past behavior/feelings to job performance. They remain controversial, but some firms use them extensively.

In behavior-based interviews you may be given a problem to solve. These vary from a simple math or reading problem to those that are meant to catch you off guard. Some problems require you to read a simple scenario and then to advocate a position—a clear attempt to rate your communication ability.

Situational

A variant of the behavioral interview, the situational interview is one where the bulk of the interview is conducted around a case study or a particular business issue. Candidates are given a document or a verbal briefing and then given time to study the issue and formulate a response. You might be asked to take the document home and write a memo. When you present your findings, the interviewer might challenge your assumptions or change the scenarios slightly. You may face "what if" questions. Be careful. The issue may be a problem the interviewer is grappling with in real life; be respectful of the solutions he or she may have already tried. For example, use qualifying language such as, "You probably tried an idea like XYZ already, but if not, I recommend investigating it from the following angle…"

If asked for a memo or a briefing, remember these tips about composing memorandums and presentations:

> ➤ Tell the audience precisely what you are going to address, then say it, and then summarize what you've told them

> ➤ Be precise and to the point

> ➤ Use bullet points or numbered lists

> ➤ Don't use crowded or busy slides; they breed confusion

> ➤ Use charts and graphs instead of words

> ➤ Do not misspell anything

> ➤ Organize main points into separate paragraphs

Group

In the group interview, several interviewers usually meet with one or more candidates. Occasionally, the firm may stream the interviewers into the discussion (like a tag team wrestling match), where they slowly build a panel. Introducing a new person into the mix every so often can add additional pressure; so keep calm. Some interviewers may even call in.

Make certain you look at each interviewer and give each equal importance. Also, recall that the one asking the questions may not be the most influential in the group. Answer each question as if the group collectively asked the question—because they did.

There may be junior members present along with a more senior person, and the experienced interviewer may defer to the juniors for background questioning. The senior may sit and listen, and then ask a probative question. For example, the junior member may ask questions about "soft areas" such as your hobbies,and then the senior questions the relevance of your answer to your career interests.

At other times, all participants may ask technical and soft questions at random. In many instances, each person has an assignment to hone in on a particular area. This is especially true after an initial interview. The interviewer could have feedback from an earlier interview and intend to dig deeper into a specific area.

Group dynamics are hard to read, so don't play games. Be straightforward. Treat each question as an important one. One method used by group interviewers is to use a good cop, bad cop routine, where one person asks a particularly difficult question, and the other person coaxes you a bit, sympathizes with the difficulty of the case, and then wham! You let down your defences, and the good or bad cop pounces with an even tougher question and maybe a little attitude. So never let down your guard. Remember, don't blow smoke or play above your game. Stick to things you know. Don't dig deeper into a hole!

Interview Insights

Some firms purposefully keep candidates waiting, sometimes for forty-five minutes or more. During that time, they have a receptionist monitor demeanor and reading habits. Are you reading the *Wall Street Journal* or a gossip magazine? Are you agitated or calm? You should assume you are under scrutiny from the time you enter the front doors of the business. Always act in a manner that says, "I'm here to do business. Take me seriously, please."

If you really like the firm, you will stay until it acknowledges your presence or it is obvious someone has made a mistake. If the latter, then politely leave contact information with the receptionist along with a note like: "I apologize for leaving, but I have another appointment at [time] and must leave now to ensure I make it. I would definitely like to reschedule. Have a great day. Signed, date, time."

Within a short interview, a firm may use time pressure and your anxiety over a tough question to see how you might react in a difficult client or business situation. Take a breath, understand the question, collect your thoughts, pause before answering, and look the interviewer(s) in the eye, and answer the question without fudging. Don't draw out a long response to a question you know little about. If you know the answer, and have a position, then defend it confidently and politely.

Social

Candidates are often evaluated over a meal or some other event like golf, cocktail party, etc. It could be a formal or informal event. Dress and courtesies are very important. See Chapter 16 for more on personal comportment and dress. This type of interview is important for those positions where the employee will have extensive interactions with the public or for sales positions. Adhere to strict guidelines on liquor consumption.

Technical

Answers to technical questions rule the day. Other factors apply, but it's all in the bottom line and how you get the answer. A technical interview can include extensive discussions with others from constituent groups about technical topics. If you are an expert in a particular field, you may be called upon to defend positions you have taken. Concise discussions of technical reports, books, interviews, and the like are best. Let the interviewers ask questions rather than preempting them. It is possible you could present a topic they would not have discussed—and that can lead to areas you may not want to address.

Informational

The informational interview is a special category of interview. Informational interviews are meetings to learn more about an industry or a company. It may or may not be with people from your target firm. Informational interviews are terrific ways to discover inside information about what a job is really about. Treat these information-gathering sessions as if they were real interviews, but make certain the other person does not think you are asking him or her for a job. To act otherwise can destroy any willingness to give you unbiased and objective information. It can also be uncomfortable to show up under false pretenses. If you are impressive, the person you meet with will remember you and may come back to you later for an actual interview.

Informational interviews can be had with lower-order employees; a senior executive has little time for these kinds of appointments—unless he or she is doing a favor for a colleague or friend. Again, treat these interviews seriously. Be prepared—you won't get much from these if you just show up and say, "Do you like your work?"

Remember to follow up these interviews with a thank-you note. Surprisingly, this little courtesy is too often ignored and is a great way to get noticed.

Interview Insights

Media-based interviews require special handling. Prior to using any technology, familiarize yourself with its use and have a fallback plan if the technology fails. Also, delays in transmission can cause confusion as participants talk over each other. This can be handled with experience. The same goes for the telephone or standard videoconferencing. Try a few calls on Skype (www.skype.com) to become accustomed to the tool. It is a computer-based service that allows you to see and hear participants from your own computer. To use the service, you will need a computer, webcam, and Internet access.

Dislocated Interviews

The dislocated interview, sometimes erroneously known only as an online interview, is conducted remotely where the participants do not see one another but are connected via technology, or they do see one another via live video. This is a broad category characterized by the type of connecting technology. The interview occurs over the telephone, via videoconference, or over the Internet using such tools as Skype. It can be used in any of the interview categories above, such as a group interview via videoconference.

Asynchronous interviews are those where the data is sent one way at a time and hence participants do not have to be online concurrently. Depending upon the setup, e-mail can give the candidate time to research an answer, but this is rarely the situation unless it is a case or business problem to be analyzed. Unplanned delays in responding could signal to the interviewer that you are in fact looking up the answer.

Many of the same rules discussed above in the other six categories of interviews apply to this type. But you should pay particular attention to differences such as transmission delays, avoidance of rapid hand movements that cause blurring on video, or speaking over other participants, for example.

These media-based interviews are becoming more commonplace for a number of reasons:

> ➤ Improvements in technology

> ➤ Leveraging time and number of interviewers

> ➤ Reducing travel costs

> ➤ Increasing volume of candidates interviewed

> ➤ An effective screening device

> ➤ Distance and location is not an issue

There are ongoing issues with these, however, for both the interviewers and the candidates. Some are:

> ➤ Sets up an artificial, impersonal environment

> ➤ Screens out capable people because of technology issues

> ➤ May not be as effective as a face-to-face interview

> ➤ Harder for candidates to convey discussion points without being seen

> ➤ Leaves a track record of candidate responses

> ➤ Reaches a wider, unknown audience

> ➤ Candidate answers can be fact-checked more easily

> ➤ Hides a candidate's hidden strengths (gravitas, personality, etc.)

Online interviews using the Internet via chat technology or e-mail require special handling. At least using video, you can see your inquisitors to a degree. There are a number of considerations when asked to participate in this type of interview as a candidate:

> ➤ Use proper grammar and spelling! Lack of a spell check is no excuse

> ➤ Make certain answers are correct—firms have more time to check

> ➤ Use bullet points to summarize key comments; think snappy, and then fill in the blanks verbally if on the telephone

> ➤ Be succinct, not flippant; don't write a novel in response to a question

> ➤ Avoid popular symbols and abbreviations—it's not appropriate to use a L, for instance

> ➤ Avoid using humor, since you are not in a position to see the reaction of your chat-mate, e-mail interviewer, etc.

> ➤ Wear interview clothing—even though you won't be seen. It will make you feel more professional

> ➤ Practice with the technology ahead of time, if possible

> ➤ Know who is online, on the call, or reading your transmissions

Treat each media-based interview as you would an in-person event, including doing your research and using other techniques. If you participate in a videoconference interview, be aware of what's behind you! The webcam will pick it up. Sometimes these interviews are conducted from your home, and that mess in the corner of your study will show up.

A Word on Psycho Exams, Braniac Tests, and Push-ups.

As part of all of these types of interviews, you may also have to take a screening or qualifying examination. Some firms cling to the notion that preinterview exams are a good idea. Somewhat controversial, these tests purport to align your characteristics against a set of job requirements. They range from simple physical tests (drug tests, for instance) to tests of mental acuity.

In some cases, the firm or test developers have determined a set of predictors that they believe point to prospective employees' success. Some criticize these tests as a failure of hiring managers to make wise choices; they rely too much upon test results to justify their actions. Such tests, if reasonably constructed, can provide a valid defense in case of litigation by disgruntled, rejected job candidates, however. Hence, more and more firms seem to be using them. The bottom line for you is that you may encounter one. If so, check with the U.S. Equal Employment Opportunity Commission (EEOC) at www.eeoc.gov for the latest information on these exams and issues surrounding their use.

According to a 2008 EEOC fact sheet on employment tests and selection procedures (modified in August of 2010), these tests come in many flavors:

➤ Cognitive tests: Assesses reasoning ability, memory, perception and accuracy, and basic arithmetic skills and reading comprehension, as well as knowledge of a specific job or function

➤ Physical tests: Measures the ability to do a particular task specific to job requirements or strength of certain muscle groups, as well as overall conditioning in terms of strength and stamina

➤ Sample job tasks: Performance tests, simulations, work samples, and realistic job previews are given to assess performance and aptitude of particular tasks

➤ Medical inquiries and physical examinations, including psychological tests

➤ Personality and integrity tests: Assesses the extent to which a person has certain traits or dispositions (dependability, cooperativeness, safety). They try to forecast the possibility a person will engage in certain conduct such as theft or absenteeism.

➤ Criminal background checks

➤ Credit checks

➤ Historic performance appraisals

➤ English proficiency tests

Some screening tools listed above, such as the credit check, don't require your active participation. Obviously, you should strive to get the highest score possible in the months leading up to your job search. The credit card companies often offer tips on how to raise your scores, which include such advice as paying bills on time and being well under credit limits.

Written Exams

If faced with an exam requiring written answers, try these hints to optimize your performance:

➤ Decide if the job is worth undergoing the exam

➤ Relax

➤ Read each question carefully

➤ Read each answer carefully

➤ Determine if each answer logically makes sense on its own

➤ Strive for consistency in your responses

➤ Answer truthfully

➤ Don't practice psychiatry (just answer the stinkin' question)

➤ Eliminate the obvious answers first

➤ Move on; don't get hung up (Let's see, I know I remember what the third differential equation is, uh…?)

➤ Answer as a reasonable, rationale, kind, loyal, smart, insightful, creative, positive-thinking, amazing, politically correct, athletic wonder leader

➤ Do not answer as a moronic, lazy, dumbfounded, antisocial, angry, provocative, delusional, perverted, stupid, bigoted Neanderthal

Many times at least one answer on a multiple choice exam can be thrown out immediately because it is absurd, answers the opposite question to the one asked, or takes a logical or incorrect path to an answer. Find out if there is a built-in penalty for guessing. In some cases if there are four possible choices, and you have no clue, then guess b or c. Some people believe those occur at a higher incidence than a or d—take that with a grain of salt.

One trick is to read the question, do the problem in your head, and then look for the answer in the choices. If your answer is there, then there is a good possibility you are correct. Also look for disqualifiers, or those questions that say "always," or "every time," or "never" or words of that sort. That may disqualify several answers immediately if they violate the "always" stipulation in the question for instance.

Push-Ups and Such

For some jobs you may need to pass a medical examination or a test of your physical skills such as hand-eye coordination, strength, and stamina. If so, make sure you get a good night's rest before the exam. And if you know the type of physical exercise to be performed, then you should practice that exercise prior to showing up for the exam. You don't want the actual test to be the first time you try doing a crawling exercise wearing a 60-pound knapsack! Many such tests are given through public placement announcements, and the physical requirements are well known so you should be well practiced in those. For some professions (firefighter, military, or police) physical exam requirements and training programs are listed on websites.

If you are required to take a cognitive exam, and it's been some time since you have been in school, then obtain an SAT study guide for college-bound students, a GRE/GMAT study guide for graduate school entrance, an LSAT law school entrance exam, or any of the other exams for the professions. These guides offer test-taking tips, practice exams, and explanations. They can help bolster your test-taking skills and confidence prior to taking one for a job. Also, there are many commercial websites, such as www.princetonreview.com or www.testprepreview.com, that give test instruction and online practice exams.

Unrealistic Expectations

Experience has shown that many candidates, even many seasoned professionals, expect one thing, but experience another during interviews. The same is generally true for many career changers.

A recapitulation of the résumé or a discussion of a person's life events may serve an HR person well; but to someone who runs a business, other issues are more important. Many HR people have never had profit-and-loss responsibility and are more concerned with verifying your background and discussing nontechnical issues.

Faced with someone other than an interviewer from HR, the interview sometimes catches candidates by surprise. Their preparation has been haphazard or seemingly nonexistent. In some cases they can answer the usual soft questions, but fumble when asked a question that digs into technical competence or challenges their choices or tries to uncover their ability to analyze facts quickly.

Interview Insights

For some jobs, especially those in academia, daylong interviews occur. The candidate may have to engage with ten, twenty, or more people of assorted backgrounds at one time. Having gone through an interview like that myself, I can tell you that this type of interview is most exhausting. In my case, parents, current and former students, faculty, the interim and former president, board members, and administrative staff were all present.

As with a marathon, pace yourself, otherwise toward the end of the day your brain turns to mush. Ask for five- to ten-minute breaks. During longer breaks, engage with one or two people and establish some personal rapport. Make use of a notepad. Do not be afraid to refer to your earlier answers if a redundant question arises. Don't be surprised if the interview is recorded.

The Rules of Engagement

There are definite rules in play for interviews. The following, I believe, are aggressive and sensible yet professional:

➤ Be on time.

➤ Watch your posture, which should be relaxed but not slumped.

➤ Do not overtly embarrass another candidate.

➤ Do not be condescending—not to another candidate or to the interviewer.

➤ Upstaging usually backfires. Second-guessing the interviewer, or, worse, trying to prove the interviewer wrong is not a ticket to paradise.

➤ If you disagree with a point of view, then say so politely. State your objection, present your facts, and articulate a position. Do this, but do it respectfully and without disdain or arrogance.

➤ Monitor your rate of speech. Speak slightly slower than normal. Many people use the irritating word *like* or phrase *you know* too often. It sounds immature and shallow. Also, take care with the upward, sentence-ending lilt that is common to many in the current generation. It can be condescending to the interviewer—it sounds as if you are questioning the listener's intelligence.

➤ If you're part of a group interview, listen closely to questions and answers; it may be your turn next to answer the same question and you don't want to be repetitive or inattentive.

➤ In a group setting if another candidate disputes your answer, remain calm. When given the opportunity, acknowledge the person's position, but diplomatically reiterate your strength of feeling that your answer is equally credible.

➤ If waiting outside, don't listen to rumors spread by other candidates. They can be conniving little you-know-whats, and remember they want the job too.

➤ Don't try to be funny, just be smart and correct.

➤ Be a team player. Interviewers may be looking to see how you might work within a team, so be ready with examples of how you used teammates to solve a problem. That shows leadership and problem-solving skills. If you're in a group interview, be the orchestrator, facilitator, mediator, or whatever it takes to make the group functional.

Don't worry; everyone thinks the others did better!

Help the Interviewer Out

Obviously, the interview provides a significant opportunity to show what you can do for the prospective company. Your goal should be to convince the interviewer that you can help grow the bottom line of the company and can positively impact your training class or your group when you get on the job. Consciously or not, most interviewers want someone who can relate to their clients, but they seldom see it portrayed overtly in interviews. They have to guess at it—and that is an uncomfortable feeling for the firm and the hiring manager. Make their job simple. Show them they can put you in front of their clients or other staff. The way you do this is by creating a growing feeling within the interviewer that the meeting is not an interviewer-to-candidate conversation, but a prospective client-to-employee discussion (see client context discussion below).

Create Awareness

Make the interviewer believe that what he or she is experiencing is how you would act once on the job. In other words, if you showcase a talent that is a client-oriented skill, you are acting like one of the interviewer's team members. The talents used by top client relationship managers invoke listening skills, interdependent thought processes, and the ability to tie what the client is saying to the capabilities of the firm. Show these skills and you go a long way toward an offer. Make certain you blend discussions like this in a subtle, sophisticated manner, and not awkwardly like you were in a classroom.

Interview Vocab

The client context is a special professional relationship that exists between a client and an employee of a firm. It is the dynamic that exists between the two where the client is receiving the product or service for which he or she pays money. It is a commercial relationship but entails aspects of trust, accountability, reward, and perceived value. In an interview, the candidate mentally treats the interviewer as if he or she were a client and the candidate acts as though he or she is already an employee.

The Client Context

By creating a client-oriented context during an interview, a job candidate can convince the interviewer that he or she has the potential to contribute to the firm's success. The interviewer has a glimpse of what the candidate might actually do as an employee. If done effectively, creating the client-oriented context starts to answer the million-dollar question: Can this candidate help the company or me make money? The best thing you can do is create in the interviewer's mind a sense that you are already on the team, and what the interviewer is witnessing in the interview is what the client will see once you are on the job. If the client likes what he or she sees, then a product sale may occur, and the company makes money (or is successful).

Most candidates don't know how to create this context. Read on and you will learn how.

To create the client context, try these tips:

➤ Listen very carefully to what the interviewer (client) says, then refer to his or her comments later.

➤ Ask questions of the interviewer (client) about the firm's (client's) needs and objectives.

➤ During the conversation, link what the interviewer (client) says to what the firm produces.

➤ Use concise summations to characterize key elements in the discussion, especially surrounding the firm's (client's) needs.

➤ Tie your experience to what the interviewer (client) reveals are the firm's (client's) goals and strategies, especially to problem areas.

➤ Prove your integrity and trustworthiness; establish an understanding in the interviewer's (client's) mind that he or she can trust you.

➤ Admit your mistakes and fix them.

➤ Be an advocate for your client.

➤ Concentrate on mutually shared interests.

The company needs talent that can help fulfill its mission of maximizing value to its shareholders or stakeholders through new client acquisition and business expansion. The basic issue is whether you convince that person across the table, the interviewer, to make the right purchase decision—to purchase your talent. A sale needs to be made, and creating a client-oriented context makes it easier for the interviewer to envision you as part of his or her team.

Interview Insights

Can you convince the interviewer that there is a match between what the company wants and what you have to offer? Do a skills inventory and match yourself skill-for-skill against the articulated needs of the company. Is the need appropriate to the product? You are the product for sale, and if you do not package yourself correctly, the odds of a sale go down. Part of the packaging is putting together a personal brand that says, "You need this and this, and my skills match those perfectly." What is your personal brand?

Ready, Set, Jump!

Let's see. You put a power résumé together, now what? Have you considered what your chances are for actually getting the job you want?

Each person possesses different strengths and weaknesses, and each job has unique characteristics and requirements. Do you have a realistic understanding of your chances of getting a job based upon an in-depth assessment of your skills and deficiencies?

Begin right now to think hard about that question from an earlier chapter: Just how fast is your jet? Or in other words, how high do you need to jump to get over what's in front of you? It's that obstacle between you and the job you want, call it the hurdle, and it represents the size of the challenge. The next chapter focuses on this critical concept.

Chapter Homework

1. Think about creating a client context. What kinds of questions could you ask that would leave this impression with an interviewer? What kinds of answers?

2. Take a sheet of paper and write one paragraph that is a statement to an interviewer about your brand.

CHAPTER 10

 # Preparation: Obstacles to Success

---

In This Chapter

➤ Components of the hurdle

➤ Offset strategies

➤ How high is high?

➤ The personal assessment grid and exercise

In this chapter you continue with step one of the dynamic interview training model: preparation. You will develop your personal employment rating by assessing your comparative strengths and weaknesses. You will also discover ways of dealing with shortcomings. (Reader warning: This is a long chapter, but an important one!)

You Are Unique

Your DNA is different from every other person's on the planet. As a consequence, you are special, a distinctive character brimming with potential—like all of us—you merely need to capture it.

However, there are traits, characteristics, and weaknesses you possess that will be obstacles to realizing your potential—hard to accept in this era of feel-good political correctness. To overcome any obstacles, you need to understand how high the hurdle is and why it reaches that height. Only then will you be able to determine if you can vault over it or not. The obstacle is sitting there staring you in the face—it stands between you and the job you want.

What do you do?

Key Topic

The competition is what stands between you and the job you want, and you will have to out-compete everyone else regardless of your deficiencies. Both your shortcomings and your strengths compose your personal brand, your public image, and your marketability. Did you describe your brand earlier? Read it again. If you were on a shelf, what would consumers (interviewers) see? Is it compelling enough for them to buy?

The Hurdle

No one is perfect. You can train for the perfect interview and have a terrific background, but you are human and have weaknesses. Some shortcomings you can do something about, others you cannot.

We each possess a unique personality, background, and set of talents. While you are different from every other candidate, you are also a member of an affinity group: workers looking for a job. As a result, some generalizations can be made. You are motivated, intelligent, energetic, ambitious, and interested in optimizing your employment opportunities—you bought this book, after all.

The differences that make you unique are those that also set you apart from other candidates, for good or for bad. Simply stated, your mission is to highlight the positive differences and offset the negative ones.

As you face the job market, you are confronted with a daunting challenge. Economic issues, job availability, your capacity to wait for the job you want, and your ability to secure an interview are all-important. But the biggest challenge is to present your case in the best possible way relative to others. To do that, let's consider that obstacle analogy again: the height of the hurdle (Figure 10A).

The hurdle is the sum of a set of factors that describe who you are and what you can do, relative to competition and a firm's expectations. Some of those factors are personal, while some are externalities caused by factors outside your control. As Figure 10A depicts, you compute the height of your personal hurdle, and then you devote yourself to overcoming it.

The "Hurdle" - represents the obstacle in your pathway to success

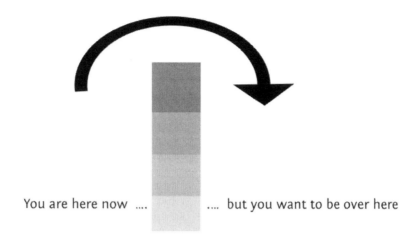

You are here now .... but you want to be over here

Figure 10A

Hurdle Factors

The hurdle is composed of a set of building blocks. Each block depicts one of four categories describing a person's competitiveness. Within each category (block), there are a number of factors that further describe a person's abilities, characteristics, and background. The cumulative impact of these factors portrays the difficulty faced by a job candidate. When combined, the four blocks build the height of the hurdle, the net impact of all the factors.

Interview Vocab

The interview hurdle is the graphic depiction of the difficulty of obtaining the job or position you want—the net sum of the positive and the negative attributes you possess.

Again, imagine you are on one side of the hurdle and the job that you want is on the other. You possess a set of experiences and affiliations that either enhances or limits your ability to achieve your objectives, and the sum of those constraints determines the height of the hurdle. A thorough assessment of these factors is necessary to create a personalized strategy to overcome weaknesses, thereby lowering the hurdle.

The factors are essential elements of an analytical tool, the personal assessment grid (PAG), you will use later in this chapter to assess your competitiveness rating. The rating will focus your efforts in addressing your shortcomings and enhancing your employment opportunities.

Diagnosis versus Prognosis

Your personal factors—both positive and negative—will be readily apparent to the experienced interviewer. You should analyze these ahead of the interview (diagnostic process) and then do something about them (proscriptive process).

Careful preparation to understand and ultimately conquer your personal hurdle will work to your advantage in obtaining an interview, performing expertly during the interview, and getting a high-quality offer after the interview.

Are there cases where someone has the family connections, charm, and wit to get a job in spite of their obstacles? Life happens. The best strategy is to work hard at overcoming your own impediments and influence those factors that are within your control.

The PAG Assessment

The PAG assessment and its offset strategies are the foundation blocks that undergird much of this program. Each negative grade has a counterpoint, an offsetting strategy that if diligently implemented can increase your employment outlook.

As you go through the PAG, think creatively. For instance, if technical skill is an issue and you want to work as an analyst in consulting, then drill down in your problem area and develop an improvement program such as spreadsheet work, mathematical modeling, and econometrics.

Interview Vocab

The Standard Industrial Classification (SIC) code is a four-digit code established in 1937 as part of the general classification system used by the U.S. government to describe industries. It is slowly being replaced by the North American Industry Classification System (NAICS) but is still used by some federal agencies such as the Securities and Exchange Commission.

If you plan on specializing in light manufacturing, investigate the SIC/NAICS codes for that industry and study automated assembly processes, foreign markets, and competitors' products. This research will serve you well in interviews with strategy-based consulting companies. Likewise, if your interest is in finance or brand management, then enroll in a course specializing in that area—if necessary via the Internet. For finance in particular, the New York Institute of Finance offers a variety of online courses that are readily accessible 24/7. Your ingenuity and time are the only things holding you back from offsetting weaknesses.

The hurdle is situational in that an impediment in one industry or company could be a positive in another. The PAG is dynamic and should be completed multiple times as your strategies begin to take hold.

So How High is Your Hurdle?

Figure 10B depicts the four categories (blocks) of employment-based attributes. They are:

> ➤ Personal

> ➤ Academic/knowledge

> ➤ Competitive

> ➤ Professional

Each category has its own factors within it. In all, the four categories have sixteen factors. The personal category is particularly interesting and has subcomponents describing various personality traits.

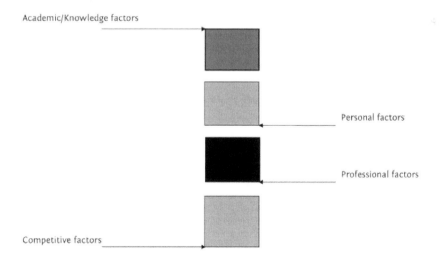

Figure 10B

Bias, Prejudice, and Stereotypes

Let's be realistic. Bias, prejudice, and stereotyping exist in the minds of some interviewers. For instance, some may think that a woman shouldn't be on a factory floor, or they may believe that a person with a disability can't do a particular job. Some may have latent racial biases or they may believe people over forty-five are slowing down. Opinions like these are wrong, but they still might increase the height of your hurdle if an interviewer succumbs to them.

It is often prudent to preempt such opinions and deal with them up front, either directly or indirectly, as it is often unwise to let them simmer and sway an interviewer's judgment.

For example, if you're an older candidate, you may want to emphasize early in the discussion that you run marathons, or are active in some other way, to destroy the idea that older candidates can't keep up. But avoid saying something like, "I trust my age will not impede my chances of getting this job, right?" Rather try something like, "I recall working on a project last year dealing with the same issue you just described. I traveled extensively, worked weekends, holidays, whatever it took. I'm glad I work out six days a week!"

Develop discussion points around objections based on bias and those that can impede the extension of an offer. Don't be confrontational, though; be pleasant and factual. Again, you can only influence those factors that are in your control and mitigate the impact of those that aren't.

The PAG is not a discrimination assessment tool; it does not attempt to list every source of bias, prejudice, or stereotyping. As you conduct the exercise, if you feel there are other factors crucial to your specific employment chances, you should substitute freely. For instance, if gender factors are not applicable but you believe race, national origin, or orientation might be, then you should rate those in place of gender.

A Final Note on the Subject

The firm may be perfectly fine and have serious programs to confront such issues, but the individual interviewer may harbor the bias. You can confront it directly if you really want to work at that firm, or you can move on to a different firm. What often makes it difficult is that you may not be able to spot the bias. Use the PAG and subsequent tools to help you think through the issues.

Interview Vocab

Bias is a mental leaning or persuasion.

Stereotype is a fixed or conventional notion or conception, as of a person, group, or idea, held by a number of people allowing for no individuality.

Prejudice is suspicion, intolerance, or irrational hatred of other races, creeds, gender, regions, etc.

Offset Strategies and Action Plans

This is where you begin to fight back, to knock down the hurdle. After you assess each of the sixteen factors, you must develop an action plan to do something about any deficiencies you uncover. These countervailing, offsetting strategies are what make you more competitive, and the fact that you develop them can be used during your interview to showcase your tenacity and seriousness. Remember: Progress on the action plans is what eventually lowers the height of your hurdle.

Start today or as early as possible to address the issues. What possible strategy could you develop to mitigate age or gender bias? Perhaps you could show that being a woman actually provides key advantages when dealing with certain client segments that prefer dealing with women. Or you could show that age can be a definite advantage by telling a story about how leadership, experience, and maturity helped you solve a problem more rapidly than less experienced people.

Interview Insights

An interviewer once asked, "This job will require intense motivation and stamina. Are you up to the task?" The candidate knew that it was a reference to his age and ability to compete with younger managers. He responded that his hobbies, power lifting, martial arts, and tactical shooting kept him sharp. The interviewer got the picture, and the candidate got the offer.

Interview Insights

A man looking for a career change was concerned about his lack of private sector work experience. So he developed a countervailing strategy to moonlight at a venture capital company. He asked what bottlenecks they were experiencing—it was boom time in the 1980s. They were flooded with solicitations for funding new business opportunities. So he became their deal screener, for free. During the experience, he developed a software program with embedded deal criteria to support a screening tool to sift through the deluge. They got some great deals, and he got terrific, relevant experience. Now, that's a good offset strategy example.

How Do You Create a Countervailing Strategy?

This is an open-ended question because circumstances vary so widely with candidates. In general, look at an area that builds the height of the hurdle and develop a program to mitigate its effects. Usually it involves additional training, reading, volunteering, and the like. It may be that you need to develop a different mental perspective. Perhaps you find that you are short on people skills. You must force yourself into situations where you deal with people—that is, unless the job doesn't require you to interact with people (like working on the North Pole!).

Many motivated individuals have found that such personal attribute-based exercises give them a chance to take stock of where they are and if their skills remain relevant or not. Periodic assessments from peers throughout your life will help you stay up with the times and make you all the more marketable in your career.

The PAG Exercise

The Smart Guide personal assessment grid (PAG) is a diagnosis of the personal and environmental factors relating to your specific situation as you prepare to launch a job-seeking campaign. As you know, there are sixteen areas, or factors, you should evaluate. Some of the factors listed in the PAG are within your power to control; others have already happened and are part of your history.

The fifth factor contains a major section on character traits. This is important because your motivation, discipline, and potential must be in synchronization with the requirements of the job, or neither you nor your employer will be satisfied.

This exercise will provide fuel for your story and will fold directly into your discussion material at the interview. Retain this grid and build it out over the ensuing weeks as you simultaneously develop your action plan. To ensure an honest evaluation, enlist the aid of your trusted agents to help you fill out the grid.

The Personal Assessment Exercise Scoring System

Instructions: Assess your talents against a high standard of performance. The numbers and color codes will help you determine needed areas of enhancement. The higher your score, the higher your hurdle and the more you will have to do to enhance your chances.

Within each factor you have strengths and weaknesses. Evaluate your relative strength in that factor by balancing weaknesses against strengths. For example, under leadership, you may have never been in substantial leadership positions, yet you always seem to be chosen as a leader in discussion and work groups or in community organizations. Balance out the weaknesses and strengths and put down a score that reflects your potential, neither too high nor too low. The stronger you are in an area, the lower the score should be. For example, a 1 or 2 in an area would be very strong; an 8 or 9 would be very weak, representing a higher hurdle for you.

What the Scores Mean

Guidelines to the scoring system are as follows:

➤ Scores of 1–3: Very positive. For example, your relevant experience is excellent with no obvious shortcomings identified by trusted agents or your own assessment. You are a self-starter, take initiative, and have excellent communication skills. You are adaptive and obviously have a command of the technical aspects of the job. You present a professional image to clients.

➤ Scores of 4–6: Generally average to positive. For example, your analytical ability has been acknowledged as being good in previous jobs or in school. You can achieve a first-rate level of quality output or performance with little or no supervision, but you have certain limitations, which constrain the amount or quality of your work. You have the ability to work with others on projects. You would not be selected for advanced training or as a leader when others are available. You may have reached your ceiling. Areas of improvement are apparent but mostly can be overcome through diligence or assistance. Peers notice weak areas. Others may have to do tasks that otherwise might be assigned to you, if you had the necessary skills. Career progression could be or is hampered. Competitive pressures make the weakness an issue at times, but you win some and lose some.

➤ Scores of 7–10: Fair to poor. For example, your teamwork skills have never been developed or demonstrated. You prefer to work alone and generally achieve your results without interacting with others. You have little to no experience in the activity, possess a very limited capability to achieve unsupervised results, and may have been counseled or admonished about performance or lack of leadership in this area. Core skills are suspect. You need additional training. You have some deficiencies in advanced competencies and in core skills in some areas. Jobs requiring a factor where you rated 7–10 perhaps should be reconsidered. Your personality traits are disruptive at times and cause friction.

Color Grade Matrix

In order to provide a visual cue, please fill in each factor with the color assigned to that score.

➤ 1–3 : Green

➤ 4–6: Yellow

➤ 7–10: Red

If you are conducting a realistic exercise, your grid should have multiple colors. If your factor score is rated a green, then this may be a quality to emphasize in your interview.

Be certain to build this into your story with examples of your performance or experience. If your factor score is rated a yellow, then before you discuss this issue you will need to enhance your ability or your explanation. If your score is rated a red, then you have serious issues to offset. This is a vulnerable spot that an experienced interviewer will use against you. You will need to address this thoroughly before the interview.

For example, a fifty-year-old may downgrade her rank on the age scale because in her industry anyone over fifty is considered to be too old. However, since she is applying for a senior management position, solid experience and a superb work history is an asset. Therefore, balancing the two aspects, she might rate herself a score of 6 and a code yellow. That's about right. She may want to explain her relevant work and current work habits to overcome worries about her willingness to work hard. She may need to refresh her knowledge about recent developments in her field to indicate growth. She should be able to attain a green in short order.

Personal Assessment Grid: The Factors

The following factors cover many of the attributes interviewers and firms assess when looking at candidates. No doubt there are others you can think of. Do not include other factors that skew the grading in your favor! The categories are broad enough that you most likely can include aspects of other attributes within them.

Age

Are you over thirty-five or under twenty-five? If the job requires stamina and exertion and you are older than thirty-five, then it would be a negative unless you can show you are extremely motivated and a fitness buff. For an offsetting strategy, start a serious fitness program if medically cleared. If you're under twenty-five, show that your youth is offset by tenacity and motivation.

Numerical Score	Color Score	Offset Strategy

Gender

Careers in some industries are notoriously tough for women to break into; some are tough for men. This is improving, but gender still may be a negative unless your specialty is in great demand, your experience is in that area, or you have a niche strategy pursuing certain client segments that prefer one gender to the other. Have a serious answer to show why the fact that you are male should not be an issue if you want to join a firm run for and by women. If gender is not an applicable issue, substitute another issue you have that might cause an impediment.

Numerical Score	Color Score	Offset Strategy

Personal Traits

The numbered scale below represents a range of personal characteristics that define your public persona. Your answers will largely determine the impressions an interviewer will have of you during your interview—and those impressions are formed very quickly. The interview is an environment where people exhibit their knowledge, ignorance, bias, accomplishments, hubris, charity, judgment, communicative skills, and other positive and negative factors. Egos can clash and personality conflicts occur. Yes, even in a thirty-minute interview.

With help from your trusted agents, rate where you are on the sliding spectrums below. Being on one end or another of the scale, increases the odds that you will run afoul with the interviewer (a person who may have his or her own hang-ups).

The best place to be is near the center of the spectrum, a 1 or a 2. But most of us tend to crowd toward the sidelines. The center spots point to well-balanced attitudes and behaviors not characterized by extremes and those to which you should aspire. Only you will know the outcome so be honest with yourself. If you are on the sidelines, then you need to develop an offset strategy to move toward the center.

Ego

Insecure 10—1 Self-Assured 1—10 Arrogant

Social Skills

Awkward 10—1 Comfortable 1—10 Fawning

Appearance/Courtesies

Sloppy/Rude 10—1 Tasteful/Polite 1—10 Flashy/Stiff

Presence

Dull 10—1 Gravitas 1—10 Haughty

Knowledge

Lightweight 10—1 Learned 1—10 Preachy

Life Experiences

Isolated 10—1 Mature 1—10 Gadabout

Professional Focus

Distracted 10—1 Centered 1—10 Consumed

Cultural Sophistication

Provincial 10—1 Well Rounded 1—10 Elitist

Average all your scores from the spectrum and assign one grade for the personal traits factor. We will count it twice at the end.

Here is a breakdown of the traits:

➤ Social Skills/Ego: At a job fair or reception, do you go to the VIP in the center of the room, or do you head to the bar and wait for others to come to you? Do you struggle with conversing with strangers? Can you make cold calls? Do you have a temper? Would people consider you aloof and arrogant? What are your peer-to-peer assessment ratings in your last firm? Are you basically introverted or extroverted? Are you hard to work with? You want to be self-assured: confident but not cocky.

➤ Appearance/Courtesies: Do you dress like the company's executives? How do you look in a suit? What is your best color combo? Do you have a dress consultant? Are you fit? Are you well-groomed? Do you have good table manners? Are you deferential to senior members? Do you return correspondence or phone calls in a timely fashion? Were you ever chosen as spokesperson? Why not?

➤ Cultural/Professional: Are you comfortable with other cultures and well traveled, or are you divisive, condescending, or naïve about the world? Are you well rounded with a balanced life, or are you so consumed by work that you have little to add to other conversations with clients?

➤ Presence/Knowledge: Do you have stature and are you noticed when you come into a meeting or a conversation? Do people seek your opinion on a range of topics? Do you have depth, or, as some would say, lots of grey matter? Are you learned in the sense that you can speak about the physical world, political issues, history, and other topics that make you interesting?

➤ Life experiences: Are you well traveled, well read, broadly educated or do you have a pedestrian, limited scope of experience without a global perspective?

If your average is close to the middle, then overall your personality is a strength. If you tend to the extremes, you have more work to do to offset weaker areas. Give yourself a green (3) if you are close to the middle. Assess a red (8) if you are near an extreme on either side. Grade a yellow (5) if you are in between. Allow your trusted agent to grade you without fear that you will retaliate! Note: Score this factor twice to show its importance.

Numerical Score	Color Score	Offset Strategy

Teamwork

Have you worked as a valued team member within the last three years? How would your peers rate you as a colleague? Were you adaptive or did you need rigid organizational guidelines? In your last team-based project, did your team develop a plausible solution? On the whole, would you say you are a person most reasonable people would want on their team, or are you considered tough to work with and difficult? Did anyone on your last team think you were a troublemaker or a know-it-all?

Numerical Score	Color Score	Offset Strategy

Leadership

What is the largest organization or group for which you had direct authority and responsibility? Can you describe your leadership style? Do people naturally follow you wherever you take them? Were you elected or selected for leadership in your last position of authority or did you assume the role? How have you performed under crisis or periods of prolonged stress for the firm, you, or your team? Do people consider you autocratic, participative, democratic, or consensual in style?

Numerical Score	Color Score	Offset Strategy

School or Company Reputation

Is your school or company not in the Top 10 of the *USNWR* or *Business Week* surveys, or *Fortune*'s list of admired companies, or similar lists from other major publications? Give yourself a downgrade. Is your school an industry powerhouse? Then give yourself an upgrade. How many firms in your industry come to campus? What are the starting salaries relative to the Top 10? How does your company rank in employee satisfaction surveys or other metrics such as sales, return on equity versus industry benchmarks and lead competitors.

Numerical Score	Color Score	Offset Strategy

Technical Skills

Are you an engineer or is your field in heavy math, science, or IT? Do you work for a tech company in a tech capacity? How good is your Excel ability or your portfolio? Do you have skills or specific knowledge relevant to your industry of choice? Did you make As in your chosen courses relevant to the industry? If not, then a downgrade. How did you do in corporate finance, or operations management, or accounting (or a similar benchmark course in your program)?

Numerical Score	Color Score	Offset Strategy

Analytical Abilities

How much case study work do you have? Have you worked for a consulting company or do you go to a school where casework is the standard? Can you handle an impromptu logic question, commit to practice the case method, or fine-tune your quantitative skills? Try some puzzles that hone your logic or math skills.

Numerical Score	Color Score	Offset Strategy

Communication Skills

Do you have written and oral evidence of your ability to present ideas, articulate positions, convince unbelievers, summarize key concepts? Do you have prior experience in dealing with the public, management, constituent groups, advocates, or internal groups? How did your ability cause positive change and impact a group or company? If you are weak in this area, then write letters, memos, and notes to improve. Try speaking to volunteer groups. Join a debate club or teach a course. Do anything to get in front of people and communicate.

Numerical Score	Color Score	Offset Strategy

Relevant Experience

Do you have unique, specific company or industry experience? It has already happened or not, so not much you can do except show how your history may translate to the new level of responsibility represented by your degree. If changing careers, it is especially critical to show how sales skills, age, network, and other factors can easily translate to the new industry or company. This must be a major part of your story. If the job requires teamwork or leadership, then highlight areas where you stand out; try to obtain some experience through volunteer work, internships, or part-time moonlighting. Do you have soft versus hard skills issues? If so, then bolster the weak areas through self-study, professional certifications, online coursework, etc.

Numerical Score	Color Score	Offset Strategy

Social and Business Network

Can you name five key executives at a major target company? Can you call five contacts that are in the business world and ask for opinions? Do you have anyone in your family who is connected? Do you belong to professional or social organizations that could offer interview possibilities? Can you call five prospective clients? Have you leveraged your network for business purposes; have you been leveraged yourself?

Numerical Score	Color Score	Offset Strategy

Internships or Expert Status

If you are in school, consider the quality of your internships. If you are not in school, then rate the number and quality of your experience with professional publications or research; and include active membership in relevant associations, trade groups, or conferences.

Students, did you get an internship? If not, then give yourself a 9 or 10. If you got one, how did you do? Did you get a tentative offer of interest? If not, then give yourself a middle grade; you have some work to do. What shortcomings were noticed? Did you discover what areas you really like? How would you rate the quality of the firm for which you worked? Is it nationally recognized?

Professionals, how widely accepted were your publications? Are you a noted expert? Are you asked to speak at conferences? Are you asked to consult on specific projects in your industry? Are you asked to chair task forces? Are you called to testify as an expert witness? Were you elected to a professional position of leadership?

Numerical Score	Color Score	Offset Strategy

Sales Skills

Have you worked in a sales capacity before? If not, did you sell your ideas within the organization effectively? Were you recognized as a salesmanship award nominee? Have you been called upon to advocate a particular position to higher-level management or clients, and did you win the day? Can you describe your last product to the uninformed so they conclude that you have a quality offering? Do you utilize a process to sell a product?

Numerical Score	Color Score	Offset Strategy

Overall Strength of Résumé

Can you plausibly defend each item on your résumé? Is every point on your résumé relevant to the particular job you want? You should be able to connect each point with some aspect of the job position you want. For example, if you list language proficiency, then point out that it shows your affinity with other cultures, and that you used your overseas experiences to broaden your ability to understand other economies and their people. Have you padded your résumé or is your experience real? Is your résumé full of industry-specific jargon or have you translated it for the reader?

Numerical Score	Color Score	Offset Strategy

Rivals: A Key Element

Do you know the level of competition? Is the firm a global, first-rate firm? How many people is it interviewing? Do you expect the competition to be fierce, and for how many spots are they hiring?

Students, is your school a primary or secondary visit for the firm? If the firm usually visits only elite campuses, then you should err toward the negative range if you are from a school outside of the Top 10. If you are from the West Coast/East Coast Top 10, then you must consider the stiff competition within your own school. If you are at the top of your class, from a quality school with ample exposure, then this should be a strength for you.

Nonstudents, how many candidates is the firm seeing? Is the job broadly advertised or is it advertised only through elite search firms? Are you trying to enter a new career field? Note: Score this factor twice to show its importance.

Numerical Score	Color Score	Offset Strategy

Other Factors

Are there other factors you should apply to this evaluation? Have you sold a business, do you have overseas experience, have you been involved in professional athletics, do you have foreign language capability?

Numerical Score	Color Score	Offset Strategy

It's the Net that Counts

To summarize, in each category you may assess that you have strength in one area of that factor, and you may also have a weakness in another aspect. It is the net score that is important. For instance, in school reputation you may believe your school has an outstanding reputation in a particular field or region but may not be ranked particularly high in the customary surveys nationally. You can give it a high grade for the one and a low grade for its lack of national prominence. One more example: under Factor 8, analytical abilities, an engineer may assume that he or she is first rate, the assumption being that analytical ability means technical knowledge and judgment. On balance, however, because the case confronting him or her pivots upon a keen insight into human factors, that same engineer may be blind to the people-related questions involved. This is what situational grading means.

Keep in mind that the job you are pursuing determines whether a particular factor is critical or not. Therefore, you should review this scorecard for each job or firm you pursue.

To conclude the exercise, net the strengths and the weaknesses for each factor and arrive at your factor scores. Recall that if the net is a 1–3, then assign it to green. If the net is 4–6, then assign it to yellow. Finally, if the net is 7 or more, then assign it to red.

Your Total Score

For the numerical scores, start by adding your factor scores (there should be eighteen) to get your total numerical score, which will be less than 180. If after adding up your net scores, your total is higher than 126 (an average of greater than 7 per factor), then you are generally in the yellow to red zone and have serious issues to work on. If you fall between 72 and 125, then your average score is greater than 4 and less than 7 per question, and you need to start an enhancement program soon. If you fall within 36 and 72, that's trending green and you should feel that you are very competitive but might work in a few specific areas. Scores of less than 54 may merit a second self-assessment to verify the grade.

The next step is to give the assessment tool to a few trusted friends who will tell you the truth. They should use the PAG tool to assess you, and then you can compare your numbers with their total. Remember, like golf scores, a low score is better and means a lower hurdle to get over.

The good news is that you can start doing something about overcoming your weaker areas, but you have to start immediately.

Use the grid below to guide your own self-assessment on color. You could, for instance, have sixteen green scores yielding as little as 16 points (an unbelievable average of 1 per factor), and only two red scores yielding 14 points, for a total of 30 points—green. But, if the two red scores are in particularly important areas for the job in question, you should say you are a red overall.

Number of Green Factors	Number of Red Factors	Number of Yellow Factors	Assign Overall Color
≥11	≤2	5 or less	Green
≥11	>2	4 or less	Red
<11	≤2	6 or less	Yellow
<11	>2	5 or less	Red

If you have less than 60 percent green (11 of 18 factors), then you may not be as competitive for the higher end firms as you thought. You should concentrate on the yellows and reds very seriously over your preparation period. If you have over 60 percent green, then absent any serious red issues, you are a green overall—but you still should start work immediately in developing your integrated story.

Your overall color code is _____

Personal Assessment Summary

Category/Factor	Score #	Color
Personal		
1. Age		
2. Gender		
3a. Personal traits		
3b. Personal traits		
4. Teamwork		
5. Leadership		
Academic/Knowledge		
6. Technical Skills/Competency		
7. Analytical Abilities		
8. Communications Skills		

Category/Factor	Score #	Color
Professional		
9. Relevant Experience		
10. Social and Business Network		
11. Internships		
12. Sales Skills		
Competitive		
13. Strength of Résumé		
14a. Rivals		
14b. Rivals		
15. Other Factors		

Number Score _____ Color Score _____

A Complementary Explanation of PAG

In the investment banking business, analysts use a tool to analyze a firm's positioning through a lens called a strength, weakness, opportunity, and threat (SWOT) analysis. The strength and weakness sections are very similar to what you went through in the PAG. The opportunity and threat analysis offers additional perspective, however, by looking at skills versus a specific job posting.

SWOT intensifies the comparison of strengths over weaknesses, and in the end you should consider any opportunity within a decision framework that addresses risks and opportunity costs.

Interview Vocab

Opportunity cost is the value of a choice that is foregone by choosing one alternative's benefits over another. Opportunity cost is sometimes described as the cost of the next-best choice foregone by picking the best option amongst a field of mutually exclusive alternatives. Opportunity cost is a key concept in the study of economics—and in interviewing.

Using SWOT with PAG - that's a mouthful

Keep your PAG analysis and let's begin to look at the job opportunity (O) in a different way. First, write out the basic job functions related to the position, and look at it from a skills-based approach. Then in a parallel column, list your own skill set. Start a matching exercise where you pose the job functions as questions. For example, a job function may be one where travel and sales skills are important. Try to match your skill set with that characteristic, such as relating well to people and being a great listener.

A second skill may be that you are adaptable in new situations and cultures. That may be a very good match with the travel requirement. If, on the other hand, you list as a skill that you are active in a local charitable network and that you are in with the local entrepreneurial crowd, that experience may not be as relevant to someone who needs to rely upon extended markets in order to be successful.

Interview Vocab

Stretch skill is a skill that exceeds the norm for a person of a particular experience level or position, for instance, an administrative assistant who also can fill in for a salesperson if necessary. People are usually cross-trained in a variety of skills as part of a contingency plan—a definite interview enhancer.

The opportunity should support your skill set and your stretch skill set, and your entire complement of skills should support the opportunity. That means that if your current skills do not neatly align with those required for the new position, then the odds of success go drastically down. Volunteer for cross-training opportunities in your current job whenever possible. Look at the matching example on the next page.

Skills Set versus Job Requirements

Many people do not conduct a realistic skills inventory test. By matching your PAG factors with the opportunity, you will get much closer to developing a point of discussion in your interview. You will show the interviewer that you really know your stuff by connecting an analytical tool to the actual requirements of the job you are seeking.

Remember in grade school where you had matching tests? Try to do the same with your job preparation. Match a list of your skills to those required by the job you are seeking.

This drills down to the skill level and gives a detailed look at areas where you are very competitive and those where you may not be. You should construct a matching exercise like the one below. Use the same PAG factors from before, but match them as best you can against the job requirements.

Sample Skills Set

> ➤ Personality: Great interpersonal skills; outgoing; good listener; empathetic; controlled temper and ego

> ➤ Technical Skills: So-so numbers oriented; basic computer skills; little logistics

> ➤ Sales Skills: Salesmanship awards; commission based; adequate closer

> ➤ Leadership: Numerous project leads; elected head of troubleshooting team; good follower

> ➤ Teamwork: Broad assignments; cross-border projects; firm's solutions fix-it team

> ➤ Communication Skills: Toastmasters; road shows; have copies of memos

> ➤ Experience: Internship in field; sales process similar; varied; international

> ➤ Network: Member/professional organizations; head of local charity group

> ➤ Motivation: Worked through MBA; graduate assistant; eleven informational interviews

> ➤ Academic Knowledge: Good coursework; broad based; mix of soft and hard

> ➤ Analytics: Case oriented; analyst experience; good research skills

> ➤ Gender: Male—should be N/A for this job

> ➤ Age: Went back to school as older student; could work against; seniority issues at forty

Job Opportunity: Sample Requirements List

> ➤ Effective communication and written proposal/authorship and advocacy skills

> ➤ Head of critical team supporting leaders of major revenue-producing groups

> ➤ Able to persuade internal groups of positions

> ➤ Must negotiate union contracts

> ➤ Desire to succeed and progress in tough internal, external environment

> ➤ Compensation commensurate with ability to help sales staff grow revenue

> ➤ Some international and domestic travel

> ➤ Reports directly to senior staff including Chief Financial Officer

➤ Public relations savvy

➤ Situational analysis of markets and technical knowledge of products is critical

➤ Self-starter with impeccable integrity

Now, cross-match your skills to each of the job requirements. Try to match as many as you can; in other words, link the firm's position description and task requirements (often listed in a search announcement) with a required skill set composed of your best factors. In the example above, people skills (listening, empathy, etc.) and communications skills (public speaking, etc.) connect nicely to negotiating union contracts (one assumes that is difficult). This is an effective way to showcase your suitability. How would you rate this person's chances?

Industry Choice

The choice of industry and job may impact whether a factor is a strength or a weakness. There in all likelihood will be strengths and weaknesses within each factor. For example, in the aerospace and defense industry you may be seeking a job as a cost analyst on a new aircraft project. Is the fact that you are a CPA a relative strength or not? It definitely shows specialty knowledge, and probably professional experience. But by itself, is it relevant to the job you are seeking? The answer may depend upon whether your experience was narrowly defined such as in oil and gas accounting. It may be a detriment unless you can show a relationship between common analytical skills and knowledge of depreciation methods in manufacturing systems versus depletion methods. Likewise, if you are looking for a consultant job but your experience has been in teaching, then you should assign your experience as a weak point unless you can tie your explanatory and communication skills to the case method and analytical frameworks used by consulting firms.

The Threat

This portion of SWOT is pointed directly at the competition. If possible, you should try to get a sense of the type of individuals the firm plans to interview. You obviously should try to discuss this with an insider at the firm who may have been hired in a similar position. If you are a student, your placement office may be able to help. If all else fails, ask the HR coordinator organizing the interviews. You might say something like the following: "I am very interested in this position and want to put my best foot forward. I believe I have a very competitive résumé, but would you mind giving me a general picture of the type of individuals, and their schools, who are also interviewing for this position?"

If you are a student, find out which other schools the firm is visiting, and analyze the particular features of that school's curriculum. Determine what advantages you might have. Don't mention any competitor by name, but you can highlight the features of your program over elements of the competition's school.

Review the list of attributes that make you less desirable. Perhaps it could be that your compensation requirements are high, or you feel that the prospective firm may want you to move to a location you find unattractive. Build a list of showstoppers and a list of negatives that pose a significant impediment to an offer. This list should be rolled into your story and used to build a better negotiation position later. Offset strategies are all about turning weaknesses into strengths. Say that out loud—it's that important!

What about a Red Hurdle?

The PAG assessment shows where your strengths and weaknesses are based upon your history. The SWOT analysis is forward thinking by matching your PAG to the opportunity and expected threats.

The height of your hurdle shows an initial assessment of your challenge. It should change over time and you should see your scores improve. At the start, and as a general rule, if you are in the green, then feel pretty good about where you are at. Does that mean you have the job in the bag? No, of course not. It means if you diligently apply yourself to the process, you ought to do well.

If you are like most of us and your PAG shows that you have a yellow hurdle in front of you, then you have work to do in the preparation and practice phases that follow in this book.

If you have a red hurdle, then seriously consider reevaluating whether or not the job you desire is the right one for you. You might reconsider your work and life choices—it is better to admit that now than waste time and resources on a fruitless pursuit of a dream that most likely will not happen. The dream may not be impossible to achieve, but a red hurdle indicates there are serious deficiencies in the topical areas of the PAG and/or a mismatch in SWOT between skills and job requirements. Those areas were selected to help determine whether you are competitive or not. Better to be a green in another field than an overmatched red.

Chapter Homework

1. Begin the Smart Guide personal assessment grid (PAG) exercise. Save your answers.

2. Develop an implementation plan for PAG offset strategies to include specific activities and projected dates. Update as necessary in the coming weeks.

Quotable Quotes

"In this world man must either be anvil or hammer."

Henry Wadsworth Longfellow

CHAPTER 11

Preparation: Fighting the Competition

In This Chapter

➤ There's a long line of people

➤ It's combat out there!

➤ How good are they?

➤ Amazon woman

➤ Good on paper, but…

In this chapter you will appraise the competition. What are you actually up against? Remember the question, How fast is your jet? Well, how fast is theirs? Just how good are the other people standing in line with you?

The Other Team

The truth is that the external environment has a major impact upon your ability to get a new job. Factors such as inflation, unemployment rates, interest rates, government intervention, and global competition are major influencers upon your search. Even in good times it can be tough to get the job you want. But someone is going to get hired, and that person is your major threat. So what will you face on the battlefield?

Especially in times of economic distress, jobs can be hard to come by. Companies put hiring freezes in place or can afford to be more selective, choosing from a larger pool of applicants. Congress has to put its nose into your affairs, of course. Uncertainties in U.S. monetary and fiscal policies, including its tax code, cause many businesses to institute layoffs, delay hiring, and/or reduce benefits. As a result, many small businesses are reluctant to hire as they anticipate increases in tax liabilities to cover the nation's rising debt.

As unemployment rates increase, the competition for available jobs also increases. Companies lay off good people, and those people look for jobs. In late 2010 the unemployment rate was a persistent 9.8 percent. In that environment good jobs do not arrive by accident—you have to go to them.

Have you ever been in a meeting with someone who thought he was the smartest person on the planet? Insufferable, right? Some of those people in line will try to get the job by reminding the interviewer repeatedly how good they are. But everyone is not a Michael Jordan or a Tom Brady, although some come very close. Just remember that you can control only those factors that are under your influence—like turning weaknesses into strengths.

Interview Insights

A young man, call him Ivan, once interviewed in New York for an important position as a banking associate. He entered the room, dressed very stylishly (actually more on the far right of the spectrum), and then immediately slumped into the interview chair. Over the course of the ensuing thirty minutes, he mentioned at least ten or twelve times how it would be a mistake not to hire him. His temperament reeked of entitlement, and he was, in a word, insufferable. If you had walked into the room as the next candidate and showed the slightest bit of humility, you would already be way ahead. Just remember Mama once said, "There's always someone bigger, smarter, stronger. Be a little humble." Good advice.

Is It Really a Numbers Game?

To some degree the interview process really is a numbers game. The more interviews you have, the greater the likelihood that you will eventually get an offer. However, with a higher than normal unemployment rate, an increasing number of graduates from colleges and technical schools, and a large number of people changing career fields, the odds may appear to be stacked against you. But don't despair.

Mr. L told of a recent advertisement announcing an open audition in New York for a coveted position in the chorus of a popular show. Arriving at the appointed hour, he expected hundreds of aspirants. He was pleasantly surprised to see only about fifty people waiting in line. The point is that although advertised to a broad audience of candidates, only a few showed up. Many others thought the odds too daunting and didn't bother to get out of bed at 7 am on a Saturday to compete.

At first glance, the number of people looking for jobs may seem daunting. And then you hear about the constant stream of new entrants to the job market from campuses around the country. In fact, enrollment in colleges and universities is on the upswing. That means that every year there are a host of new entrants into the labor force.

When economists talk about the employment reports, they mean the number of new jobs the economy must generate in order to accommodate these new entrants—entrants who may be standing in line for the job you want.

Not all of those folks in the employment line are ten feet tall and braniacs—many are mediocre at best. And even more perform poorly in front of an interviewer. In fact, in my experience many will not be as competitive against people who train for interviews by engaging in a program such as this.

Employment and the College Graduate

If you are a college student, you are no doubt aware of the variances in program quality offered by universities. Floods of people are getting degrees, many from less-than-sterling programs. Increase that by the number of international students looking to relocate to the United States, and you have a large pool of potential competitors for that job you want so badly. Each year there are approximately 150,000 students engaged in the process of finding a job to pay off exorbitant B school loans.

Having a quality degree will help in your job search. But you still need to assess the landscape to determine what edge you might have—that little, or big, something that will push you over the top and beat out the competition for that job. Even though bloated, the numbers show there are a lot of fresh new entrants into the labor force—and they are not all from degree mills.

The data below tells the story of the access people now have to advanced education. A similar phenomenon is occurring in community college and trade and technical school attendance. All graduates will not immediately hit the labor market, but enrollment is increasing as evidenced in the table below.

The following table shows total real and estimated fall enrollment (in thousands) in degree-granting institutions from 1970 through 2019 (Table prepared October 2010).

Total fall enrollment in degree-granting institutions 1970-2019

Year	# of students
1970	8,581
1980	12,097

Year	# of students
1990	13,819
2000	15,312
2001	15,928
2002	16,612
2003	16,911
2004	17,272
2005	17,487
2006	17,759
2007	18,248
2008	19,103
2009	20,428
2010	20,550 Projected
2014	21,669 Projected
2019	23,448 Projected

Source: US Dept. of Labor, National Center for Education Statistics. NCES website, Fast Facts, 2011.

The Data for New College Graduates

According to the National Center for Education Statistics (NCES), "from 1998–99 to 2008–09, the number of bachelor's degrees awarded by public institutions increased by 29 percent (from 790,300 to 1,020,400 degrees), the number awarded by private not-for-profit institutions increased by 26 percent (from 393,700 to 496,300 degrees), and the number awarded by private for-profit institutions more than quadrupled (from 16,300 to 84,700 degrees). Despite the large gains made by private for-profit institutions, they awarded 5 percent of all bachelor's degrees conferred in 2008–09, while public institutions awarded 64 percent and private not-for-profit institutions awarded 31 percent of all bachelor's degrees."

The Data for Graduate Degree Holders

The NCES data also shows large increases in the number of master's degrees awarded and for trade and technical colleges. The point is that more and more people are obtaining advanced education and training.

The Baby Boomers

Baby boomers are the sons and daughters of World War II's generation. There were actually 76 million births in the United States from 1946 to 1964, the nineteen years usually called the baby boom years. According to the U.S. Census Bureau, as of 2000 there were roughly 80 million people in the United States between forty-five and sixty-four years of age. Any way you cut it, that's a lot of folks. And some unknown percentage of those still work—out of necessity. That means many people in that age group are also looking for work, and they have special needs.

We already covered the fact that an employer can't discriminate based upon age—but some still do. So what can a fifty-six-year-old AARP member and red-blooded worker do to combat unfair interviewer behavior? Most of the techniques in this book apply to you if you are in this age group. In addition, try these interview enhancers for the older worker:

➤ Compose a personal story around age as a positive attribute.

➤ Be fit and look like it (dress appropriate to your age, but take care to be stylish, well groomed, and able to fit in).

➤ Use current workforce vernacular (read *Harvard Business Review,* for example).

➤ Be computer savvy (use computer lingo, like *cloud computing*).

➤ Translate any question into an answer with energy and creativity.

➤ Don't relive the past—think about and articulate solutions for the future.

➤ Don't be apologetic, be enthusiastic.

➤ Try government jobs—government employers are sticklers for Equal Employment Opportunity Commission EEOC rules and regulations.

➤ Start a home business—consulting can be a lucrative ticket.

➤ Don't be defensive; you have a lot to offer.

➤ Be willing to start over.

➤ Take distance learning courses or residence programs to learn new skills.

Preinterview Competitor Intelligence

Having preinterview intelligence of competitors vying for your desired job is highly desirable. That is not easy to do, as most firms will not give you any information. But there are ways to gain a hint or two from various sources, and like building a mosaic, you can piece the information together to get a better understanding of the picture. Talk to an HR person, an assistant, a former employee, a current employee, a friendly headhunter, someone at a competitor's firm, or look online for a job posting. Try a social networking site and ask, anonymously, if someone knows someone at the firm, befriend that person, and then ask if he or she has heard of the job search and who is being interviewed. Exercise caution about revealing true personal information.

Each little bit of information you gather will give you better insight as to who you are up against.

If you understand the competition, you can exploit your strengths and discuss key areas where you know you hold the advantage. For example, let's say you are a recent graduate trying to land a job as a teacher and you know the district is interviewing people who have more than ten years of experience. You need to stress your knowledge of up-to-date teaching methods, energy, and a willingness to learn new things. It's possible that your competition is out of touch, unwilling to listen to new ideas, and offers little creativity.

The Seemingly Tough, Well-Qualified Competitor

You should prepare for the possibility that someone out there actually does have all the requirements listed in the job posting. Should you be discouraged? Not in the least. There is more to winning a job than what's on a résumé.

To underscore the point about competition, consider several composites of people who were looking for jobs. They represent highly motivated individuals. But take heart; as great as they are, they have holes in their armor. Can you spot their issues?

➤ Amazon Woman: Some years ago, a woman came to New York for first-round interviews. Her résumé went something like the following: Jr. Olympic kayak champion; amateur mountaineer; founded a cosmetics company in high school; chemistry major with honors at a tony West Coast university; biochemistry masters at an Ivy League school; sold cosmetics company while in school for substantial gain; volunteered for the Peace Corps; member of hometown opera theater; pianist; fluent in four languages; perfect SAT score; Phi Beta Kappa; Mensa member; worked as vice president for product development at a Fortune 100 company before getting a Top 10 MBA. WOW! A slam-dunk hire, right?

➤ Gigabyte Man: A man worked for ten years in the IT industry. He graduated from a good Midwestern school in engineering. He was an accomplished sales person after heading up a technical development group. He had ascended through the ranks and progressively moved up the corporate ladder. He received a part-time MBA from a Top 30 business school. He was recruited heavily to join a strategy-consulting firm. A combat veteran, he was a former Special Forces officer in the U.S. Army and was still in the Army Reserve. He was a marathoner and fluent in three languages, including Arabic. And he was married with three children. What were his concerns?

➤ Supercarb Guy: Another man was an auto mechanic with twelve years of experience in heavy diesel engines. From a lower-middle-income family, he received a GED, then an associate's degree, followed by a bachelor's degree in engineering at a local university. He continued to work for the family business, heading up the heavy maintenance shop. Eventually, he received a master's degree in mechanical engineering. After twenty years, he decided a change was needed. He wanted to work for a major aeronautics or construction company. Can you list his obstacles?

These people are extreme cases, right? Not really. The NCES studies show that access to education in the United States means a proliferation of degrees and technical training in the general population. The studies point to an increasing level of achievement accomplished by many people from many categories, all looking for work.

Amazon woman could be your competition. Beyond her listed achievements, she was nearly 6 feet tall, blonde, and beautiful. She was from California, listed surfing off Australia as her hobby, and was training to run the Boston Marathon. But she had a weakness. Have you spotted it yet?

It's Combat Out There!

There is a famous scene in a well-known Vietnam war movie where the crusty platoon sergeant is describing the Vietcong, also known to in-country troops as Charlie. The combat vet is talking to a set of brash, new recruits. The entire time he's addressing the seated, bored youngsters, a Vietcong defector has quietly infiltrated the barbed wire fence behind the unsuspecting men and is slowly sneaking up on them. All at once, the sergeant says to the recruits, "Turn around. Meet Charles." The shocked wunderkinder turn to see a grinning Vietcong guerilla 6 feet away and pointing a weapon at them. Point made.

Many people work hard to achieve their dreams. Do not underestimate tenacious people, who like Charlie or Supercarb Guy, are working hard to take that desired job away from you. You may be a high achiever, but top jobs are few and the discriminating firm has the luxury of passing you over for the person it thinks it wants. Your task is to make the firm understand that it wants you!

Interview Insights

Keep in mind that good on paper yet disappointing in person still loses. Let's face it, some people pad their résumés to look good. Padding is never a good idea, unless you are in the furniture-moving business. Many people are overrated, it's true. Don't be one of them.

If you are like most average folks, remember the tortoise and the hare. Many times managers would rather hire someone who works hard, is dedicated, reliable, and honest rather than a brilliant, arrogant, untrustworthy talent. Ask Charles, diligence and effort make up for a lot.

Again, Imagine Amazon Woman

You remember her—you know, the kayak champion. Even she had a weakness. Did you spot it? She didn't get an offer, by the way. First-rate firms know how to ferret out weaknesses. Nearly every one of her prized accomplishments was a solo achievement. How do you think she ranked in personality and teamwork?

By the way, the interviewer was ready for the interview to end after five minutes—she had a very combative, entitlement-based personality. Entitlement-based attitudes are notoriously famous these days. Trust this: Most times that sort of attitude will sink your chances! Confidence is important, but there is a line toward arrogance that you do not want to cross. Be hard-nosed, not snotty-nosed.

The point is that everyone has a hole in his or her armor. Don't let the competition wear you down before you even get on the court.

By the way, Gigabyte Man worried about spending hours away from his family, after so much time away on deployments for his Army Reserve commitments. Strategy consulting means many things, and all the opportunities seem to involve travel. And what about Supercarb Guy? He confronted a dilemma facing many people, regardless of qualifications: being the ripe young age of fifty-one.

Key Topic

Competitive pressures and the complexities of globalization have forced firms into a culture that uses matrix-based, layered, and virtual spontaneous teams. Globalization of business has spawned an enormous push inside companies to hire people who can work easily with other smart people to inspire coordinated, integrated solutions across many boundaries—organizational, cultural, demographic, product, and geographical. Can you relate simultaneously with teammates from Hong Kong, Australia, Ireland, and Poland to solve a problem for a client in Buenos Aires? It happens.

Hard-Nosed Performance

People are depending upon you. You need to move ahead, or you need a job. The days of firms giving you a job because you went to XYZ school, through an MBA program, or have come from ABC firm are largely gone. While a prestigious sheepskin is still important, it is just the key to open the door; you have to walk in and perform during the interview.

The Lighter Side

Ivy-covered walls, crisp autumn air, and vibrant colors punctuated the interviewers' exhilaration at visiting a famous Ivy League business school. Mr. Y was at this university to interview MBA students for a vice president position in a wealth management firm in New York. His own graduate experience had been a wonderful journey of the mind, and proved to be the seminal intellectual experience in his life. So, he was naturally upbeat about returning to an Ivy League university on a recruiting event for a famous Wall Street firm.

He had been forewarned these students were among the best and brightest. They were each expecting multiple offers from competing firms and were highly coveted. The interviewer was also told he was under the gun and was given a not-so-subtle warning from the head of human resources to uphold the sterling reputation of the firm. The pressure to make a great hire began to mount. What a surprise he had waiting!

Mr. Y's customary interviews were admittedly tough. He was there as the representative of an elite firm to meet students at an elite school, and they were interviewing for a coveted position. So, he gave them what could easily be described as a major league interview. At the salaries and bonuses and other perks these folks would be given, the firm deserved brilliant performances. What my friend found was surprising. The students were lacking basic interview skills—and they were better prepared than many of you thinking about buying this book!

During interviews, Mr. Y would usually employ scenarios involving markets, clients, and a problem. He would role-play a typical client and give a realistic conversational overlay to the interview. It was apparent these students had not given a lot of prior thought to situations they might actually face while working in the positions for which they were interviewing. They were out of touch with current events, key indicators within the investment markets, and some very basic business common sense.

Mr. Y shared this notorious example of dialogue he experienced:

Interviewer: So, what would you like to do at the bank?

Candidate: Well, I am not really sure at this point. I was hoping you might shed some light on that.

Interviewer: OK, let me try another approach. You know the type of job we are offering. Does that fit your skill set?

Candidate: I suppose. Frankly, I'm not sure I want that. What do you think? Do you have anything else?

Sadly, this isn't a joke. It was a response from someone who had a few years of work experience prior to business school, too. What a waste of time. Needless to say, Mr. Y passed on the candidate. The point is that like Amazon Woman, people can look good on paper and in person but can still perform poorly during an interview for a variety of reasons. Remember, lack of preparation and practice are two common, glaring mistakes made during interviews. In the case with the candidate above, the mistake was a lack of preparation leading to uncertainty about goals and objectives.

Know who you are and what you want before you enter the interview room. Know for certain what it is that you want to accomplish at the company. The interview is no place to discover yourself. It is definitely not the time to have the interviewer help you make up your mind. Be decisive; be directed. Do not go into an interview in a quandary about what position you want. Decide what position is attractive to you, and then do the research to support the effort. Few things dissuade as easily as a person who does not have a reasoned, clear picture of what he or she wants, and a plan for how to get there. It is frustrating to interviewers to speak with someone who is uncertain about career goals. The next person in line probably knows exactly what he or she wants.

Use Your PAG Assessment

Discover key elements of the position you desire and decide specifically what you want to do. Use the PAG process to help uncover your areas of interest. Mention to the interviewer that you have engaged in the PAG as evidence of your serious effort to match skills with the job's requirements.

And remember, you are implementing an action plan that culminated in the conversation during the interview! That alone is an important point to make to anyone who is trying to learn about your analytical skills.

What to Do?

How can you convince someone in an interview that you can fulfill his or her requirements?

Remember your time is short; Amazon Woman is waiting next in line, and you have an overworked, savvy, short-tempered senior executive in front of you. What do you do? Platitudes and superficiality will spawn bored, even angry responses.

Be more like Gigabyte Man—be a personable, dedicated individual willing to go the extra mile for the firm and your teammates. Be willing to show you can still learn new tricks and are hungry to get the job done. You have what some call fire in the belly. That's right! You must show you have fire in your belly!

Along with your other skills, working hard, leading by example, and being up-to-date, commitment makes money in the long run—the million-dollar way. Have this attitude and you go a long way toward being memorable.

In writing fiction, new authors often hear from editors to show, not tell. In other words, tell a story through examples, not narration. In the interview, it is not enough to say you have fire in your belly to be successful. Convince the interviewer through an example like the following.

Mr. X tells the story of a long-anticipated business trip to Boston from New York. The plan was to catch an evening flight, and then have dinner at a hotel to prepare for the next day's planned meeting. A blizzard ensued, all flights canceled! Without hesitation, my friend wheeled about from the airline ticket counter, sprinted to the rental car agency, and got the last car available. He drove at 15 miles per hour all night long and arrived in Boston the next

morning at 7:30 am. The meeting was to be at 8:30 am. He changed clothes, grabbed a pastry, and drove to the prospective client's office just outside the city. The prospect was so stunned to see such dedication that he signed papers on the spot and began a long-term profitable relationship with Mr. X's firm.

Now, that is fire in the belly. Use a story like that, and you show commitment.

Quotable Quotes

"Let us be thankful for the fools. But for them the rest of us could not succeed."

Mark Twain

Chapter Homework

1. Continue to refine offset strategies from the last chapter.

2. Create a realistic appraisal of Amazon Woman in your industry. What attributes define such an amazing competitor? Refine your understanding by conducting at least two informational interviews.

3. Begin your weekly job search game by awarding points for your activities in accordance with the table provided earlier. Set targets and start work on a weekly schedule of activity.

CHAPTER 12

Preparation: Getting Ready for the Job Interview

> ## In This Chapter
> ➤ Expectations
> ➤ Things to do right now

This chapter addresses expectations you and a firm have about one another. Another step in your preparation is to understand that the challenge confronting interview candidates is their exhibited performance during the interview versus the hiring firm's perspective about potential performance on the job. In addition, the chapter recognizes there are a number of mundane items that need to be considered now because they take time to accomplish.

Not Everyone is a Rock Star

The interview objective is simply to match a firm's evaluation of candidates' interview performance and its judgment about potential with its requirements and expectations. Sadly, in some cases, expectations are so mismatched by both parties that the interview is DOA.

On the one hand, some firms, aware of their world-class business, look to fill their needs with the best people they can find, real rock stars. By comparison, many candidates believe they really belong on a metaphorical stage and are high-velocity achievers. As such, they rate their history as superb and all they need is for an evaluating firm to appreciate their talents. It gets uncomfortably crowded in a room full of supposed rock stars.

But the reality is that everyone is not a rock star. Some programs, firms, and students truly stand out, but a much larger percentage is average at best. The question for you is how to differentiate yourself enough to increase your chances of being hired by the firm you want, one of the few that shines, regardless of the type of interview that is thrown at you.

Know Both Sides of the Table

Know who you are and what you want before you enter the interview room. For certain, know what it is that you want to accomplish at the company. The interview is no place to discover yourself. It is definitely not the time to have the interviewer help you make up your mind. Be decisive. Be focused. Be definitive. Do not go into an interview in a quandary about what position you want to go after. Decide what position is attractive to you, and then do the research to support the effort. Few things dissuade as easily as a person who does not have a reasoned, clear picture of what he or she wants, and a plan for how he or she will get there. It is frustrating for interviewers to speak with someone who is uncertain about their career goals. The next person in line probably knows exactly what he or she wants.

Following are some desires and expectations you as a candidate may have:

- ➤ Desired working hours
- ➤ Compensation requirements
- ➤ Access to additional training
- ➤ Transparent career progression
- ➤ Fair performance appraisal process
- ➤ Clear reporting lines
- ➤ Frequency of travel
- ➤ Responsibilities and authority
- ➤ Definable benefits package
- ➤ Desired location
- ➤ Work environment, acceptance, and other cultural factors
- ➤ Degree of management/supervisory support

Employers want and are looking for the following in their employees, depending upon circumstance, industry, experience, and position:

- ➤ Competency
- ➤ Performing as advertised
- ➤ Initially worth the money
- ➤ Loyalty and commitment
- ➤ Learns new tasks
- ➤ Not disruptive

➤ Reliability

➤ Team oriented

➤ Punctuality

➤ Commitment

➤ Responsive

➤ Leadership potential

➤ Quality oriented

➤ Disciplined

➤ Visionary

➤ A role model

➤ Honesty

➤ Communicative and articulate

➤ Lucrative

And the firm hopes to assess all this in an initial thirty-minute interview? At least the interviewer would like insights into these areas so he or she can dig deeper in subsequent discussions.

So, it is imperative that expectations are set accurately on both sides of the table. You should know as much about the job's requirements as possible, and the firm needs to understand who you are and what you can do. Therefore, your resume, with an adequate cover letter, needs to clearly communicate your skills and objectives. If mutual expectations are not set properly prior to the interview, confusion will ensue and the interview ambulance will roll. These mismatches can be so bad some candidates have been asked if they had bothered to read the job placement announcement.

Interview Insights

Mr. A once interviewed a man for a position as an associate relationship manager for ultra-wealthy clients of a private bank. Early in the discussion, the candidate asked, "What does your business group do?" It turns out he wanted a job in either mutual fund operations or as a marketing representative for a pharmaceutical company. The interview was a waste of time for both people. The candidate should have known ahead of time what the business was all about.

You should be certain what the job entails and what you want to do before the interview. If you do not know what you want, don't expect the interviewer to help you decide. For the purposes of that interview, on that one day, know exactly what you want, what that job does, and how you can communicate your interest. Otherwise, cancel the meeting.

Rising Expectations

If a person is about to graduate from a small town high school and another will soon receive a prestigious MBA from an Ivy League school, they will soon share a common experience. This may be the first time both have interviewed with their newly minted credential.

So what? First, the firms' expectations will rise because you are institutionally certified to know something—you hold a diploma saying so. Second, your expectations will rise because you believe the firm will recognize what you know—you hold a diploma certifying your value. Can you see a possible train wreck?

Interview Insights

How do you handle situations where there are negative voices about your performance? Perhaps they are unjustified, but they could scuttle your chances if a firm hears a lukewarm comment here or there. One senior executive, who has hired hundreds, believes it best to confront any such issue head on during the interview in a professional, calm demeanor. At least you will have done your part to deflect potential criticism. It is unfortunately hard to prove if someone is intentionally undermining your efforts. The alternative is to hope that the person hasn't spoiled your chances. In that case, if you don't get the job then you are left wondering. Pick positive references, but preempt any possible issues up front.

Things You Need to Do—Early in the Process

There are a number of items that need sufficient lead time before an interview. Locate a good tailor or a dress consultant now. Don't take your sweetheart to help decide on your interview clothing and accessories—he or she may think you look great in everything or may be reluctant to tell you that you don't!

Start right now lining up references for the interviewing firm to speak to about your personal character, professionalism, work history, or other qualities. You should first obtain the person's agreement to participate either via phone call from the firm or via letter or e-mail. Social networking sites also have referral sections where people can write testimonials about your work and character. Use this with great care and make sure the words your reference's use are positive and targeted.

Here are a few rules you should consider when supplying references:

> ➤ Make certain the person is comfortable giving a reference on your behalf.

> ➤ Ask if you can write the reference letter to save the person's time.

> ➤ If a former supervisor is not available, find someone at the old firm with whom you worked closely to take or make the call or write the letter.

> ➤ Make certain the reference person's contact information is current when you supply it to the requesting firm.

> ➤ Ask the person to let you know if the firm contacts him or her about you.

You may never know what the person actually says about you, so pick your references carefully. That said, they should not just be close friends either; they need to objectively give a strong evaluation. In fact, in contacting possible references, you may stumble across additional job leads from them.

Chapter Homework

1. Get pictures of people in your target industry and company. Take those pictures to a first-rate department store (suggestions are in chapter 27), tailor, or dress consultant. Skip ahead to chapter 27.

2. Write down your expectations for the job of choice.

3. Jot down possible references and start tracking them down.

CHAPTER 13

Preparation: Beginning to Craft Your Interview Dialogue

In This Chapter

➤ Your personal scripts

➤ Filling out your dialogue

➤ Connecting facts and figures

In this chapter you analyze information necessary to become a world-class practitioner in your chosen field. You also begin to prepare the scripts, or dialogue, that will comprise your interview discussion. Thus far, you know who you are and what challenges you may face, and now you begin to compose what you will say. And then, looking ahead, the next chapters will help you practice how you will say it.

Personal Scripts: An Exercise in Creativity

When a Hollywood film director plans the movements of actors around a set during a scene, he or she utilizes a charting method called storyboarding. The devices used are boards that visually depict the movement of actors and the flow of the plot action during a scene. They are also known as graphic organizers or serial illustrations. They are used in many ways in both business and the arts.

Where a script simply calls for an actor to enter a room, the storyboard pictorial and attached dialogue tells him or her precisely how to do it—right down to facial expressions, lighting, sounds, environmental effects, etc. It is a snapshot of what the actors will see during the scene. It is a physical manifestation of the plot.

For example, instead of simply directing "enter stage left," an elaborate storyboard may say, "walk through the door with anger on your face, trip over the flooring, then recover by flailing your arms wildly, and move menacingly toward the other actor at center stage. Then point a finger at him. Hold it for five seconds, and then shout, 'You can't do that to me!' The storyboard is more descriptive and visual.

Interview Vocab

A storyboard is a graphic representation of a scene in a movie, screenplay, business presentation, or live drama; it is often tied to a script and its associated action. A storyboard is sometimes portrayed with dialogue and pictures of the actors. Hundreds of storyboards are used in making a movie or Broadway play. Walt Disney Studios is generally thought to have originated these in the 1930s in the making of cartoons. Nowadays, storyboards are widely used in movies, other media, and business.

In other words, storyboards are a method where the details of movements, expressions, and nuances come alive before they hit the big screen. The actors internalize the storyboards so the characters' actions become second nature and believable.

Remember that the actions and reactions of all the actors in the scene, in total, create the product that viewers will see.

Interview as Screenplay

When you think about it, an interview is very much like a live drama or feature film. So it follows that it needs a counterpart to the storyboard—a form of personal script—to depict the dialogue you will use as well as an illustration of the scene itself.

Think of an interview, then, as your own Hollywood debut complete with a context, an environment, actors, and a script. You are one of the actors, the interviewer is another, and others like the receptionist are supporting cast members. Really, anyone with whom you interact during the days prior to and during the interview is an actor in your movie.

The way you orchestrate this epic will impact the quality of the playgoers' experience. Either you choose to direct it or it will steer you in a direction that may not benefit you. For example, if an actor (the cab driver) doesn't arrive on time to take you to the interview setting, then your play could change from live-action to full-fledged drama.

The Dialogue

What exactly will you say during your interview? Personal scripts are similar to storyboards in level of detail, but they cover a broader and deeper scope of content. If done properly, they hold the knowledge and methods of implementation that will yield an Oscar-winning performance in your feature film entitled *The Perfect Job Interview*.

When you develop the personal scripts (later in this chapter), you will first develop the knowledge base, the content. Then you will compose the actual words to fill out the ebbs and flows of the dialogue based upon that content—that is the art of delivering a fine performance. It is imperative that the personal scripts-based dialogue you deliver is not stilted or mechanistic. It should be written with a smooth actor's delivery in mind.

For example, assume one topic you list on a storyboard relates to teamwork skills. You should play with your dialogue and concoct dialogue. For example, your first attempt might look like this: "I have experience working and leading teams under critical deadlines. I recently guided my five-person team through a redevelopment project dealing with our city's recreational parks. We came in ahead of schedule by two days, the council was really thrilled, and our plan was adopted by the council and important citizen activists who were really upset over delays."

Then edit, edit, and edit to become even more succinct, more hard-hitting. The second cut, for example, says, "Citizens were upset (convey sense of anger) over delays in parks development. My five-person team crafted a revision two days ahead of deadline, and the plan satisfied the council and citizens' advocacy groups when they came to a meeting."

Finally then, "When citizens' groups berated (convey sense of anger) the council over delayed park improvements, my team's two-day response calmed everyone. The new plan was enthusiastically approved."

The first edit is shorter, conveys the same basic information. The final one is shorter still and leaves room for further explanation. You will want to play with dialogue throughout the following personal scripts process and edit ruthlessly: Get it to memory-ready form.

Interview Insights

You don't need to be a Hollywood graphic artist to draw a rendering of the interviewer's office or the cafe or the conference room or the cocktail reception hall. Sketch the scenes, then attach the sketches to each applicable storyboard and its content. You will be surprised at the power of visualized dialogue.

Personal Scripts Components

There are four major components that comprise your personal scripts or storyboards. Each component section will have its own personal scripts storyboard composed of topics and subtopics. Feel free to build out additional storyboards for selected subtopics. The information contained in these boards will allow you to compose actual dialogue in response to questions by the interviewer, just like in the parks example above. The four components are:

➤ Technical

➤ Personal information

➤ Opening and closing

➤ Connectivity

The Technical Component

The information in this section concerns the knowledge that you must have to answer questions about your competence to do the job. Of course, you will want to astound the interviewer by knowing much more. Pack the personal scripts full of detail, as much as you know. This is your core competency!

The Personal Information Component

This is information about your background, experience, likes and dislikes, and such. It is information that allows the firm to get to know who you are as a person and what your values are. Many ethics questions concern how you handled a previous situation and it is from this category that you draw an example to support your answer. Here you also address your responses to contingencies, or those things that could surprise you or not go as planned.

Opening and Closing Component

The opening statement is the way you first meet and greet the interviewer. Poised, confident, and professional are the key features to keep in mind. The closing statement is the clincher, the reason you should be hired. It is when you make the statement the interviewer will always remember!

The Connectivity Component

This information highlights ways to tie seemingly independent topics together to present an integrated response to a question. This section is so important that more will be presented on this topic later in this chapter.

Constructing Personal Scripts

Consider an important question. I call it your statement of intent and conviction. How would you finish the following statement? "I want to be a world-class
_____."

Your answer becomes a statement of intent. It's also a statement of conviction, showing your intensity of feeling.

For example, "I want to be a world-class teacher" is a powerful statement. It is supported by your skills assessment work and an in-depth analysis of your strengths, weaknesses, and offset strategies from your PAG worksheets.

Take a piece of paper and write down your initial thoughts about being a world-class _____. Once done, you have paid a deposit on getting that new job!

Now, ask yourself what skills and knowledge does it take to become a world class _____? What do you need to know? What skills and knowledge do you need to attain such a position?

As a start, draw a structure like that shown in the following schematic (Figure 13A). The structure illustrates a drill-down approach to content construction. Start at the top and dig deeper to the lowest level of detail you think is necessary to show you know your stuff.

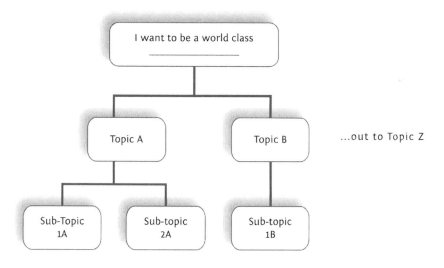

Personal Scripts Architecture

Figure 13A

This is a simple two-level chart. The ones you will actually build will have many more topics and subtopics (depicted as out to Topic Z).

Addressing Topics, decide on your answer to the question about becoming world class, then answer the following: What skills and knowledge do I need to be a world-class (fill in the blank)? Fill out each block with a major topical area that a highly competent person occupying the job should know about. For instance, someone who wants to be a world-class teacher should know a lot about a primary subject area, history, for example. History would be Topic A. But a world-class teacher ought to know a few other things, too. What about parent-teacher-student communication skills or, organizational skills or, behavior control skills or, computer and research skills? Each area should have its own Topic block. In our teacher example, for instance, communications skills would be Topic B, etc.

Another example might be: You want to be a world-class brand manager in the consumer products area. Topic A describes product features; Topic B might be major competitors.

Add as many topics as necessary to fill out each of the four components described earlier (technical, personal, open and closing, and connectivity).

You should use the same logic for the subtopics, except drill down and add substance to the knowledge base you are building. For example, in the teacher case, under Topic A History, you would add U.S. Colonial as subtopic 1A. Under communications, you would add parent-teacher coordination as subtopic 2A, etc. Under each subtopic, you should specify important details of your knowledge in that area.

For the brand manager case, for example, under Topic B Major Competitors you might add information on Kellogg, General Mills—their strengths and weaknesses, as well as their primary lines and recent trends.

Note that knowledge of the state of a nation's economy should be a major topic on everyone's list under the technical component. Remember, capture data for the personal scripts on every topic and subtopic important to the new job, and deposit that information in its own computer file. You can't cover all aspects of what you know; use those you believe might be discussion points in an interview or those that you want to be discussion points.

How Many Topic/Subtopic Areas?

Some jobs may require more topical areas than others. As job complexity and responsibility rise, the number of topic areas and the corresponding subtopics also increase. And there is no limit on the number you can research. It's dependent upon how many your brain can hold and use. What is the optimal number? It depends upon the job, naturally, but you should use the rule of thumb that any area that comes to your mind should have a block of information. You will probably add, consolidate, and delete subtopics as you proceed.

A rule of thumb is to ask yourself the world-class question: what areas would a rational person who either works in that industry, is a client using the product, or is a competitor competing against your target company naturally be concerned about?

Your goal is to compose multiple personal scripts that are your weapons, tools, solutions to counter the twists and turns of the plot that runs your feature film. It's what your hero (you) needs. The twists are the contingencies that develop just prior to the interview and during it.

For career changers, you definitely want a personal scripts storyboard concerning your ability to translate your prior experience into something relevant to the job at hand. Your explanation may be the most critical element in the entire conversation, so you must have a concise, believable tale to tell.

Interview Insights

For professional jobs, the technical-based blocks probably number from ten to fifteen. The character, personal experience and circumstance blocks number around four to six. The opening and closing should each have one. And connectivity is dependent on the other sections, but around nine to ten is a good estimate. So, in total that's around twenty-five to thirty-three blocks. It's more manageable than it sounds. You will probably consolidate some. Remember, you want to be expert and world class.

More on the Subtopics

Other examples of possible subtopics are listed in the table below for four selected occupations:

Job	Topic	Subtopic
Pharmacist	Organizational skills	How to track/compose detailed drug dispensary reports
Real estate leasing agent	Research	Knowledge of applicable national occupancy rate databases, new development projects by region, and computer skills
Litigation attorney	Communication skills	Sample summations, case histories, winning over juries
Assistant brand manager for consumer drinks	Sales and revenue factors by product	Sales histories vs competitors by region/age, etc., for each product; focus group surveys; growth rate projections

Personal Scripts Presentation

You should implement the personal scripts by constructing physical manifestations of the material. I suggest that old-school poster boards—one or several for each major topical area should be constructed and ultimately placed on walls in a quiet room of your house or apartment. Review and update associated subtopic data weekly. You want the constant visual impact of wall-mounted poster boards to take root within your mind.

Using a computer to consolidate the material is fine, but you lose the power of sweeping visualization if the personal scripts are not constantly visible as you move around a room, sit at a table, etc. You are creating a panorama, an epic movie.

Importance of Connectivity

Connectivity is where you will outshine the competition. It is where the personal script idea shows real power. As mentioned, we live in a global economy where a company in Phoenix with a client in Milwaukee sells its product manufactured in Italy with its ongoing servicing provided by a call center in India. If there is a problem, then a virtual team could gather with representatives from all those locations, and perhaps additional ones as well, to conspire on a solution. It is into this type of environment that a firm wants to hire you.

Show you can work across the organization, borders, and products. If necessary for the job, prove you can work with disparate personnel and cultures to solve the client's problem. How is the hiring firm going to know with some degree of confidence that you are the right person for this job? If you are not a global organization, then replace global with domestic or local, whichever applies. The point is that businesses want people who can do their job well and within a larger context.

Connectivity is a way of showing how to do that, how you approach problems. This is especially true if you are given a case study or scenario to solve. Using a connectivity perspective, you can deliver integrated, interdependent answers to multivariable problems.

How Connectivity Works

You should fashion a connectivity argument that establishes the relationship between key functional topics and their subtopics. It is the interdependent nature of these elements that you want to find and to articulate in the interview.

For example, if an interviewer poses a question covered by a subtopic, you can ease the discussion from just the single issue to include its interdependent cousin under another subtopic, perhaps under a different main topic even. This opens up the discussion to a wider array of information and can highlight a particular area of expertise you own.

To further illustrate, perhaps you are the best mechanic of carburetors known to humans, but the questions are focusing on tires. If you can establish a smooth connection between tires and poor carburetor performance and your ability to fix them, then you show how you think to solve problems; you become a troubleshooter for the client and you might fix two problems instead of one. The client is happy and your boss is happy (the money question again).

Key Topic

The underlying structure of the personal script is based upon content preparation and interdependence. Use the structure in a down-and-across pattern. In other words, if someone asks a question, then mentally locate the proper box at the topical level, drill down that channel until you discover your answer within a subtopic, and then find a logical connection to another subtopic underneath a different topic. Then use the knowledge there to give a comprehensive response. Fortunately, it is simpler in the doing than in the telling. Remember, drill down for the answer, move across to another subtopic for the connection.

Connectivity is what high-end professionals in the field do every day, and if you can do it during the interview, then you go a long way toward answering the million-dollar question; remember, it's the one lurking in the interviewer's mind.

Personal Scripts Example

Let's illustrate personal scripts construction by using an example of someone preparing for an interview in the financial services sector. If you are from another industry, it is not important that you know the terms in this example; replace them with those germane to your situation. The point is that you need a level of detail that shows you know your subject matter really well.

Sherry is looking for a job with a financial services firm in Chicago. She is a recent graduate from a regional MBA program in the Midwest. She is twenty-six years old, with three years of work experience as a marketing representative for a consumer products company. She wants to work in financial services. She has an upcoming interview with a managing director of a large, regionally renowned wealth management company. She ponders what she will say and uses personal scripts to build out her content.

Below you see her initial attempt. She highlights topic areas in bold and jots down subtopic elements for each topic. She knows there will be additions and deletions over time but thinks this is a good start. She commits to learning in detail about each subtopic, and then she begins searching for connectivity.

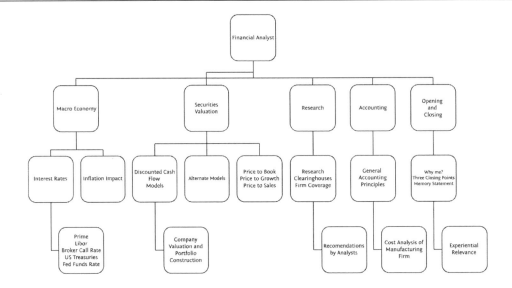

Figure 13b
Personal Scripts Financial Services Example

Statement of Intent and Conviction

First, Sherry composes a statement of intent and conviction. She believes the following topics comprise the knowledge base it will take to show an interviewer she has what it takes to be a world-class financial advisor in private wealth management/FatCats Bank/Chicago.

Under Technical:

Topics	Subtopics (needed information/thoughts)
Interest rates	Discount rate, money rates, broker call, labor, fed funds target rate, prime rate, shape of yield curve
Macroeconomics	Inflation; trade and budget deficits, inventory levels, productivity, unemployment, oil/commodities prices, GDP, retail sales numbers, etc.
Bond Markets	Municipal bond rates; duration and convexity; valuation methods; spreads over US treasuries/ high-yield and emerging markets; asset allocation; distressed 1-yr, 10-yr, 30-year US treasury yields, market-leader views
Alternative Assets (AA)	Private equity and venture capital, allocation, valuation methods, trends, major players
Hedge funds	Part of AA/deserves separate section; types, performance, regulatory issues, global macro vs merger arbitrage vs directional vs event-driven vs etc., major players

Equity markets	Market indices; YTD returns; trends; P/E valuations; dividend discount models; value vs growth; allocation to stocks; favorite stocks; sectors; alternative valuation methods, i.e., momentum vs growth, etc., forecasts
Foreign exchange	Purchase power parity; dollar vs major currencies; interplay trade deficit and interest rate environment; impact on specific industries, etc.; current government policy
Commodities	Allocation, gold, oil and gas, futures markets
Estate planning	Major issues, estate tax legislation, basic trust structures/role in wealth plan, family governance issues, coord w/investments
Passive vs active investment	ETFs vs indexing vs active portfolio management. Alpha generation?
Risk measures	Ratios: Sharpe, Treynor, beta, default, bank risk, STD deviations, BIS benchmarks
Real estate	Allocation, the role of REITs vs direct investment.
Credit	Labor, prime, broker call rates; other lending rates; advance rates; use of leverage for wealthy investors; spreads and credit
Art and collectibles	Allocation, current market. [Note: read Worth magazine articles]
Music and the arts	Know a little about major composers and major works of art; major cultural centers in the United States and abroad: opera, ballet, and symphonies. Read Vintage Guide to Classical Music or some other guide to classical music
Firm information	Top management profiles, strategic direction, annual report, recent news, analyst reports, stock price and forecasts, major business elements and competitive edge, key employee departures/hires, key challenges to products, product gaps, financials versus benchmarks, balance sheet, customers
Competitor information	Positioning, platform differences, competitive advantages, new product offerings, recent news
Industry macrofactors	Trends and key issues, industry structure, earnings growth, regulatory issues affecting industry
My client experience	Typical client, client segmentation, new business development issues, opportunities for cross selling, advertising campaigns, relationship management
Legislative, tax and legal environment	Recent legislative initiatives, SEC and SRO issues, outstanding litigation? Hedge fund disclosure issues, etc.

Under Personal Information, Sherry writes down topics, including some from her résumé, but she goes well beyond those. She includes:

Topics	Subtopics
Educational choices	Why MBA? Why U of B?
Job choices	Why leave consumer products?
Hobbies	Why soccer? Trekking?
Reading Interests	Why novels and business mags?
Leadership	Project X and Team Red leader
Teamwork	MBA case team, basketball
Sales experience	None, but Smart Guide BD model!
Work relationships	Mentorship program at fmr firm: BK Products
Values/ethics	Conflict example at BK
Travel and language	Study abroad plus French
Decision making	Product crisis at BK!
Charitable work	Food bank volunteer
Life and work goals	Want partnership, good balance
Employment location	Need Chicago only
Last job issues	References? What would they say? My counter?
Career aspirations	Committed to financial services
Professional certifications	Working on CFA, Need Series 7 broker license
Life Lessons	Travel and volunteer work in clinic
Disability	Overcoming adversity—my handicap
Lack of experience	Desire, judgment, examples

Under Opening and Closing Statements, construct your third set of personal scripts storyboards around your opening and closing statements:

Topics	Subtopics
Intro statement	Thanks and comment on time, schedule, excitement, comment on what else?
State of the markets	Intro comment on day's markets
Commitment	Express desire to work at FatCats Bank
Three summary closing points	Desire, quality of work, teamwork???

Great impression	Life lessons (disability) with hard work and overcoming adversity, success oriented, quick study, million-dollar question: must show how to get a new client!!!
Skills vs requirements	Empathy and listening to client needs
Closing phrase	Develop memorable good-bye phrase: "I can do this job if you give it to me" ??? (Maybe not. This subtopic is critical: needs work)

Under Connectivity, Sherry relates key topic/subtopics to others to stress abilities (Key Topic):

Questions about Topics/Subtopic	Connected to
Interest rate knowledge	Valuation methods to credit to foreign exchange to overall economy (inflation, unemployment)
Hobbies	Art and collectibles, music to travel to client stories to relationship management ability
Knowledge of firm	Competitors to differences in platforms to reason I want the job at FatCats Bank
Employment history	Desire for education to choices to job search to reading interests to career
Leadership skills	Consumer brands to a project to teamwork to private banking to solving client issues?
Commitment	Volunteer work to values to ethics example
Hedge fund knowledge	Performance to macro economy to communication ability to client relationship skills
To be determined - need more	

By using stories like these, connected via the personal scripts storyboard, Sherry can weave a logical, coherent argument to almost any question posed by the interviewer.

Single-dimensional answers are often superficial and shallow. It is not what major league firms are looking for, but it's what they usually get from candidates. For example, Sherry believes if she gets a question about relationship skills with clients, she can lead it back to her knowledge of hedge funds, thereby showing the interviewer a comprehensive understanding of private banking. She would first tie her knowledge of a client's specific case to her practice of regularly communicating with clients via modern media, and then she would connect her media savvy to her use of technology to gain insight into the economic environment. Finally, she would show that certain hedge funds are just what the client might need to solve his or her problem in that kind of investing environment. Bingo! The million-dollar answer.

Personal Scripts Connectivity Analysis

Now, get a legal pad. Take a moment and think of your target industry, firm, and position again. Even a gardener in the Sahara Desert can come up with personal scripts topics and subtopics—every job has them.

So, after writing topics and subtopics, and connections, what have you accomplished? You've thought rigorously about key issues, the details of those issues, and then tied them together with the details of other key parameters. Now you are not operating in the vacuum we described earlier but weaving a coherent argument connected in ways that listeners— clients—can understand. You are thinking globally integrated, complex interconnections— wow! That's powerful stuff when you think about it. People will say, "Now there's a thinker!"

Important Areas to Cover

Don't forget everyone will have four components of personal scripts: technical, personal, open and closing, and connectivity. Somewhere under those components ensure that certain critical areas are covered. They may not be asked, and in some cases they should not be asked. But, if they are, and you decide to respond, make sure you are ready with a great answer that puts the question to rest (see chapter 28). Some special topics Sherry should consider are:

➤ Explaining unusual circumstances (arrest records, for instance. Check the Equal Employment Opportunity Commission website, www.eeoc.gov, for more information. Expunging criminal records is complicated and varies by state. Consult an attorney for this possibility. Surely this is not applicable to Sherry!)

➤ Unusual gaps in work history

➤ Frequent job changes (a sign of trouble to employers)

➤ Sudden departures (story must be convincing and professional)

➤ Career changes

➤ Layoffs (don't be embarrassed; this happens often these days)

➤ Age (for the youthful and the older hearts)

➤ Relating your experience to the job at hand

➤ Last employment experience

➤ An example to answer the million-dollar question

➤ Questions for the firm

➤ Compensation

> ➤ Disabilities

> ➤ Sexual orientation (if you want to be preemptive and open)

> ➤ Physicality (weight, height, etc., if you think it is an issue)

Defending Your Personal Scripts

When you are finished, give your initial personal scripts attempt to your trusted agent or interview buddy for review. Give that person a quick outline sketch about the job you want and take his or her input. Then go through your boards and defend why you think the points are germane to the position. Your trusted agent/interview buddy should carefully listen for these from you:

> ➤ Gaps in logic

> ➤ Confusion

> ➤ Inconsistent arguments

> ➤ Lack of knowledge in an area

> ➤ Shallow explanations

Sample Jobs and Topics

Listed below are other selected industries and jobs with some but not all major topic areas one would need to cover to be a world-class worker in that industry. This is just a start, whereas *The Occupational Outlook Handbook* is a good place to look. For not-for-profit jobs, search www.guidestar.org, a site offering information filed by private foundations, charities, churches, hospitals, schools, etc.

Investment Banking:

> ➤ Valuation methods and models

> ➤ Specific industry and company analysis

> ➤ Macro economy

> ➤ Recent deals in industry sector and opinions

> ➤ League tables

> ➤ Case work

> ➤ Competitive dynamics

> ➤ IB process and underwriting dynamics

> ➤ Regulatory framework

> ➤ www.careers-in-finance.com/ib

Real Estate:

> ➤ Discount rates
>
> ➤ Comparables
>
> ➤ Commercial vs industrial vs retail
>
> ➤ Major deals, major player's books
>
> ➤ Location and specific market issues
>
> ➤ www.careers-in-finance.com/re

Brand Management:

> ➤ Competitive position
>
> ➤ Advertising spend
>
> ➤ Current outlets vs brand
>
> ➤ Brand identity
>
> ➤ Case work
>
> ➤ www.careeroverview.com/brand-management-careers

Management Consulting:

> ➤ Specific industry structure and competitive dynamics: products, pricing, platform, strategy, etc.
>
> ➤ Presentation and communication skills
>
> ➤ Case work
>
> ➤ Major issues
>
> ➤ Macroeconomic and industry-specific threats
>
> ➤ Analytical ability
>
> ➤ New business orientation
>
> ➤ Teamwork
>
> ➤ www.careers-in-business.com/consulting

Production Management:

> ➤ Case work
>
> ➤ Logistics and inventory models
>
> ➤ Cost models

➤ Production drivers

➤ Specific process/line issues

➤ Overseas influences and outsourcing issues

➤ Labor issues

➤ www.bls.gov/oco/ocos016

Retail or Wholesale Sales Representative:

➤ Specific industry and competitor information

➤ Distribution and production issues

➤ New product introductions

➤ Sales goals and sales channels

➤ Travel and logistics

➤ International and new markets

➤ Product features

➤ Sales techniques

➤ Computer skills

➤ www.education-portal.com/articles/Retail_Sales_Manager

Not-for–Profit Organizations (NFP):

➤ Tax-exempt disclosures and requirements

➤ www.guidestar.org

➤ www.capitalresearch.org

➤ www.taftgroup.org

➤ Capital raising

➤ Specific knowledge of issues driving chosen type of NFP

➤ Demographic influences including philanthropic trends

➤ Grant process

➤ Government funding channels

Teaching:

➤ Sample lesson plans

➤ Grading policy

➤ District policy

➤ Parent interaction

➤ Continuing education

➤ Problem students/discipline in the classroom

➤ Challenged students

➤ Teaching methods

➤ www.careeroverview.com/education-careers

Medical Sales:

➤ Sales experience

➤ Sales process

➤ Product knowledge

➤ Customer relations

➤ Economy

➤ Pricing models

➤ Management interaction

➤ Compensation

➤ www.globaledgerecruiting.com/specialties/medical-products

www.career-overview.com is a good place to start for personal scripts-type of information about many other careers.

Practice Personal Scripts

You most likely have a target job or industry to which you aspire. If you are undecided, then use one of the above and practice the personal scripts process. Again, the *OOH* handbook should help. At least you will know how to do the routine later when you get a call from a headhunter!

Steering the Interview

In order to steer the interview the way you want it to go, lead the conversation toward a personal scripts storyboard. It takes practice, but you can do it well with repetition. For example, suppose the interviewer asks you a simple question such as, "What hobbies do you enjoy?" Connect your personal interests personal scripts to the personal scripts subtopic on business development. You could say: "I enjoy golf," but instead, try this: "I enjoy golf, and I find the game gives me the chance to interact with clients who also enjoy the game. I can play golf, relax, and learn more about what really interests them. I can more accurately assess my approach to their needs. I get to understand them better and vice versa. I find it also helps my sales numbers. For instance, I recently closed a deal on a new Model X1 on the twelfth tee!" Ka-ching Ka-ching! The money answer!

In this way, you connect a lay-up question about a hobby to a business purpose. It also shows you can connect a question a client may ask to what your company actually does. Mr. Y once turned a question about an interest in football to a discussion about satisfying the client's desire to help his alma mater's athletic program, which was accomplished through an inventive charitable structure developed by Mr. Y's firm.

Play a Game

To practice the use of connectivity, play a training game to help react to prospective client objections to a sale, or in your case during an interview. Call it the listening-connect-the-dots game. Try this over the course of the next week or so.

Connect what you see in your everyday environment to your chosen field of interest in business. For instance, as you sit in a restaurant and you overhear a conversation at the next table about (pick a topic), construct a conversation in your own mind as to how you would connect it to your business. In other words, how does the topic of the conversation relate to what you do for a living?

For example, if you see a sign on a bus advertising an upcoming rock concert, connect it in your mental conversation to something you will do in your new business. If you practice this enough, you will be able to connect almost anything that someone is saying to what you do for a living, and make it work to your advantage in an interview.

Best Practices Sales Technique for the Interview

The point is that with enough practice, you can connect almost anything to what you do for a living. Practice the little connecting game and you will be able to connect what the interviewer is saying to what you want to highlight as one of your core skills.

The best sales people—and for the purposes of the interview you are a sales professional—connect the dots with ease to enter salesmanship clubs and the like. If you can master this technique, you could be on your way toward a successful sales career. The interviewer will certainly be very impressed.

Chapter Homework

1. Recreate the listening-connect-the-dots game over the next week. In fact, I suggest you adopt it as a routine.

2. Review your topics/subtopics exercise and begin to fill in the detail under the subtopics.

3. Come up with an example to answer the million-dollar question like Sherry did.

Quotable Quotes

"The creation of a thousand forests is in one acorn."

Ralph Waldo Emerson

"Why can't somebody give us a list of things that everybody thinks and nobody says, and another list of things that everybody says and nobody thinks?"

Oliver Wendell Holmes

CHAPTER 14

Preparation: Writing a Script Worthy of an Oscar

In This Chapter

➤ How you write dialogue

➤ Refining the script with style

➤ Exercises in creativity

In this chapter you refine the script that will guide your dialogue and develop the plot to end with a job offer.

The Script

Scripts are the guideposts that direct a plot through time. A movie is complex and so is the interview. It's your interview, so write it like you own it.

One advantage you have over most actors is that you get to write your own script, your personal scripts, and the closer the interviewer resembles a character in your script, the better off you are.

Personal scripts are a self-constructed remedy for poor organization, muddled thinking, and a wandering interview. Combined with your personal delivery techniques, personal scripts become your dialogue. Remember that a personal script represents your ideas of what will be discussed in your interview. We will handle deviations from the script shortly, but for now let's get on with the process of writing your award-winning screenplay.

The Dialogue

Obviously, the interview will have dialogue. And what you will say is mostly dependent upon what questions are asked and what lines of discussion you want to invoke. If you were thorough in you preparation, your personal scripts contain your answers to those questions you believe might be asked and the conversations you wish to initiate.

The first task is to refine your personal scripts and make certain you include any information from a daily journal. A journal is a logbook of ideas and impressions you have each day. These thoughts can occur while standing in line at the grocery store, while sitting on a subway, or any place. Review these entries each evening and incorporate them into your interview preparation and practice.

Start by retrieving the pads of legal-sized paper you used for previous chapters where you listed topics and subtopics. Write down sentences that deliver the actual language you will use to describe the topics and subtopics. Build short, choppy sentences that are easy to memorize. Make notes around emphasis areas, specific gestures, etc.

Interview Insights

If actor Johnny Depp only relied on dialogue, even he might be rather boring. It's that face—the wonderful distortions, playful eyes, grimaces, and other physical manifestations that make him the terrific actor he is. His physicality is what brings richness to the dialogue and makes him believable and memorable. Using these techniques during an interview can help underscore key points in your argument and create an important moment. In addition, these mannerisms can emphasize your strengths and that you are a credible player in the interview game.

Elements of Style

What makes a great character in a movie? Depth. The character has something that captures viewers' imagination. The best characters intrigue, resonate, and create a sense of familiarity (both good and bad). They are also believable. An honest portrayal is what is often heard from critics when they describe an actor's fine performance. What does that mean to you?

In the interview, it means you need to accurately portray your skills and your objectives. It only breeds trouble later on if you don't. Interviewers believe they will get what they see. They trust that you can deliver what you say you can do.

As the director of your movie, you have the luxury of telling at least the lead actor (you) what needs to be done and how to act. Imagine you were really directing an interview movie. What would you tell the candidate to do?

The musical score that accompanies an award-winning movie often is a multi-movement piece of music utilizing the entire ensemble of instruments. Like your interview, your script should have the equivalent of a virtuoso first violin, a resonant timpani drum, a quiet flute, and the rest. The conductor invokes nuances within the music by getting the right instrument to play at exactly the right time to support the action in the movie. You must do the same to create a virtuoso interview performance with the instruments at your disposal—your personal scripts.

The personal scripts provide the content for your interview discussion and are drawn upon as needed. You connect a point here, a point there, and like a movie director you weave an integrated, compelling personal story.

Using the same legal pads containing sentences about your topics and subtopics, adapt and integrate them into trial conversations you might use in an interview. Blend what you learned to your needs, and practice it over the coming weeks using as much of your personal scripts information as possible and within a mock interview setting. Use your video camera again to see how they look from an interviewer's perspective. Remember less is more, but showing nothing is worse.

Bodies in Motion

Your body language, style, movements, and tempo of your speech convey the heart and soul of the scene. You can exhibit Depp-like believability if you use emphasis points in your responses. Make emphatic hand gestures, thoughtful looks, conveniently timed nonverbal responses. They should all be blended into your dialogue.

One of Newton's laws of physics states that a body at rest or in motion tends to stay that way unless an outside force acts upon it. Well, as a job candidate, you are a body that should neither be completely at rest or constantly in motion during an interview.

Control your movements in the interview. Be natural, not stiff. You should not be a stone memorial, but that does not mean that you turn into an animated Dutch windmill, either. Your gestures and other body language should be natural and add to your dialogue but not become the center of attention.

Body language is suspect science to some, but it is undeniably important as a method of emphasizing key points, indicating understanding, and showing interest. Here are some tips:

➤ Simple head nods show interest and agreement

➤ A furrowed brow indicates disagreement or confusion

➤ Crossed arms indicate resistance

➤ Pursed lips and constant smiles just look silly

➤ Hands on hips indicates rigidity, stubbornness

➤ Jingling pocket change shows lack of confidence

➤ Darting eyes creates suspicion

➤ Forefinger to lips shows intellect

➤ Slumped shoulders show indifference, fatigue

➤ Too many gestures indicate you failed body language school

➤ Crushing handshakes mean aggression or overcompensation

What Did You Say?

Scene-stealing dialogue captures the listener's imagination and makes the plot sizzle. Here are some tips to try when you write yours:

➤ Write lots of words to describe your topics and subtopics.

➤ Edit those words, then edit again until they are short and sweet and able to be memorized.

➤ Give emphasis to certain words in your dialogue.

➤ Make points that lead to others; use transitional phrases.

➤ Use moderating language, such as "Another possible alternative might be…".

➤ Coordinate gestures with your narrative.

➤ Gestures should be limited and used tactically.

➤ Good scripting poses interesting questions and generates two-way conversation.

➤ Use scene-stealing action language (active verbs, up-and-down variations in voice and tempo).

➤ Use complementary conversation (additive to interviewers' points; politely contrary when necessary).

➤ Be pointed, not pointless.

➤ Award-winning dialogue is not a constant broadcast.

➤ Listen to great dialogue in movies, and then write yours.

Quotable Quotes

"I not only use all the brains I have, but all I can borrow."

Woodrow Wilson

Chapter Homework

1. Finish working on personal scripts worksheets and concentrate on what it is that you are going to say and how you will say it.

2. Watch a favorite movie, one that you know very well. Pick a character. Mimic scenes of dialogue complete with the gesticulations and body language portrayed by the actors. Watch the way the actor conveys ideas through hands, arms, legs, and face. Watch for turns, crossed legs, pen holdings, eye movements, greetings, squints, smiles, and entrances. Do it exactly the way the actor does it. It might make you laugh, and that's OK. Keep practicing. You won't act that way in an interview, but this exercise will give flavor and texture to your dialogue.

3. Take the movie in #2 and go to the most compelling, most powerful dialogue. Why does it work? Find five key points why it works so well. Take your subtopics and begin writing your dialogue incorporating as many of the key points as you can.

4. Extra Credit Homework: You are directing a documentary entitled *A Man for all Ages* about a dynamic interview between a fifty-four-year-old worker in the auto industry and General Motors. Write a short screenplay, including possible questions and answers, and an outcome. Now, get a few friends together over perfect pizza and make a short movie. You are the director, so tell the protagonist what to say and how to say it using the screenplay and script you wrote. Make the actor deliver an honest portrayal. Orchestrate the set—make the setting believable. You are the set director, so put the props together, a desk, chairs, a restaurant scene, or a cocktail party, for example.

The interviewer should be a young hiring manager, skeptical and slightly condescending but with a need to hire someone. The second cut could be with a different type of interviewer. The candidate can play any of several types as well. Use your video recorder, and replay it to the group over laughs and the last of the pizza. Discuss what you learned.

CHAPTER 15

Preparation: Research Sources and Methods

In This Chapter

➤ Research methods

➤ A research framework

➤ Hard sources

➤ Soft sources

➤ Useful websites

➤ A recommended booklist

In this chapter you dig into research about your job opportunity and explore a useful framework from which to approach data gathering. Preparatory research comes in both hard and soft varieties and the chapter gives details about each.

Research: You Can Never Know too Much

The act of preparation for most candidates involves the uncovering of a few incidental facts about the company. Perhaps they look at a website, see what the firm does, and look at a brochure. Then they call it quits and think they are ready. That is called inadequate research.

Instead, world-class research efforts must go well beyond the norm. Research means among other things, uncovering firm strategy, what others say about the company and industry, key management initiatives, product features, and the list goes on. It means discovering corporate weaknesses, culture, competitive pressures, financial data, acceptable appearance, and on and on until your brain gets tired.

Researching a company usually means finding out financial information (balance sheet, stock price, various inventory and production ratios), facts about management (name, background, press releases), and information on the firm's products and markets (description, customers, location, competitors, complaints). It also means uncovering the firm's marketing strategy, regulatory issues, merger and acquisitions activity, and other business combination issues.

If you are interviewing for a job as a clerk in a candy store, you still should know what brands of candy are sold, right? How about pricing information, discount availability, closest competitors, rankings of brands and shelf space, distributor relationships, and promotions? You will know all there is to know about the candy store if you want the job badly enough.

Interview Insights

Researching a competitor of your target firm can also provide valuable information. Competitors hear about your target firm from their own clients and those of your target firm. This way, you gain insight into your target firm's products, services, and strengths and weaknesses. Also, you come to understand the firm's reputation as seen through a competitor. Find a friend of a friend who works for a competitor, and take him or her for coffee.

A Research Framework

Below is a simple framework for research and a small sample of questions for which you might want answers. Remember the framework by the ludicrous, but usable, acronym, 4Ps, a CFO, and a Mickey Mouse Government (PPPPCFOMMG). The framework is:

➤ Product (P): What products are the firm concerned with? What are the characteristics, strengths and weaknesses, features of the products? Is there room for growth? Is the firm mature or emerging? What is the firm's R&D pipeline? What is the quality and reputation of the firm's products?

➤ Price (P): What is the firm's standard margin (price over cost)? Is the firm a price follower or price setter? Is there room for price increases? How are the firm's prices relative to the competition? What are the production costs?

➤ People (P): How long do key personnel stay on the job? Who have been the recent departures and hires; do they have a defined career path? What is the morale of the employees? What is the firm's promotion policy, turnover, and training? What are the reporting lines, accountability, and sanctions?

➤ Platform (P): What are the firm's operating efficiencies? What type of IT support and infrastructure does the firm have? Does the firm have support-to-line personnel? What are the administrative issues? What about procurement and sales support?

➤ Competition (C): Who are the firm's prime competitors, and what is their product array? How does the firm rank in industry rankings by a third party? How strong is the firm's rivalry with other companies? What advantages does the firm have?

➤ Financial (F): What are the firm's balance sheet issues, debt coverage ratios, capital structure, lead banks, stock and bond information, recent securities issues, quality of earnings, inventory and receivables management?

➤ Organizational (O): What is the firm's structure? Is it flat or is it hierarchical? Who makes the decisions and allocate resources? What is the company culture, size, reporting lines, and strategic?

➤ Market Information (M): What so analyst reports say about the firm? What's the firm's macroeconomic elasticity, client segmentation, domestic vs overseas ratio?

➤ Media (M): Research press releases and news reports both negative and positive. Check out the firm's video history, Internet site, and use of next generation social media.

➤ Government (G): What is the government's extent of regulation and exposure? What are the government oversight bodies for the firm? Have there been SEC inquiries, Wells letters, etc.?

Information versus Data

Data is easy to find, but information is different. You need to sift the data and understand it before it becomes information. Then you need to synthesize it and figure out what to do with it and what it could mean to you.

For example during your PPPPCFOMMG research, let's say you found that the head of human relations and the chief financial officer both left the company within the last few months. Absent any direct information to the contrary, you should triangulate that data to find out what it means. Check with people at rival firms, read analyst reports or press releases and commentaries to find out where the pair

Interview Vocab

Triangulating data means to find two other sources to confirm or deny the facts.

went after they left the firm. Did they go to a rival? Did they resign or were they fired? Once you get the data and confirm it, you can make judgments about whether it matters or not.

Information Gathering

Use public sources on the Internet as well as at the library. Government sources, such as the Department of Labor *Occupational Outlook Handbook* (*OOH*), lists jobs by six-digit NAICS code and four-digit SIC code. If you recall, these codes classify industries and companies and categorize them accordingly. They eventually direct you to information about specific occupations. In the *OOH* you can find information concerning various types of jobs, employment statistics, experience needed for specific positions, job growth forecasts, knowledge requirements, etc.

Speak to people in the industry to gain better insight. Use the alumni network; go to trade shows where competitors might give insight. Try to use their product, or try to talk to people that do. Speak to friends in the consulting world who specialize in your target company's industry. Many times the major consulting and accounting companies issue white papers on industries, trends in the global economy, regulatory and company-specific issues. Call them and ask for the papers or visit their websites.

Hard Sources

Hard sources involve the discovery of information through technology or media. Begin by listing relevant sources of information and a method of capturing and formatting the data. If you are a student, your career center can be a great place to go to get information from online databases about industries, companies, prior interview sessions, etc. It will have access to most of the databases that provide company and industry information.

Put the firm on a watch list for stock price, valuation, analyst views, product innovations, news articles (utilize a news retrieval alert list), and other key factors. You can do this through any online brokerage company. Get an annual report, 10K report (issued by the company), and other required disclosures to discover financial and other strategic data (ye old public library has access to these). CNBC also has a helpful website you can check daily for commentary.

Alert Notifications

Decide must-know information points and keep the information flowing automatically. Would you be alerted if there were an invasion of South Korea or a terror incident or a meltdown in major stock markets? It would be embarrassing to walk into an interview and not know that a major event had occurred that has potential impacts on your target company.

News retrieval services like Bloomberg (www.Bloomberg.com), Fortune magazine (www. Fortune.com), The Wall Street Journal (www.WSJ.com), Thomson Financial (www.thomson.com) have excellent company information, as well as debt and equity capital markets information, including investment banking league tables. Forbes magazine (www. forbes.com) is an excellent all-in-one site for general business news, global issues, and markets-related data, including an analyst ranking by industry. Most of these types of sites have alert messaging capability.

Harvard Business School Press (www.hbsp.harvard.edu) also has a site filled with the latest thinking from leading business authors. The Harvard Business School Case Clearing House (www.hbr.org/case_studies) and the School of Law (www.law.harvard.edu) also have excellent sites where cases and texts concerning public and private issues can be purchased, including some excellent readings on negotiation. Stanford University and the University of Chicago do likewise. Plus, most retail brokerage firms such as Schwab, Fidelity, and E*TRADE have websites with research about industries and companies.

As of this writing Edgar Online, Inc., maintains SEC mandated information on over 14,000 U.S. firms and over 30,000 worldwide. The information contains SEC filings, director information, initial public offering (IPO) information, and at least eight years of quarterly financial data on U.S. companies (see www.freeedgar.com). Edgar is a U.S. government–mandated data handling service that provides investors with information about specific companies and their filings. Edgar Online and Free Edgar are not affiliated with the SEC's Edgar service.

The Government and Other Thinkers

The U.S. government also has other helpful sites such as the Library of Congress (www.loc.gov); the Department of State (www.dos.gov); and the Central Intelligence Agency (www.cia.gov); The World Fact Book at CIA is an excellent compilation of country-level information. Although not part of the government think tanks, the Rand Corporation (www.rand.org) or the Hoover Institute at Stanford (www. hoover.org) publish white papers regularly on issues of our time, including economic matters. Think tanks are great

Interview Vocab

A think tank is a research-based, nonprofit organization dedicated to analysis of public interest topics. Some are partisan organizations; others purport to be nonpartisan, objective institutions. They are great sources for information on foreign affairs, environment, taxes, unemployment, jobs, defense, education, and many other topics.

sources of useful information and events in particular about key issues that might affect a particular company or industry, such as the nuclear energy industry. Check out hks. harvard.edu for a long list of think tanks. As with all sites mentioned in this book, test the information before you act upon it.

Soft Sources

Research on soft sources involves meeting with people who know about the company. Those people could be from the press, the chambers of commerce, competitors in the industry, or academia. Attend corporate luncheons, where people from that industry gather, and ask what attendees know about company XYZ. This is particularly helpful for the energy, technology, defense, and health care industries.

Gain HUMINT

In the world of spies and spooks, soft sources are known as human intelligence, or HUMINT. If the company is an open forum, such as a museum or retail establishment, then go there. Ask employees how they like working there. Listen to the interplay between the employees and how they interact with customers. Engage with an onsite manager by asking questions a customer might ask.

About one month ahead of the interview is the time to extract information from key players in your network. These networks will help to refine background information and studies of target firms.

Extend your social and business network to people beyond your standard web. Ask for referrals. Remember the six degrees. Get to people who know the company or have interacted with it. Former employees are great sources of information—they may have an ax to grind, so be aware.

Basic Research: Try the Product

Try the company's product, if possible, as well as those of its competitors. What better way to know the firm and how competitive it is? Every piece of intelligence is important when strung together into an understandable pattern. Think of building a mosaic of bits and pieces of information and then sewing them all together for a more complete picture. Using a company's product gives insight into what its customers go through and what its competitors might think.

Job Search and Other Helpful Websites

The websites listed below in the table are separated into four basic categories but all have elements that will help you in your job search. Some offer free services, others might require a subscription fee. Some of the sites offer free trial periods for only the price of registering your name and e-mail address. In some cases, very robust sites such as www.mergent.com are almost institutional in nature and may only be available through a university, library, or research institute. They do provide top-notch research databases on public and private companies, important executives, corporate actions, etc.

ALL-PURPOSE SITES	GOVERNMENT & OTHER USEFUL SITES	INDUSTRY & INTEREST-SPECIFIC SITES	BUSINESS SITES
theladders.com	usajobs.opm.gov	lawjobs.com	hoovers.com
jobrap.com	dcjobsource.coM	selectleaders.com (real estate)	forbes.com
ivyexec.com	governmentjobs.com	topschooljobs.org (education)	nytimes.com
linked-in.com	govjobs.com	journalismjobs.com	foundationcenter.org
resumerabbit.com	federaljobs.net	defenseindustrycentral.com	bloomberg.com
tweetmyjobs.com	americajob.com	accountingjobstoday.com	uschamber.com
trovix.com	jobsfed.com	burryman.com (freelance writers)	guidestar.org
snagajob.com	cia.gov	bloggingpro.com (bloggers etc.)	thomasnet.com
careerbuilder.com	sec.gov/edgar	healthcarejobsite.com	nawbo.org
beyond.com www.elance.com	edgar-online.com dol.gov	airlinejobfinder.com	zapdata.com (phone and mailing lists)
indeed.com	www.everest.com lexisnexis.com	agjobs.com (agribusiness)	employment911.com
simplyhired.com	realtor.com ehow.com	talentzoo.com (media related)	employmentguide.com
oodle.com	thepaperboy.com (International and national newspapers)	jobsinlogistics.com (logistics)	dnb.com
jobster.com	commerce.gov	telecomindustryjobs.com	skyminder.com (Business intelligence)

ALL-PURPOSE SITES	GOVERNMENT & OTHER USEFUL SITES	INDUSTRY & INTEREST-SPECIFIC SITES	BUSINESS SITES
monster.com	fool.com	prjobforce.com (public relations) www.backstage.com (acting jobs)	manta.com (Information on small businesses)
jobcentral.com	hrhero.com	engineeringjobs.com (engineering)	history.com
vault.com	historyplace.com/ speeches	rigzone.com (oil and gas)	cfr.org
jobing.com	foreignpolicy.com	schoolspring.com (teachers) agcareers.com (agribusiness)	businessweek.com
jobengine.com	history.com	constructionjobs.com	worklifepolicy.org
jobfox.com	Bing.com	jobs.prsa.org (public relations)	metacrawler.com
college-recruiter.com	foreignaffairs.com	sciencejobs.org	csis.com
aftercollege.com	heritage.org	hcareers.com (hospitality industry)	ask.com
dice.com	hoover.org	jobsinsports.com	economist.com
employmentguide.com	ebizmba.com	nursingjobs.org	informationweek.com
jobs.aol.com	resume-resource.com	martindale.com (law)	international-business-center.com
jobBankUSA.com	definitions.net	traveljobwire.com	economywatch.com
IMDiversity.com	ask.com	careerchange.com	fortune.com
jobslinenetwork.com	concierge.com	salesjobs.com	crains.com
www.zoo.com	*craigslist.com*	*www.workinsports.com*	*www.womenforhire. com/advice/professional dress and appearance*

Interview Insights

If you're a really serious candidate, develop a book selection list like the one offered in this chapter—pick those relevant to your desired job. Many are business and economics books that will help you understand the macro-environment in which you are seeking employment. Some also will help you understand how to better market yourself. Others help you understand how firms operate, how to be a great leader, and other topics of interest. Such reading will provide a backdrop or a lens through which you can construct a view of the world and a thoughtful articulation of your perspectives.

jobsandmoms.com	smallbiztrends.com	cranes.com (construction)	ala.org/rusa

A Business-Oriented Book List

The following is a reading list you may find helpful during your research.

Beckwith, Harry. *Selling the Invisible*. New York: Warner Books, 1997.

Chernow, Ron. *The House of Morgan*. New York: Atlantic Monthly Press, 1980.

Collins, Jim. *Good to Great*. New York: Harper Collins, 2001.

Evans, Phillip and Thomas S. Wurster. *Blown to Bits*. Boston: Harvard Business School Press, 2000.

Fisher, Roger and Alan Sharp. *Getting it Done*. New York: Harper Business, 1998.

Fox, Jeffrey J. *Customers and Clients*. New York: Hyperion, 2000.

Gladwell, Malcolm. *Blink: The Power of Thinking without Thinking*. New York: Little Brown and Company, 2005.

Guiliani, Rudy. *Leadership*. New York: Hyperion, 2002.

Hastings, Hunter and Jeff Saperstein. *Improve Your Marketing to Grow Your Business: Insights and Innovation that Drive Business and Brand Growth*. Upper Saddle River New Jersey: Wharton School Publishing, 2007.

Hayward, Steven F. *Churchill on Leadership: Executive Success in the Face of Adversity*. Rocklin, Ca: Prima Publishing, 1997.

Koegel, Timothy J. *The Exceptional Presenter*. Austin, Texas: Greenleaf Book Group, 2007.

Levitt, Ted. *The Marketing Imagination*. New York: The Free Press, 1986.

Weissman, Jerry. *Presenting to Win: The Art of Telling Your Story*. London: FT Press, 2006.

An Inspirational Book List

The following is a reading list to raise your spirits and inspire.

Ambrose, Stephen. *Undaunted Courage: Meriwether Lewis, Thomas Jefferson, and the Opening of the American West*. New York: Simon & Schuster, 1997.

Donald, David Herbert. *Lincoln*. New York: Simon & Schuster, 1995.

Isacson, Walter. *Kissinger: A Biography*. New York: Simon & Schuster, 2005.

Kasal, Brad and Nathaniel R. Helms. *My Men Are My Heroes: The Brad Kasal Story*. Des Moines: Meridith Books, 2007.

Luttrell, Marcus and Patrick Robinson. *Lone Survivor*. New York: Little, Brown, Co., 2007.

McCullough, David. *1776*. New York: Simon & Schuster, 2006.

Other ideas include reading a good biography of a great historical figure; read a travel book about another culture or region such as in China, India, or Brazil; read a Pulitzer Prize-winning novel; study an overview book covering the great masterpieces of literature.

Interview Vocab

The whole-person concept was offered first by Twentieth-century American philosopher Mortimer Adler, who reportedly said, "Whole Persons are engaged in a lifetime quest to achieve balance and congruity in all aspects of their lives and continually seek to develop their full human potential." A whole person is one who understands the importance of a broad-based education and a grasp of the world's treasures. The term as used here refers to one's educational reach—the expanse of one's intellectual curiosity—and a desire to be well rounded.

Whole person does not mean someone is less than human if he or she does not ascribe to this concept. And it does not attest to a person's development as a kind and decent human. The term does not insinuate a mental incapacity or deficiency either. **Whole person** is simply not a pejorative term. Now is that politically correct or what!

The Whole Person Concept

By developing your overall fitness you can be more relaxed and self-assured. The whole-person concept makes you a well-rounded person who would be an interesting teammate or person to have dinner with a client. With a higher job level, a higher level of cultural and social sophistication is usually needed. A well-rounded person shows an ability to converse at some level on most topics that are issues in society: history, art, politics, music, sports, etc. Think of what might be discussed around a dinner table or over a cocktail or at a sports event with those who might hire you. Don't be the only person who doesn't know what the discussion is all about. You don't need to be an expert, just be aware. The PAG Assessment will help as will the reading lists provided in this chapter and in Appendix D. Research other topics that could help you become well rounded.

Using Your PAG Assessment in the Interview

Earlier, you used the PAG to uncover areas of interest and your strengths and weaknesses. In fact, you should mention to the interviewer that you have engaged in the PAG as evidence of a serious effort to match skills with the job's requirements.

For example, if the interviewer asks, "Tell me a weak area you have." You can say, "I recently went through a personal analysis on that topic and found that I needed a plan to develop a broader range of interests that could also impact my business. For instance, as part of my reading program, I read a book recently about communications techniques ministers use to inspire their flocks. There are some outstanding sales tools at work there that could help my business. I now ask my subordinates to develop a similar game plan to fix their shortcomings."

After all, you are implementing the action plan that culminated in the conversation in the interview! That is an important point to make to anyone who is trying to learn about you.

Chapter Homework

1. Pick a company and utilize the PPPPCFOMMG framework.

2. Make a selection from the book list and begin reading it. Can you apply concepts in the book to your experiences or your business?

3. What example do you have to show commitment and dedication? Are you an interesting person?

4. Try out several of the websites, especially the megasearch engines like www.metacrawler.com

CHAPTER 16

Preparation: Time is and is not on Your Side

> ## In This Chapter
>
> ➤ Time marches on
> ➤ Phases
> ➤ What if time is short?

In this chapter you learn about a timeline of activities to ensure you move steadily toward your goals and cover all the bases prior to an interview.

Time Phases

Time is relentless. In some cases, you will have weeks or months to prepare for an interview. In other cases, especially if you are a career changer, you may have only a few days of warning before an interview. You take them when they come, right?

Therefore, it is a good idea to build a schedule that parses the time prior to the interview into discreet phases filled with activity. Depending upon the amount of time prior to the interview, build a six-phase approach.

If the time is compressed, the phased approach will help ameliorate the effects of a surprise interview and ensure you don't neglect key activities. If you leave your planning to the ad-hoc approach, industry-specific research, practice sessions, and other preinterview tasks such as intelligence gathering may be shortchanged. You can begin many of the activities described below before you know you have a specific interview. Then, when you get the notification, you will already be well down the learning curve. So, start basic PPPPCFOMMG-type analytical work now in case you are surprised by a compressed time schedule.

The phases below illustrate a recommended approach, but you should customize it to meet your needs.

Phase One: General Preparation

Phase one should ideally start thirty to sixty days out from your interview. In this phase conduct core PPPPCFOMMG research. Uncover background information on the firm's business, its sector, key executives, its product mix, competitive positioning; research reports from Wall Street, key industry dynamics, and other articles written about the company by third parties. For example consult a website like www.bloomberg.com or www.zoominfo. com (information on over 5 million businesses and 50 million employees in 2011) for key information about a company and its industry. There you will find:

➤ Recent news on the industry and the company

➤ Recent press releases

➤ Snapshots of earnings, employees, and stock price history

➤ Pertinent articles about specific industries (retail, energy, finance, consumer goods)

➤ News about key regulatory or legislative issues affecting the company and industry

Reminders and other Phase One Activities

➤ Set e-mail alerts

➤ Continue work on your PAG

➤ Start work on offset strategies

➤ Develop a contact network

➤ Get informational interviews

➤ Find an executive mentor who is interested in your success, and keep him or her apprised of your efforts

The Daily Journal

Start a daily journal to record information and other facts and ideas as they come to you, such as ways of illustrating your experience or observations about the economy or new laws. You can purchase journals from your local bookstore. If you prefer, use your laptop and start your journal there. Review your entries each night, record your thoughts and plans, and start to incorporate these observations into your movie. Carry it with you—you never know when you might have a record-breaking insight.

Use the following as an example:

Date and Time	Comments
January 12th Barney's Coffee Shop on Maple Street	Overheard conversation about a job at Widget Co. Two employees discussed working environment there. Great culture, benefits, and they thought a new job was opening in purchasing. Check out website.
January 16th Dr. Pope's waiting room	Read an article about using stories to describe your life. Good interview technique??? What about my trip to Japan and China last year—learning the language, tell the story in Mandarin??
January 20th Shopping	Saw a new suit at Benton's Apparel—$800. Check on Buy.com. Put it on hold 'til tomorrow.
January 25th Meeting with suppliers at work	Discussed the new IT infrastructure project—volunteered. Could be great for the résumé. Tell the boss I want it.
Feb 27th Heard interview on radio; also, heard earnings from ABC Corp weren't very good	Heard politician about economy—expects higher inflation and more unemployment. Yikes! Check out his blog—cross-check on Forbes.com and others about Widget Corp. What's wrong? Sales? Product?
January 28th Heard about website and opportunities at State Dept. from Prof. Thomas in Poli Sci class	Check out www.cia.gov and state.gov for info on countries, etc. Call about foreign service exam.
Feb 3rd Spoke to Linda	Wants to work on personal scripts—get coffee together!!! She can hear my life story! And weaknesses too—ugh!

Start a Reading Program

Indulge in readings specific to your industry about trends, major players, new products and technologies, strategic elements, personnel moves, etc. If you are in school and don't have time to read a broad array of material, try summary services or reading book reviews in lieu of reading entire books.

Regularly read the standard magazines and newspapers: *The Wall Street Journal, Business Week, Forbes, Fortune, The Economist, Financial Times, Barrons,* and your industry's trade journals. For instance, if you want to work in construction, substitute some of the above with McGraw Hill's *Construction* for news about people, projects, and current affairs related to the industry. Also *Construction Outlook*, an annual report, offers information on economic data, forecasts, trends, and regional information.

Other industries have journals similar to *Construction Outlook.* PhRMA is a consortium of member pharmaceutical companies advocating on behalf of the pharmaceutical industry.

It publishes *Profile,* a report on key factors affecting the industry. Use a search engine like Google to discover other such periodicals for different industries.

Interview Insights

The Economist magazine issues its annual *Global Outlook,* a world roundup of economic statistics by country. This is extremely useful preinterview reading, especially if your target company is a global enterprise.

Phase One Schedule

Begin this schedule as far in advance of the interview as possible. The sample schedule of activities below is for a professional position. While the reading portion may not be appropriate for some positions you are targeting, there is nothing wrong with everyone broadening their understanding of economic issues facing the country. This schedule should start during phase one and continue throughout your program.

Modify the schedule as you see fit with magazine and news articles that are specific to your industry or chosen trade or profession. Engage in a reading program (either print or online editions) similar to the following:

➤ Every weekday: Scan a newspaper like The *Wall Street Journal, New York Times,* or the world news and business sections of your local paper for economic data, world affairs, and financial data. Read the *Financial Times* (www.FT.com) for a global economic perspective. Listen to or download CNBC/Fox Business/Bloomberg News for background commentary on the economy, trends, and the financial markets.

➤ Monday: Visit news-based websites such as www.fortune.com; www.businessweek.com; www.foreignpolicy.com.

➤ Tuesday: Read two chapters from a book off your reading lists

➤ Wednesday: Read articles from a nonbusiness magazine on sports, culture, or the arts.

➤ Thursday: Scan www.forbes.com; read one article in *Foreign Affairs*; visit a think tank website such as www.hoover.org, www.heritage.org, or www.cato.org.

➤ Friday: Scan trade magazines relevant to your industry; read two chapters in the book *Good to Great.*

➤ Saturday: Read *Barrons*; begin a novel of your choice; scan the weekend *Wall Street Journal*; scan the *New York Times* business, arts, and international sections.

➤ Sunday: Read an article in *Foreign Affairs*; scan two chapters from the nonbusiness book selection list.

After you finish reading *Good to Great* (or a substitute), choose another book and continue the schedule. The amount you absorb is dependent upon when you get started. By sticking to a rigorous schedule of reading, you can start to build a current issues knowledge base. Periodically look at the Discovery or History channels on television.

Time to Develop Your Brand Presentation

In phase one, further develop your personal brand and the stories that support it. Capture tales about your experience, skills, etc. Work on your dialogue exercises. Consult an appearance advisor about your brand and what clothing suits you, then purchase the items. Quality tailoring takes time so start this in phase one. Be certain to try your new threads and have someone give feedback while you can still exchange them!

Phase Two: Story Development

This phase starts after your basic research is well under way and should be at least two weeks before an interview. It is time to weave together your story via the personal scripts. Other phase two activities are:

➤ Review the location, if possible—plan on visiting the site and look for possible issues around seating, lighting, drugstores, book stores, cafes, etc. And make sure of your directions and backup routes.

➤ Conduct intelligence activities on the firm and on your rivals.

➤ Practice and record mock interviews; team with an interview partner or partners.

➤ Determine the nature of the interview (group, panel, etc.).

➤ Is the interview with a preliminary round with an HR person, or is it someone senior?

➤ Develop your entrance and exit. Develop good opening and closing statements and your three main points. For example, practice the opening introductory greeting, the reason you should be hired, etc.

Questioning the Interviewer

In phase two, develop a list of substantive questions to ask the company. Questions you ask say a lot about you, so make certain they are not run-of-the-mill or ones that you could find out by spending a few minutes on the company's website. Depending upon the circumstance, position, and industry, study the following question examples:

➤ Can the interviewer describe the nature of the duties associated with this job?

➤ What are the key issues faced by the industry and the firm?

➤ Can the firm describe the current state of the economy and its effect upon the firm's business?

➤ What is the firm's strategy or business plan? (Listen carefully to the answer. Be ready to respond to questions about it.)

➤ What is the firm's commitment to your line of business?

➤ Can the interviewer give examples of employee teamwork?

➤ What are the specific resources available to your business line?

➤ What about career advancement—does the firm have a formal career progression path?

➤ Is there a formal training program? If not, what about mentoring or other suggestions?

➤ Is on-the-job training available?

➤ Will you be expected to work independently?

➤ What is the firm's profit picture (latest earnings and any balance sheet issues, etc.)?

➤ Will you have authority commensurate with your responsibility?

➤ What are the work hours and benefits, including vesting and eligibility for profit sharing, 401(k) retirement plans, health plans, and vacation?

➤ What are expectations about your goals?

➤ Who will be your immediate supervisor and what is his or her background?

➤ Are there additional duties beyond the primary job?

➤ What are the strengths and weaknesses of the firm's product or service (from the interviewer's perspective)?

➤ Determine the process following the interview—when will you get feedback?

Be sure to weave these questions into the interview discussion, and not hit them all at once.

Contingency Planning

Develop contingency plans based upon "what if" worst case scenarios. These should be developed to give you the comfort of knowing what your reaction will be if you spill your coffee on your brand-new suit, or you call the interviewer by the wrong name.

Contingencies can be categorized into:

➤ Logistics problems, including transportation, weather, hotels, funding, changes in interview venue

➤ Dress and appearance issues, including lost baggage, ruined clothing, forgotten items

➤ Content issues, including last-minute updates to information germane to the interviewing firm or candidate, unexpected Q&A, unanticipated changes to job requirements

Planning for Travel

When you find that you have an interview, it is natural to wonder who pays for any travel involved. Obviously, the type of firm and the prospective position drives this decision. The higher the status of the position, the better the chances are that the firm will pay for travel expenses (transportation, hotel, meals) either directly or through a recruiting firm.

If the firm asks you to come to its location, assume it will pay, but verify that is the case. Ask the HR coordinator, administrative assistant, or other person handling your interview.

In some cases, the firm will not pay for costs. Consult your tax advisor because some job-search expenses may qualify as tax deductible (résumé preparation, travel related to interviews, relocation costs).

Other travel issues are:

➤ Find a hotel near the interview site.

➤ Leave plenty of time for travel delays to and from the airport, station, etc.

➤ Think of backup transportation modes, especially for unfamiliar cities.

➤ Locate a drugstore nearby for toiletries, newspapers, etc.

➤ Travel lightly and use carry-on bags to avoid misrouted and lost luggage.

➤ Upon arrival, locate the interview site, if possible.

➤ Keep only a small amount of cash on hand.

➤ Keep identity documents secure when traveling to unfamiliar places—use the hotel safe.

➤ Upon arrival call to confirm time and location of the interview and the nature of any changes.

➤ Take luggage with you to the interview and secure it with an assistant if time is tight following the interview.

Phase Three: Jam Time

One week before the interview is when you set important aspects of your plan into motion. This is the animation phase where you internalize your interview tactics. It is when you start to act out your mechanics and refine your personal scripts delivery. Review earlier video attempts and redo it. Set up a schedule for practice interviews. Do a live rehearsal with a trusted agent and look for your vulnerabilities. Use a video recorder and allow buddy partners to review one another's work.

Continue reading *Business Week, Forbes,* and *Fortune* especially for macro economy, numbers, and industry-specific trends. Refresh "what if" scenarios with the latest intelligence.

Interview Insights

Some interviewers take questions right out of popular magazines or newspapers. Reviewing a publication like *The Wall Street Journal* on a daily basis builds a solid foundation in international affairs, economics, technology trends, and other social issues. Generally conservative based upon its editorial page, the other sections are technical data and objective. It is an interviewer's paradise. Read it every day, regardless of your industry.

Phase three includes the days just prior to the day of the interview so develop a chain of events for the few hours ahead of the appointment. Some activities include:

➤ Continue practicing!

➤ Review updates about the company on a daily basis.

➤ Review e-alerts and messages.

➤ Review your daily journal.

➤ Build inclement weather scenarios, parking issues, etc.

➤ Try to get the interviewer's name.

➤ Confirm time, location, and format

➤ No later than one week before the interview, dry clean your interview clothing; have a backup clothing plan.

➤ Shine your shoes the evening before the interview.

➤ Have a good meal and get a restful sleep the evening before the interview.

Phase Four: Interview Day

It's game time. Eat a nutritious meal two to three hours before the interview. Studies show performance increases 25 percent with a good meal prior to stressful situations. Use the checklist in Appendix A. Other items of interest include:

➤ Confirm scheduled departure times.

➤ Check news updates: listen to CNBC, Bloomberg TV, or the radio.

➤ Review the local business section of your paper.

➤ Check sources for late-breaking news alerts on the company and industry.

➤ Check with the placement agent or other firm handler for any updates on the interview.

➤ Recheck the weather (www.accuweather.com).

➤ Take a breather and go to the gym or do something for fun if time permits.

➤ Arrive at the site fifteen minutes early—confirm that the site is where you expect it to be.

➤ Determine if the interview is on schedule.

➤ Check your grooming and appearance.

➤ Mentally review your opening and closing remarks.

➤ Imagine personal scripts topics and subtopics.

➤ Remind yourself to get contact information for every person with whom you interviewed. Don't forget the gatekeeper! Get interviewers' business cards to ensure the correct spelling of names, phone numbers, and addresses.

➤ Get your business cards ready.

➤ Review your cheat sheet of key topics, economic data, and your three main points.

➤ Remind yourself to ask about the next steps and timing. The firm owes you an answer one way or the other. Most reputable firms will let you know, but some do not. Don't let it bug you—you probably dodged a bullet with that firm anyway.

Phase Five: The Follow-Up

Start your follow-up as you are leaving the interview room. If you know you made a mistake in an answer, tell the interviewer you have some additional information you would like to send that further amplifies an answer. Then send a brief note ASAP. If necessary, slip the career center coordinator a note on the way out with the right answer and ask that it reach the interviewer. Refer to chapter 31 for more detailed information on actual follow-up activities.

➤ If you are a student, thank career center personnel for their assistance.

➤ Call the executive recruiter, if applicable, and give feedback on your performance, next steps, etc.

➤ Call trusted agents with results.

➤ Record your follow-up steps in your daily journal.

➤ Go to a pub (just joking).

Interview Insights

If you make a mistake in the interview, correct misstatements as rapidly as possible so that the interviewer knows you would never leave a client hanging with the wrong information. Incorrect information can snowball if decisions are made based upon it. This is particularly true if the client is depending upon your judgment before proceeding with a project, an investment, etc. Salespeople correcting errors quickly have won new business—it is a sign of integrity that clients like. You can't string together mistakes, but correcting an isolated error is simply good business.

Phase Six: Lessons Learned and Integrated

As soon as possible following the interview—certainly within an hour—record your insights. This phase is tied to the dynamic interview training model, so do the following:

➤ Create a lessons learned section in your daily journal; record facts, omissions, and commissions you learned about at the firm, your execution, Q&A, errors, etc.

➤ Consider what you did well and what needs more work. Roll this into the dynamic interview training model preparation and practice cycle.

> ➤ Grade your effectiveness.

> ➤ Did you get your three main points across?

> ➤ How effective were your closing and opening statements?

> ➤ Were you off-balance at any time? Were there areas in which you were not well rehearsed or researched?

> ➤ Ask your trusted agent to debrief you about the interview.

> ➤ Record technical questions where your answers seemed confusing or you were uncomfortable.

These are the types of questions you should ask yourself. Learn!

Phase Compression

What if you find out that you only have a few days before an interview? Develop a quick reaction activities list consisting of WSJ online, Internet alerts, logistics and transportation requirements, and contact information. Get MapQuest or Google maps directions to the interview site. Use Hoovers, Edgar, etc. Practice your opening and closing statements.

Chapter Homework

1. Set up your timeline activities on your laptop or home computer. Begin using the schedule of activities.

2. Determine questions to ask during an interview.

Quotable Quotes

"An intellectual is a man who takes more words than necessary to tell more than he knows."

Dwight D. Eisenhower

"What may be done at any time will be done at no time."

Scottish Proverb

CHAPTER 17

Practice: Want to Fly a Chair?

In This Chapter

➤ An exercise in imagination

➤ Muscle memory

➤ Doctors, soldiers, athletes, and conductors

➤ Mock interview sessions

This chapter initiates the second part of the dynamic interview training model, the practice phase, by using several novel techniques based upon routines utilized by military operatives, actors, surgeons, athletes, and others. The chapter also discusses how to use your trusted agents in practice sessions called mock interviews.

The Amazing Brain

Mental processes and the way a person learns interact with the physical structure of the body in dynamic and interesting ways. Your brain drives the body language you use and convey during an interview. Harnessing the brain-body interconnection has allowed many different professionals when under stress to gain confidence and project authority. It is, in short, practicing the art and craft of brain-body power—the amazing concept of muscle memory. It can work for you, too.

Quotable Quotes

"Imagination grows by exercise, and contrary to common belief, is more powerful in the mature than in the young."

W. Somerset Maugham

A Picture is Worth a Thousand Words of Feedback

The first time you see yourself on camera can be an eye-opening experience. You use gestures, mannerisms, and body language you never realized, and some of them can detract from your performance. Here is a notable parade of stars for which your trusted agents should be on guard:

> ➤ Mr. Shifty Eyes
>
> ➤ Mr. Slumpee
>
> ➤ Ms. Bangs in Eyes
>
> ➤ Ms. La Perfumery
>
> ➤ Ms. Swipe Her Hair
>
> ➤ Mr. Vice Grip
>
> ➤ Mr. and Ms. Sweaty Hands
>
> ➤ Mr. and Ms. Nodding Head
>
> ➤ Mr. and Ms. Stiff Body
>
> ➤ Mr. Stuff-His-Face
>
> ➤ Mr. Soup Slurper II

These names depict self-explanatory behaviors. However, you may not be aware of your own behavior because no one has told you. Fortunately, video replays rarely lie so get someone to record you while you eat a meal, enter a room, issue a greeting, etc. If you are afflicted with a body language malady, then you will need to train your body and mind to change your behavior.

Interview Vocab

Body language is a term used to describe the image manifested by a person's posture, facial expressions, hand usage, and other physical movements. Body language is used as a means to convey certain messages. These messages could be subliminal or overt, intended or unintended. They can be used tactically to send signals of acceptance, boredom, displeasure, anger, and many other emotions.

Mock Interviews and the Rules of Engagement

When you practice, use the unbiased opinions of your trusted agents to further your progress. Real time feedback from someone who has your best interests at heart is priceless.

Your trusted agent should possess certain attributes in order to attain the optimum result. He or she shouldn't tell you what you want to hear. Instead, an unvarnished critique about what went well and what went wrong is what you need to hear.

Get two trusted agents to help with the mock interviews. The scenarios should not always be from your chosen career field—the more you interview in unusual circumstances, the better you become at connecting the dots and fielding uncomfortable questions. It induces the discomfort you might feel when coping with an unusual question in an actual interview.

The more you simulate a real interview, the better the training benefit. Use an interview-styled room, or do it over dinner or drinks. Simulated interviewers should insert a few distractions into the game, such as telephone interruptions. Study the career fields a bit so you have some idea of the content, and do a quick personal scripts workup.

Mock interview sessions, and samples of actual or near-actual interviews are presented in Appendix B. Use the facts presented in those scenarios to formulate believable questions.

First, the interviewer should go to Appendix B and analyze the situations that highlight some of the principles that we have learned. As you, the job candidate, answer the interview questions, the interviewer should note how you use the following:

- ➤ Relevant and/or leading examples
- ➤ Steering the interview
- ➤ Great opening and closing words
- ➤ Quantifying achievements
- ➤ Opportunities to use body language
- ➤ Three summary points
- ➤ Connectivity
- ➤ Being memorable
- ➤ Creating the client context

Time for a Few Laughs

As a test, without worrying much about the questioning, set up a trial run in a mock interview environment such as over dinner, in an interview room, in a cocktail setting, perhaps in a group. Act as you probably would in a real interview. Be yourself. Then get your trusted agent to record you during the trial run. If nothing else it will be good for a few laughs afterward.

Remember, for the real interview, you need to "Train like you will fight, and fight like you trained." If you train in a haphazard manner, you will most likely perform that way. If you train rigorously, then trust your preparation and execute according to your plan.

The History of Chair Flying

Flying a chair conjures a funny image to most people, but don't worry, your feet will never leave the ground.

Interview Vocab

Chair flying is a technique used to develop almost instantaneous reaction to external stimuli; a practice tool used by those in high-stress environments to further develop muscle memory. It's an excellent practice tool for interviews, sales presentations, speeches, explosive ordinance disposals, jury summations, etc.

Back in the early 1900s, when first learning to fly the newfangled air-flying machines, pilots memorized a number of emergency procedures and made them second nature.

Over a hundred years later and even with the availability of super-sophisticated and expensive flying simulators, pilots still resort to the time-tested practice of chair flying. Why? Because it works and it's portable. The brain-body connection still works the way it did way back then. Pilots still have to react very, very quickly to certain events.

For instance, a fire may have developed in an engine during takeoff. There was an explosion in an outboard engine. What does the pilot do? Near-instant action must take place. Lives are at stake. There may be twenty steps that need to be implemented, ten switches that need to be thrown, radio calls to be made. And, oh yeah, the aircraft still has to be maneuvered while all this is taking place.

In that critical time, perhaps only five steps must be performed immediately, nearly instantaneously within a few seconds of the explosion. There isn't any time to spare. If action is not taken, catastrophic results could ensue.

Pilots these days practice for such emergencies in those sophisticated simulators where environmental conditions and aircraft status can be computer programmed. But simulators are expensive to utilize. To supplement their training, pilots use an alternative method of instilling the physical and mental reactions required to handle catastrophic events. It is called chair flying.

Making the Body Do What You Want It to Do

Simply put, chair flying is an artificial and simplistic way of practicing the body movements and mental decisions associated with handling flying activities while under stress. It is a detailed physical and mental exercise, or programmed mental rehearsal. It is perfect for practicing for the perfect job interview.

The following description may sound simplistic, almost childish. But trust the thousands of pilots who owe their lives to this cherished aviation technique.

Pilots sit in a chair, close their eyes, and position their bodies (hands, feet, posture) as nearly as possible to that held while in the cockpit. They let their imagination take off. They imagine a flying condition, in this case a fire during takeoff. As they imagine the situation, they see it in real time in their brain. They call out the required critical action steps and begin to physically move their arms and fingers to engage imaginary switches and instigate required radio calls, throttle movements, control stick movements, and the like. They do this repeatedly.

Amazingly, when confronted with the actual event in the air, pilots who have practiced the scenario often enough start to effect the proper movements nearly instantaneously. Before they consciously realize it, their brain has received the stimulus from a sensory source. Their hands begin to move toward switches, move the control stick, change throttle positions—all in a matter of a few seconds. How? The brain-body interconnection recognized the external stimuli and began to react: muscle memory.

Even the vaunted Navy Blue Angels precision aerial demonstration team uses chair flying prior to each highly demanding air show. They all sit around a conference room table, eyes shut, mimicking throttle and stick movements while the commander voices aloud what he is doing in each maneuver. Each pilot is visualizing each maneuver and moving the aircraft's flight controls and throttles to fly the aircraft through each maneuver he sees in his mind.

Interview Insights

You can train your body and mind to react almost instantaneously to external stimuli if you practice enough. Dr. David Hebb (1904–1985), a noted Canadian psychologist, studied the effects of learning and neural networks. He also studied how cells in the brain interact and create assemblies of neurons that are functionally related. Together over time, these nodes and networks in the brain seem to have a persistent effect on movement, especially repetitive tasks. Sounds like muscle memory.

Muscle Memory

The muscle memory concept is presently used in many professions where immediate and critical actions, like those in our flying example above, must be adopted often with little time. Difficult but routine procedures can be thought through and practiced until they become second nature. There is a link between muscle movement and brain activity such that as the brain stimulates the body to act or react in a prescribed, learned way, the muscles involved tend to remember the movement practiced many times before. They may not realize it, but major league pitchers use this system, as do surgeons and actors.

Interview Stimuli

If you practice with simulated interview stimuli enough, your reactions to events in an actual interview can become second nature as well. Chair flying as a method of producing near-instantaneous physical and mental reactions can help you react to external interview stimuli, and as with pilots, you can react with more confidence. Don't think that chair flying allows you to influence the outcome of the interview through playing mind games. That's not it at all. Instead, think of it as training your mind and body to act as one.

If your mind is used to thinking a certain way, and your body is used to moving in specified channels or grooves, then later they will react to external stimuli in known and predictable ways. Ask a professional golfer.

By practicing responses, both verbal and physical, a candidate can make natural those reactions that otherwise might be unnatural and overlooked. For example, you can practice your reaction when an interviewer asks a difficult question or tries to surprise you with a trick question, or you make an error.

Contingencies and Chair Flying

Don't overplay the idea, but chair flying is a method of practicing, through imagery, all the various scenarios that could happen in an interview. When combined with the personal scripts discussed in the previous sections, chair flying your responses preprograms your mind and body to act in prescribed ways when you answer questions. By using the connectivity charts in the personal scripts and playing them out through chair flying, you can create a more polished and coherent response. Chair flying is designed to shape your reactions to what-if scenarios.

Verbalize and Visualize

What is the difference between this technique and just practicing? First, practicing a verbal response only gets you part way there. It's easy to think through an answer without really putting the script together the way someone will actually hear it. And connecting an answer to other interdependent ideas requires practice. The best practice is one that allows you to verbalize and visualize. Capture the visual representation offered by the personal scripts and let your ears hear what you are saying (along with your trusted agent of course). Ideally, when you get a question, you should "see" your personal scripts and its connections.

Visualizing the personal scripts makes it easier to connect the dots between them when under the pressure of the actual interview. And combining the personal scripts and chair flying methods allows you to associate physical movements within your answers. For instance, at a point in an interview you may want to stress a particular idea with hand gestures; chair flying allows you to integrate those movements into your answers effortlessly. Practicing chair flying is about integrating your acting lessons with your personal scripts.

If you construct personal scripts, as described in the previous sections, and then sit in front of them taped upon a wall, you can build a situational context that emulates what you can expect in an interview. You can imagine the personal scripts in the interview room with you, and you will be much better able to connect the dots and present a coherent, interdependent response.

Interview Insights

An internationally known Olympic swimmer once heard the explanation of chair flying and said he used something similar to train his muscle memory as part of his routine. Of course, he didn't realize he was actually flying chairs around as he lay on his stomach and went through his strokes and motions. If it's good enough for a world-class swimmer, maybe it's good enough for the rest of us!

Flying the Director's Chair

In the exercise that follows, try to promote as much realism as you can. At first, you will probably feel silly. But if you use your imagination and get into the exercise, you will begin to see its benefits. For full effect, ask an observer to read the exercise problem to you as you proceed or have prerecord the exercise from step two. Afterward, record your thoughts in your journal, think about the process

Quotable Quotes

"Flying fighters is what God invented to show us He is a really cool Dude."

American Fighter Pilot

overnight, and then try it again a second time. Then compare the two and see if your second attempt had more descriptive detail and seemed more real to you—it should.

Chair Flying Exercise: The Race at Le Mans

Step One: Get a chair, place it in the middle of a quiet room, close your eyes, and be seated. Turn on the tape recorder (or use a reader). When you are instructed to put your hands on the wheel, do it. When you are instructed to turn on the ignition, move your hands to the dash and act like you are turning it on. The reader or taped message should read each following step verbatim.

Step Two: Imagine you are driving a race car. The ignition is on the left next to the steering wheel. Grip the wheel with both hands, and then move your left hand to start the ignition. Simultaneously, move your left foot to the clutch. Hold the brake with your right. Do it now. Do you hear the roar of the engine as it fires? Move your right hand to the stick just to the right of your right knee, and move the stick forward 2 inches into first gear.

Step Three: Slowly let out the clutch with your left foot. Move your right foot off the brake and apply pressure to the accelerator.

Step Four: As the car moves forward, look over your left shoulder for any oncoming racers circling the track. Apply pressure with your right foot and accelerate rapidly onto the tree-lined course. You are passing 15 miles per hour, and you shift into second and then third and fourth, accelerating to 100 mph.

You sense trees off the track to your left as the road starts a sweeping curve to the right. You continue to accelerate and hear the rush of the wind, the loud whine of the turbine engine, and the oncoming straightaway as you whip out of the curve, continuing to accelerate. You glance at the speedometer momentarily and then quickly look back to the track. You noticed 150 mph and it's continuing to rise.

You see another racer just ahead, a blue car with white and red checkerboard on the spoiler that extends above the back. You turn the wheel slightly to the left and accelerate with pressure from your right foot. The car ahead swerves to avoid an oil slick, and it is right in front of you! Instinctively, you quickly turn the wheel further left, and then quickly back right, narrowly avoiding a collision.

Ahead, the straightaway is clear and you push the car to its limits; 200 mph on the speedometer and the car feels light. Hairpin curve ahead! You downshift as you enter the sharp left-hand curve, and continue to decelerate into a pit area just beyond and to the right for a tire change. You continue the race without your friendly commentator. You finish the curvy, tree-lined, slick, crowded racetrack.

It is a bright sunny day with temperatures in the 30s and hundreds of thousands of spectators rimming the course. They are wearing multicolored coats and hats. They are cheering wildly for their favorite drivers. Shell Oil, Pennzoil, Porsche, Ferrari, and Nextel signs line the inside of the track, and over the hills beyond the straightaway lies the deep blue English Channel.

You see red and white sailboats dotting the horizon, and then the finish line with a man in a yellow and red leather jacket with black pants wildly waving a huge checkered flag at you as you roar past. Congratulations! You just made it through a Grand Prix race in France. A checkered flag!

Let's Get Back to Work

Now that you are back from France a winner, think about applying your active imagination to the ideal interview. Imagine it over and over, and chair fly the perfect interview. Remember to steer the interview the way you want it to go. Lead the conversation until it connects to a personal scripts topic and one of your chair fly scenarios. See yourself answering the questions just like you saw yourself shifting gears and taking that hard S-turn at Le Mans.

Chapter Homework

1. Finish your personal scripts and dialogue now, as described in the previous chapters, and put them on poster board. Tape them to a wall behind a simulated interview desk. Chair fly your ideal interview with the boards in front of you. This will help you recall them during the actual interview later. You will be much better able to connect the dots and present a coherent, interdependent response. Remember your Le Mans experience; realism is important to the exercise.

Follow these first steps to get started:

➤ Turn on the video recorder.

➤ Knock on the door.

➤ Walk into the room and stop in front of the desk.

➤ Conduct your simulated greeting to an interviewer.

➤ Sit down and position your briefcase, purse, etc.

➤ Imagine an opening question: "So, please tell me a bit about yourself."

➤ Answer the question, then make a simple one-step tie to a personal scripts topic about your skills, personality, etc.

➤ Imagine a second question: " This job is all about [XYZ]. How do your skills compare to those requirements?"

➤ Answer the question, then select a key skill and connect it to an example from your work history, life experience, etc.

➤ "Tell me about a recent work experience where you were unable to accomplish an objective."

➤ Answer the question. This is a prepared response; you will most likely get this question, so it should be easy. Get through it quickly, and then concentrate on what you learned and how that made a difference the next time you face a similar occurrence.

➤ Continue with questions from the sample question list in Appendix B.

PART THREE

Executing the Perfect Interview

CHAPTER 18

Execution: The Setting

> ## In This Chapter
>
> ➤ The Entrance
> ➤ Introductions
> ➤ Initial moments

This chapter discusses the execution part of the dynamic interview training model. The opening moments of the interview are crucial, but the time just prior is also a critical period.

Nail the Entrance

The audience is arriving, the popcorn and drinks are bought, and your movie is about to begin. Like any great script, the opening act of your interview has to be the hook that gets your interviewer's attention. What happens over the next minute or two will in large measure determine the outcome.

When you meet the interviewer, the first few seconds are key. Some seasoned interviewers claim that the first forty-five seconds will determine the outcome of the interview. If that is so, then you have to nail the entrance and the introduction. Never was chair flying more important than in preparing for the grandest thirty to forty-five seconds of your interview life.

A calm demeanor derives its source of strength from practice (chair flying). Walk with excellent posture and don't shuffle your feet or slump. Look people square in the eyes, give pleasant smiles, and present a friendly greeting. Present a firm, not crushing, handshake that lasts only a few seconds.

The Wimpy Hand Jive

Likewise, don't give a wimpy wilting waft of a wave. If your handshake turns out to be the finger-tip grasping variety, then consider one of these:

> ➤ Laugh it off and briefly refer to it by saying, "Let's try that again!"

> ➤ Reposition yourself so as to grasp the interviewer's forearm with your other hand. "Very nice to meet you. I've looked forward to this meeting for some time."

> ➤ Completely ignore it (but the recipient may not)

Opening Distractions

Seat yourself comfortably. Listen closely for an opening line from the interviewer. Put your briefcase by your side, and open the clasp (you don't want to fumble trying to open it later). If the sun is in your eyes or there is some other distraction, then correct it. Don't let something silly disturb your concentration. If you notice it, then smile pleasantly and quickly move to another seat if one is available, or ask the person to adjust the blinds, or turn down the radio. Confidently and courteously ask the person to eliminate the distraction if it will seriously interrupt the interview.

Unless you are an on-call doctor or on alert for a disaster response team, turn off your cell phone. It is disruptive and rude to have the thing go off during an interview. Would you have it on during an important client meeting?

Interview Insights

What do you say during the opening moments? A perfect opening might simply be: "Thank you for spending time with me today. I've looked forward to meeting you and I know you are very busy." It's inane, but safe. Avoid a funny or clever opening line about the weather, traffic, the city, etc. It might fall flat and set the wrong tone. *Awkward* is not the adjective of choice to describe your interview.

Opening Remarks

Customarily the interviewer will start the conversation, but if he or she doesn't, start by stating that the position is an important one to you, that the firm has an outstanding reputation, and you are pleased to meet to discuss the opportunity. The interviewer should then start by stating the company's objectives, explaining the conduct of the interview, or asking an opening question to start the discussion. If you have done the introduction personal scripts correctly, you will have several possible opening statements depending upon whether the interviewer starts right away with résumé-based information, a technical question, or a leading question about your interests. Be ready for the interviewer who says, "Nice to meet you. The floor is yours."

First Swing at the Plate

Be prepared to hit an opening discussion point or two based upon the job announcement. Listen carefully and start to tell your story using the tools presented in this text. Some opening questions are meant to soften you up and make you feel comfortable; others are intended to do the opposite. You must be ready for both. Make certain that you understand the question before you start. If you do not, don't say, "Please repeat your question." The person will think you are merely stalling and that you probably don't know the answer. Instead, restate the question as you understand it, and say, "Is that correct?"

If you are sure you understand the question, then start your answer with a succinct summary of the question as an introduction. If case-oriented facts are laid out, then have a notebook and pen handy to jot down pertinent details. To do otherwise is foolish, and the interviewer will think so as well. It is generally a good idea to summarize the facts and assumptions in the question prior to starting an answer. It is better to head off mistakes early, than to set off on an erroneous course that could derail the entire interview.

Monitor your rate of speech. Don't let your eyes wander—wandering eyes look like you are either bored, nervous, or hiding something. And don't let your posture slip.

It's a Long Fly Ball

OK, so you have introduced yourself, and the interviewer(s) have asked the first question. It is time to listen intensely to each question, and constantly try to relate it to your personal scripts. Make your conversation professional and courteous and speak with a relaxed, confident tone. Do not come across as someone who has all the answers (they know you probably don't). Most competent interviewers, especially senior ones, are not looking for that. Remember, they are trying to see if you can answer the million-dollar question. Keep that fact in mind as you progress during the interview.

In their book *Made to Stick*, authors Chip Heath and Dan Heath make the point that some ideas stick in people's minds because of six basic factors: they exude simplicity, unexpectedness, concreteness, credibility, emotional connection, and are story based. You should keep this in mind as you try to make an impression during your interview. . Your personal scripts and your ability to translate your prior experience into a credible, simple story should resonate and be remembered.

Keep your initial answers simple. Throw in a twist of unexpectedness such as your knowledge of something the person or company did. Be specific and establish your credibility with pointed references to experience or knowledge. Hit a hot button with the interviewer by establishing a bond around a mutually shared interest or goal. And use storytelling through your personal scripts to emphasize your answers. This should make your answers stick.

Show Off Your Client Management Skills

Work to develop the client-oriented context we have discussed previously. Treat the interviewer as a client. Show your client management skills by advocating a certain position, backing it up with facts, and showing why it would be good for the client. In doing so, you treat the client (interviewer) with patience, intelligence, and great care—never with condescension or arrogance. Tie your answers to specific personal scripts, thereby leading the interviewer(s) where you need them to go. Integrate the personal scripts connectivity argument, and lead the interviewer to a point in the conversation where you can connect with a personal strength or a creative difference-making idea you had in your previous work experience. Consider the following scenario where the candidate listed her love of chess on her résumé.

Interviewer: Good afternoon.

Candidate: Hello, good afternoon.

Interviewer: Helen, nice of you to come by. I saw your résumé, and I looked forward to meeting you. Before we start, I was curious about your résumé. I see you love chess. Tell me about that.

Candidate: Thank you for the time to meet today, I know you have a lot of people to see. I thought you might wonder why I listed chess as my favorite hobby. I think it is the mental aspect of the play that intrigued me from the start. The cat-and-mouse nature of the strategy is appealing. I found as I excelled at it over time that I began to see parallels with life and with business. In fact, I found it gives me an edge.

Interviewer: An edge? Please explain.

Candidate: Yes, by honing my competitive skills, I found that the game quickened my intellect and made me realize that I could see solutions more quickly than many other people could. At my last company prior to business school, for instance, I was working on a project team to solve a difficult servicing issue with a large, multimillion-dollar institutional client. The team was mired in many possible alternatives, but I think my chess background allowed me to play out the various strategies and think several steps ahead to possible client reactions and negative consequences. In the end, my solution was the one we adopted. It was simple, direct, and the client loved it.

Interviewer: Interesting analysis. OK. Let's next discuss …

Do you see how the person took a simple question about chess, highlighted her problem-solving skills, and began a line of discussion about creating value and money for an important client? She also created a hook by stressing how chess gives her an edge. The interviewer couldn't resist reacting to the hook. She steered the interview where she wanted it to go. That's salesmanship.

And although the interviewer said, "Before we start," remember that game day starts the moment you arrive at the company's building and not just inside the interview room. Everything is evaluated; at least, that is how you should conduct yourself.

As you continue to address each question, it is always a good idea to speak only about what you know. Do not tap dance. Remember to stop digging! If you do not know an answer to a direct question, especially a technical one, then admit it. Here is an example (you can substitute information relevant to your circumstance):

Interviewer: Can you evaluate the cross-currency rate between the Japanese yen and the dollar relative to purchase power parity?

Candidate: I know the exchange rate is XXX yen/$, but I am not able to tell you if that is fairly valued or not. I will look into that after our discussion, and I will be sure to get an answer back to you.

Interviewer: OK, but surely you know whether it is above trend or not, correct?

Candidate: I am not a foreign currency trader, but I do know the dollar has been undervalued relative to most major currencies. I would rather not speak out of hand unless I know specific facts, so I would feel more comfortable getting a definitive answer to you after our meeting. (Then write down in your notebook to research the answer, and get it back via e-mail ASAP).

Sometimes You Have to Know the Answers

First, unless the candidate was interviewing for a position on a currency-trading desk or in the Treasury Department, the interviewer in the example was probably testing to see how the candidate would respond to the pressure of not knowing an answer. Clients do, after all, ask questions you may not be able to answer on the spot. If this were a technical interview, then the candidate should have been able to discuss purchase power parity and all its ramifications, or else he or she would be blown out of the water.

The Set

The Hollywood film analogy is illustrative, but how does it affect your interview? Tying a visual picture of the interview setting to your chair flying sessions enriches your mock interviews and makes them more closely emulate interview conditions.

It also allows you to react to unforeseen circumstances better. For example, if the interviewer is running late, make sure you don't look bored or irritated while waiting in the reception area. Have some reading material handy in case none is available. Make certain you are busy with something productive. Some candidates sit staring into space like zombies awaiting the return of the mother ship. Be aware that wandering assistants are sent to waiting rooms with instructions to see how candidates are reacting to an overdue interviewer.

And, by the way, don't let the other candidates freak you out with their confidence. They are just as angst-ridden as you are and probably are thinking that you have the job in the bag. Actually, you can affect the soft elements of the setting by the way you appear. Your demeanor, your quiet confidence, your manner of dress, your greeting—all can affect the setting and overlay a calmer, more relaxed atmosphere to the interview. You gain these attributes through studied practice and doing your scenario preplanning.

Hit Your Marks

Remember the interview room is a stage. There are marks, or places where you physically could be called upon to stand or sit. Are there stairs? Is the interview on a trading floor, manufacturing line, or in a cutting room? Think it out beforehand.

Be acutely aware of critical environmental conditions to which your previous surveillance should have alerted you. Is there a phone in the interview room? What do you do if the interviewer takes a call on it or on a cell phone? You should probably ask if he or she would like you to step outside for a moment. Also, is the seating awkward? Is there a sofa instead of a chair? Seating arrangements can be important considerations, as some interviewers use seating as an intimidation or pressure factor. Do you sit across from one another, diagonally, or on the same side of the desk? Have an idea ahead of time what the combinations might be.

A candidate once encountered an interviewer who moved his seating position several times during the interview just to create more distance. Change along with the interviewer(s) as necessary to ensure you get in a comfortable seating arrangement where you get your message out. That is the important thing. Mind games are just meant to distract you. If you expect them, you won't be surprised.

Other factors you should consider about the actual, or hard, elements of the setting are these:

> ➤ Lighting conditions (glare, brightness)

> ➤ Media distractions (Bloomberg, television)

➤ Wandering assistants (in the interviewer's office)

➤ Reading material (in the waiting room)

➤ Other interview candidates

➤ Time constraints, artificial or real

➤ Picturesque settings

➤ Bystanders (In restaurants, be careful not to disclose confidential information if non-firm bystanders are nearby.)

The Antihero Mirror Image Technique

Let's talk about the nonverbal and rude interviewer, the person who is either trying to add pressure by not talking very much or is really bored with the whole interview process. Another possibility is that the interviewer is just overly reticent and quirky. Many times, if you feel that a person does not give you all the facts you need to answer a question or is especially uncommunicative, a technique called mirror imaging can work. Used by prisoners of war, mirror imaging is repeating back verbatim what the interrogator, or interviewer, has said. There is a sense in most human beings to resist being silent when someone asks them a question.

Salespeople use this technique in business development meetings with prospective clients. If someone gives you just a tidbit, then repeat the tidbit back exactly as it was given to you, except phrased as a question. In most cases, the person will respond to you with a little bit more information the second time around. This technique sometimes works if the person is trying to give you very little to go on and you are grasping for straws. With the little bit of extra information, you might be able to lead the questioner down a different path that gets to his or her objectives and hopefully makes him or her more communicative.

Jerks, Neanderthals, and other Semi-Human Beings

If the interviewer is acting like a jerk, then the best you can do is act politely and answer the questions as best you can. You will have to decide whether this behavior is worth overcoming to continue to considering the firm or not—is that guy typical or not? Is he just testing you to determine how you will act in the presence of demanding and rude clients?

Suggestions for how to handle various personality types are listed on the following page. The information is based upon several of the more common personality characteristics from the PAG in chapter 10 and their extreme positions on the sliding scale (left or right end).

➤ The Paranoid: Insecure; PAG sliding scale: left

Do not be overly aggressive or ambitious with this type. Give consideration to the person's position; use deferential language. The person may not be a great spokesperson for the firm. Try saying, "You obviously have been successful here …"

➤ Mr. or Ms. Walks on Water: Arrogant, self-important, overly inflated view of him or herself; PAG sliding scale: right

Don't be offended or angry. This type usually likes to talk a lot and overtake the interview. Relax. Be pleasantly assertive. Be concise and make your points. Use body language to signal you have something to say. Try nodding your head, raising your index finger, and then say, "Excuse me, that's a very interesting point you make. I recall having a situation where I (make your points) …"

➤ The Cold Fish: Awkward, doesn't interact, nonresponsive, bored; PAG sliding scale: left

Be calm. Get this type of person talking. Draw him or her out with questions about the job and the firm. Repeat back the short answers verbatim, but as a question. Be relaxed and friendly, but direct. Try saying, "I can see you are a busy person. How do you handle the demands of your job?"

➤ The Flower Child: Obsequious; socially effusive, fawning, overly friendly; PAG sliding scale: right

Stay professional. Don't mimic. Use lots of eye contact and affirming commentary. Act or react to his or her comments. Try saying, "I believe in teamwork. I can see that is a hallmark of this firm. Is that your opinion also?"

➤ The Rude Dude: Discourteous; PAG sliding scale: left

Be polite. Do not reciprocate. Try not to be offended. Maintain your presence. Disarm him or her by being empathetic. Try saying, "Are you exceptionally busy today? Perhaps we could meet at a more convenient time?" In all matters maintain a tasteful decorum and appearance.

➤ The Stiff: Overly Formal; PAG sliding scale: right

Be especially polite and refrain from casual language. Be especially cognizant of titles and position in speech and written correspondence. Try saying, "Sir (or Ma'am), I value your opinion. Would you list what you consider to be the critical drivers of success in this job?" Maintain a tasteful decorum and slightly more formal appearance.

➤ The Lightweight: Underperformer; not particularly sharp; PAG sliding scale: left

Be careful not to step on toes with your sparkling intelligence or résumé. Be friendly and respectful of the person's work. Try saying, "Can you give me your thoughts about what it's like to work here and the culture of the firm?"

Be Yourself

Regardless of the personality across the interview table, act like yourself, not like someone else. Be unflappable, but don't be a pushover. Don't get rattled. Stand up for yourself, but be diplomatic in doing so. Diplomatic? What does that mean? It means maintaining your cool, keeping the bigger picture in mind, saying what is necessary at the moment to forestall a conflict, and not reacting on impulse. Remember that the interviewer is a representative of the company, and his or her behavior reflects positively or negatively upon the firm. In the end, you too have a vote on working there. You must decide whether Mr. Stiff is indicative of the organization or an anomaly.

Chapter Homework

1. Imagine you are sitting in front of an interviewer who is acting like a jerk. Write down all of the odd behaviors and phrases a person might use. Say them out loud and think of your responses. Use the chair flying method to practice your reactions. Consider using your interview buddy to emulate the interviewer.

2. Now do the same with each of the other types of behavior listed above.

 Execution: Leadership Skills as a Differentiator

---

In This Chapter

➤ Leadership basics

➤ Traits of good and bad leadership

➤ A leadership tool you can use

➤ Leadership knowledge and the interview

➤ Leadership questionnaire

The aim of this chapter is to put leadership and its execution in a practical light, and show how people choose to be "good" or " bad" leaders. In short, you will think about leadership skills, great leaders, and how leadership applies to your interview discussion.

Basic Leadership

Ah, leadership! What is it? Some say they know it when they see it. They often mean, instead, that they can see the absence of leadership. They then disagree with what needs to be done, complaining there isn't any leadership shown by those in charge. You've probably heard someone say, "If they had only done what I wanted, then it would have worked out correctly. I should be in charge."

Quotable Quotes

"If I advance, follow me! If I retreat, kill me! If I die, avenge me!"

La Rochejaguelin

Or, have you heard someone lament, "Why don't people just do what I say? Why aren't they following me in this?"

Each of the complaints above sheds light on important characteristics of leadership—both good and bad. Can you uncover them? How about showing empathy, willingness to experience what your staff members face, self-delusion, commitment, and sacrifice. Know any leaders that show these?

Leaders are a dime a dozen, but great, moral, visionary leaders are in scant supply. So, how can you use leadership knowledge to your advantage during an interview?

Even if you have a track record of leadership excellence, in an interview you may still need to articulate how you propose to be a great leader amidst the challenges of the new firm, new people, new problems, and new customers. This is especially necessary for senior executive, or C-suite, interviews. But even if you are at a lower level, the interviewer may want you to describe how you would act in a leadership role

Leadership is Misunderstood

Leadership is an oft-touted, oft misappropriated term. As a consequence, leadership is a controversial topic. Most people believe they have what it takes to be a great leader, or they think they can recognize great leadership when they see it. Most ambitious professionals believe they are great leaders, or could be if only given the chance. There are many managers pretending to be great leaders. Others are in a position of leadership and fail to measure up to the challenges confronting them and their groups.

In truth, there aren't many of us who are Churchillian (or great enough to have your name used like that!). The trick is to be the best possible leader you can be commensurate with your position when you are called upon to exercise authority over others.

Here is the age-old question: Is leadership innate to the individual, or is it a learned skill? Does it have anything to do with moral values, or is it entirely an exercise in making people do what you want them to do regardless of core belief or moral justification?

What is Leadership and How Do You Do It?

Leadership, broadly defined, is merely getting a group of people to follow you in the direction you intend for them to go. While simple in notion, the act of leadership is a complex mixture of human emotions and physical reality that makes a simple definition misleading. Over the past years, few topics have spawned as many new authors as has the topic of leadership and its mistaken twin—the art of management.

In this section, we focus on what you can do to impact your new organizations in a positive way, in the shortest period. While you may not be a born leader, you can learn ways to enhance the organizations you work for, whether you are the one in charge or not. In fact, it is through following that many of you can initially exercise your gifts and indirectly provide something akin to leadership. For example, punctuality at meetings or a rigid adherence to quality control standards can positively influence those around you.

There have been many studies of great leaders and of various models that purport to construct an optimum form or structure for leaders to follow. As of yet, there isn't a single basic model that fits all circumstances and can direct leaders in the way they should go. Numerous theories abound that describe a fashionable approach, but theory often is left lacking when you are faced with a practical, pressure-laden problem on a shop floor or in a boardroom.

Interview Insights

There once was a manager who came into a troubled unit that was besieged with distrust and declining profits. The new boss immediately installed floor-to-ceiling smoked glass walls in his corner office to replace the long-standing clear ones. Immediately people wondered how much they cost, and assumed he must be talking about them behind those glazed windows! Not the way to introduce new leadership into a beleaguered outfit. Amazingly, he replaced the glass walls with wooden ones a few months later. At least with the smoked glass you could tell the lights were on. Obviously, the lights weren't on in the right places.

Leadership is the art of provoking creativity, initiative, actions, and behaviors, whereas management is the science of control, analysis, resource allocation, and stability. The two can exist within the same context, within the same person, and at the same time. The boundaries between the two are, in fact, blurry. But, leadership is generally dynamic and demands the application of a set of abiding principles that when applied correctly can cause subordinates to rise to meet larger challenges and to perform better than if they had been left alone. Management, on the other hand, is more static and often void of any identifiable persona or individual characteristics.

A Simple Leadership Model

Maybe what is needed is a newfangled, complex leadership paradigm that has emerged from an expensive ivory tower. No! Instead, try a simple diagnostic tool that leaders can apply to everyday challenges—a tool that captures the human attributes that drive events toward positive, successful outcomes.

Figure 19A, below, is the first part of a simple leadership tool that describes positive leadership talents and associated attributes. A group of talented executives, graduate and undergraduate students, military men and women, and people off the street were asked to describe someone they thought was a great leader. Guess what falls out?

Most described leaders for whom they worked. They had someone in mind. When presented with pictures of great leaders like Churchill, Roosevelt, Dell, Packard, and others, many of the same positive attributes were repeatedly listed. The ability to call forth on a sustained basis these talents is what separates great leaders from the others. Do you know how to call forth and apply these leadership traits when you need them? Can you call to mind situations where these traits were needed? If so, then integrate these stories into your preparations for the interview.

Showcase your leadership skills by using illustrations that point to problems where the exercise of your leadership talents resulted in positive outcomes. At the end of this chapter, you will find a leadership assessment guide. Fill out the form and give it to a trusted agent and a peer to complete. Perhaps a former subordinate or boss would evaluate the questions for you.

Look at Figure 19A again, and note the attributes that were both present and missing in situations that confronted you in your past. Write out these past situations and apply a missing attribute to see what difference it might have made had you applied one or more of them. The absence of leadership in organizations is at the root of institutional failure and is the missing ingredient that firms aspire to obtain. Provide evidence of your potential in this area and you will gain a competitive advantage.

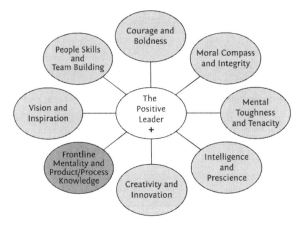

Figure 19A
Positive Attributes of Great Leaders
Source: Cavender Park Consulting, LLC.

Figure 19B below portrays a model of negative leadership attributes. In many cases, they are the countervailing characteristics to the positive ones in Figure 19A. See if you can assess your own awareness and skill level in each of these areas. As mentioned earlier, you will have an opportunity later to formally rate your leadership talent, as well as have someone else rate your ability.

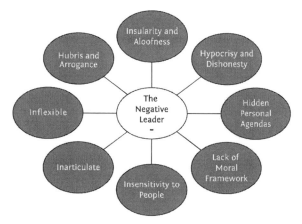

Figure 19B
Negative Attributes of Leaders
Source: Cavender Park Consulting, LLC.

Do What is Right

Do what is right. Sure, that's a copout, you say. What is right? That's a tough nut to crack. It changes. But, every great leader has to do the right thing. Why not start with a determination to choose the best behavior you can consider, and hold yourself accountable to that standard? That's not a bad prescription, is it? Especially if you have respected, trusted agents to hold you accountable. Stand for something good and back it with an articulated and heartfelt value system.

There may be traits you can think of in addition to those depicted above, but the idea is to capture and embody as many of the positive traits and recognize and consciously discard or deal with the negative ones—especially if you are ingrained with the latter.

Good Management vs Good Leadership

To be effective in an organization, you must both adopt essential leadership qualities and deploy management techniques. MBA programs offer a plethora of management techniques and coursework such as production management, human resource management, marketing management, managerial accounting, managerial finance, operations management, and technology management. Wow, how much more management could there be? Why not offer techniques and coursework in production leadership, operations leadership, and so on?

It is the ability to lead that continues to hamper many people in positions of authority. Let's try to tackle the question of how to develop leadership skills and how to do it in such a way that it positively impacts your first months and years on the job.

Interview Insights

By effectively discussing leadership skills in an interview, you can distinguish your talents from many of those that have no leadership framework from which to draw. Have examples ready. A typical interview question tries to uncover your leadership potential. Just remember that not everyone can be a leader—there must be followers, too. One is a leader by one's position, but one exercises leadership by one's actions.

History Teaches Great Lessons

It is helpful to look at a number of leaders such as Lincoln, Gandhi, Thatcher, Reagan, Jobs, Welch, and others to see what type of behavioral characteristics they have exhibited at various times, and when they have summoned, as Lincoln said in his first inaugural address, those attributes that are "the better angels of our nature."

Great leaders had their failings, but they called forth overriding principles or captured the imagination of others to a greater degree exactly when the situation hung in the balance. Their ability to discern a complex soup of events when others could not had a great effect on historic and legendary outcomes.

The Leadership Model in More Detail

Let's go around the model depicted in figures 19A and 19B, tackle some of the positive characteristics, and discuss how you can develop these traits. Some you already have, such as intelligence. The trick is not to let it spill over into hubris and arrogance. Each trait breeds its negative attribute if you are not careful. Hubris spawns arrogance, which can also lead to insular behavior. Insularity translates eventually into a lack of understanding of the people who work for you. By keeping this model in mind, you can work to counter the negative trait while implementing the former.

For example, if the situation calls for the leader to understand what impacts employees, and I say that is always the case, then you will find the leader on the assembly line floor, in the creative drafting room, in the labs, on the trading floors and desks, in the mailroom, and certainly out front with clients. Having a frontline mentality uncovers what you are putting your people through and whether the company is on track to meet its goals. Stay out of the way, but actually try to do what your employees do.

If you set targets for salespeople, for example, be willing to try and get a new client yourself so you can understand just how tough it really is to get someone to buy your products and how hard it might be for salespeople to implement those targets. As you progress upward in your organization, insist that leaders below you sell the company's products as well, or work within a project team in order to see how creative and competitive the employees really are.

Good and Bad Leadership

Leadership is best understood by looking at examples of great and bad leadership, discerning what positive and negative attributes were at work, and then learning from successes and failures.

To be certain, villains can be great leaders in the narrow definition. They get millions to follow their vision, and they lead them off a cliff as though they were lemmings. Think of a few notorious villains and each one exhibited the ability to motivate, to create, and to passionately articulate a vision. While often charismatic and tenacious, they also insanely and simultaneously employ most of the traits of negative leadership as well. So far, leadership in a vacuum has no moral framework to guide it. Some of the most notorious mass murderers in history exercised leadership talent to accomplish devilish ends.

Contrast that with the leadership of Dr. Jonas Salk, who benefited humankind and saved the lives of millions of people through inspirational, creative leadership in medicine. Next to nuclear war, polio was considered the greatest threat to the human race. Hailed by many as a gift from God, Salk oversaw the development of the vaccine that virtually eliminated the virus. He reportedly took no interest in a patent and instead believed it belonged to everyone. That's moral, principled leadership—not a bad model to follow.

Study other great role models of principled leadership, people such as Lincoln, Churchill, Eisenhower, Mother Teresa, and Luther, among others.

Read biographies and history as much as you can to understand how normal men and women became history's treasures. One great value of history is that as human beings we tend to repeat ourselves over time in all aspects of life, and much can be learned about the present by considering the victories and failings of the past.

Look at the work of a missionary teacher in a remote village in the Third World to see further evidence of inspirational leadership. Leaders must inspire and motivate people to move mountains by taking up a shovel themselves.

Interview Vocab

Frontline leadership is the leader's conscious effort to engage in activities that lower-level employees conduct. For example, a sales manager should actually engage in sales activity and get new business rather than simply issue sales quotas and mandates.

Innovation is Essential

Creativity is essential if the innovation-driven leader is to move the organization forward. You do not have to be a creative genius, but you have to foster learning and creative environments within your group if you are to beat the competition, remain competitive, and grow your business over time. Creativity breeds change and energy in an organization.

Change must be managed in the sense that accountability benchmarks, progress markers, and information systems need to be used to monitor the rate of change and its impact, but it is leadership that spawns the atmosphere that creates solutions, innovates, hires the right people, and instigates action.

When change is called for, or there are competitive issues or product failings or any number of other challenges, the leader must have the mental toughness and tenacity to remain upbeat when others are pessimistic, strong when others want to wither, solution oriented rather than problem focused, and willing to stay the course or change it when circumstances demand it.

Leadership and Morality

When the company is under stress, competitive pressures increase, or times are too good to be true, then it is the moral compass of the leader that sets the standard. It is that sense of right and wrong that sets the environment for the company to always endeavor to do the right and just thing for the client, for its people, for the country.

For some, moral codes change depending upon personal whim and circumstance. Do what you want when and how you feel like it. In other words, social standards don't matter any longer because someone or something else made them up. That results in chaos and has proven to be nonsense. Business standards are codified in the nation's laws and regulations, and those are easy enough to see and follow. People sometimes choose to overstep them, and the leader must instill a zero tolerance environment within the organization to aberrations from ethical and legal standards.

It is in the gray margins of behaviors, laws, and decisions that people and organizations can get in trouble. Here, the leader must be overt and clear about what is expected. Codes of conduct are good places to start, but they must be visible in the leader's behaviors and attitudes if they are to be part of the overriding culture of the firm.

Lifting the Organization

People skills and team building comprise human leverage. Exploiting the talents of others lifts the organization beyond itself. It starts with a value system that rewards the concept depicted by the band of brothers. By valuing the notion of camaraderie and the idea that good teams can yield remarkable results, a leader builds a consensual and sustaining culture. A culture that attracts collaborative talent, and a leader who understands his or her staff can structure teams around this concept and move his or her organization to the next level.

Crafting Inspiration

The ability to inspire others is a necessary ingredient in effective leadership. This is an easy one, yet not everyone can do it equally. People believe leaders who truly believe in what they are doing. Inspiring leaders communicate their views with passion, causing followers to inculcate the leader's excitement and energy. Without the ability to inspire, mediocrity will breed complacency, lack of innovation and creativity, and, finally, obsolescence.

The ability to motivate and inspire can be practiced. The words of inspiration are found in great speeches and great acts of behavior. For example, listen to a rendition of Henry V's Saint Crispin's Day speech prior to the Battle of Agincourt or Joshua Chamberlain's speech before his troops at the Battle of Gettysburg.

Effective Smarts

Not just intelligence but also knowledge of the company's product and process are essential for leaders. You have the intelligence, but to be effective, you must acquire the product and process knowledge that generates the value inside your new firm. This is a long-term commitment to lifelong learning and to understanding the nodes of value generation within your organization. It completely undermines a leader within the organization if decisions are made without a proper recognition of what such decisions will do to current plans, people, and products. Get to the factory room floor, in other words, and experience the business where it is done.

Going Against the Tide

Courage and boldness are traits that define great leaders under duress. In the business context it could be stress from a turnaround situation or owning up to a sense of loyalty and duty. The classic case is the Johnson & Johnson Tylenol scare—were it not for great courage, a great brand could have gone down the drain. The willingness to go against the tide or stay the course when a leader feels it is morally the right approach is the stuff from which great legends are made. To learn how one can attain such rarefied certitude, read Marcus Luttrell's book, *Lone Survivor*, and Michael Useem's *The Leadership Moment*.

The courage of your convictions starts with a value system that will not abandon you when times are rough—again, it's not the absence of fear or timidity, but the willingness to overcome it. "Courage is fear hanging on a minute longer," according to General George Patton. So, persevere for a minute more and make certain of your facts, your convictions, and your values. Then stick to your guns. Tenacity follows conviction and courage, so be right and be tenacious.

The Leadership Context

The context of leadership, the contextual leadership model if you will, helps you discover which attribute must be at the forefront at any particular time. There are situational models, behavioral models, and autocratic models—enough models to confuse the issue. The leadership context is, however, stressed by false stories. These incorrect views or opinions of circumstances may in their own time present legitimate leadership challenges, but in the interim mislead, contort, and pressurize the situation currently confronting the leader. The issue for the leader is to discern what is real from what is not, and deal with that at the moment.

Interview Vocab

The contextual leadership model uses the hub-and-spoke concept where positive and negative attributes surround a leader who is immersed within an organizational reality or context. The model arms the leader with a set of positive traits to draw upon when he/she sees or senses a particular environment. The context changes over time and can be distorted, so the leader must continually revisit the attributes to ensure he/she is using a positive attribute and suppressing a negative one.

Figure 19C below depicts a leader immersed in multiple situations within a patchwork quilt of competing influences. These distortions within the context that surrounds the leader at any moment persuade, pressure, and confuse the leader. Every leader is constantly pulled and pushed by both real and counterfeit forces competing for resources, judgments, and time. The buildup in tension within this context may force actions and reactions that may not result in the leader's desired outcome. What is the correct story and who is telling it? Are there hidden agendas at work that seek to undermine strategy and cloak real intentions?

Torsion within the system can be managed, but a disciplined leader must be devoted to the conscious application of the positive leadership traits illustrated earlier in order to control it. The leader looks through a cloudy lens distorted by these pressures (Figure 19C), and can sway the decisions he or she makes and can move the organization off course.

The real test is whether a great leader can look through "the fog of war" and have the ability to see the core issues, the critical ones that will mean the difference between success and failure. Can he or she apply the right leverage of talent, courage, perception, and inspiration to get other good people to achieve more than they otherwise would without the leader?

Can the lens remain clear enough to see through the arguments, personalities, false crises, disruptions, and competitive dangers to get to the one or two key issues that drive the desired outcome? Regardless of an individual's view of the Iraq war, for example, everyone surely sees the leadership talent of the military officers who came up with a new defining strategy to win that conflict. Most credible authorities view his achievement as miraculous. Try looking at Abraham Lincoln during the Civil War years through this model and see what new insights you gain. Did either of them suppress innate emotions or reactions to swirling events in order to accomplish a greater good?

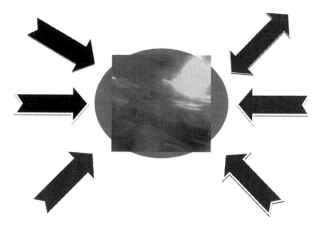

Figure 19C
The Distorted Context as Viewed through a Leader's Lens

Reality and the Leader

Some information may seem true but are not really facts at all. People working at cross-purposes distort reality to such a degree that a leader's initial task is made more complex by the malleable context within which he or she must operate. By contextual leadership then, we mean the ability to know when and how to exercise your positive talents as a leader, and then when to be a follower. This is especially true in the new global economy where virtual teams are spread across the world and organization as problems or challenges emerge and change. Dynamic models that allow for change in the leader-follower structure are critical to the ability of adaptive organizations to survive and flourish over time.

The Leadership Assessment Guide

Here is a short questionnaire to help you gain insight into your leadership style and how to articulate it during an interview. Fill out each question in detail. Recall examples from prior experiences, self-assessments, and friends' or employers' observations. Be honest about your assessment.

Leadership Assessment

1. List jobs in which you were called upon to exercise a leadership role.

2. In your most recent job, did you have direct authority to influence the work of others? If yes, what did you actually do to demonstrate leadership in this function? Did others consider you a good leader?

3. Were your leadership talents stretched in your last position? If so, list the reasons why you were tested to such an extent.

4. Were you able to define the objectives in your last job and correctly perceive solutions to the problems confronting your group?

5. How many people did you have as direct reports, where you acted as team leader or supervisor? Did you determine their compensation?

6. If you were a supervisor, were there employees who especially challenged your leadership talents? How did you cope to get the job done? If you were unsuccessful, what would you do differently now?

7. What personal traits inhibited your performance as a leader in your last several positions?

8. Would you consider yourself a flexible leader or one who sticks to a pattern of leadership that has worked previously?

9. If confronted by a situation involving an ethical problem with your most productive employee, what would you do?

A. Confront the person, and if so, why?

B. Ignore the possible problem until such a point it actually materializes. Why?

C. Attempt to understand the core of the ethical dilemma and rationalize the problem until the problem goes away. Why?

10. What leadership talents do you most admire in leaders you have encountered? What do you do to emulate those leaders? If you have not done so, what new steps can you take to ensure you implement such attributes in your next job?

11. Do you believe leaders are born, or are they made? If the latter, what specific steps have you taken to learn those traits that turn managers into leaders?

12. What differentiates a leader from a manager or supervisor? Do you exhibit both positive and negative traits of a leader? Which ones? In what areas do you lack the training, knowledge, or capability?

Behavioral Assessment

1. Would you characterize yourself as flexible? If so, how would you handle a chronically late employee who also happens to be one of your best people?

2. Would you publicly admonish a person who makes a mistake or would you always praise in public, criticize in private?

3. Do you believe you need continuous feedback on your performance or are you oblivious to performance evaluations anyway?

4. If your personality does not allow you to be a leader, how can you overcome this shortcoming?

5. If you have a temper, how do you control it when your frustration level hits a new high at work?

Chapter Homework

1. Think about your leadership style and describe it as you would in an interview.

2. Fill out the leadership assessment guide. Note deficiencies and develop a plan to address each one.

Quotable Quotes

"So much of what we call management consists of making it difficult for people to work."

Peter Drucker

 # Execution: Relationship Management as a Second Differentiator

> ## In This Chapter
>
> ➤ Clients are everything
>
> ➤ Essential skills
>
> ➤ Cross selling is a sales skill
>
> ➤ Why CRM is an essential interview skill

In this chapter client relationships take center stage. Just as leadership can help differentiate you from competition in interviews, understanding how to deal with clients can also provide additional spark. The chapter addresses which essential skills are needed to be a world-class client relations professional and how to discuss those skills in an interview.

Clients are Everything

Clients are the lifeblood of an organization, and nurturing those relationships is key to long-run, sustainable growth.

Every organization and each employee has clients. You may be in a sales or service role, or you may be in a support function like research and development; it doesn't matter, you have clients. They may be internal such as other staff people, a committee, or a supervisor. People who are expecting you to deliver something to them are your clients, and you need to keep them satisfied with your product and service.

If you are in a service role, you realize you have clients or customers. You may have a few select, recurring clients or you may serve the public at large, but the firm-client relationship is critical if the firm is to grow. Clients and customers provide the revenue that makes everything else possible. Without customers and clients, the firm withers and dies.

Client Relationship Management

The ability to work with clients and keep them buying from you and your firm is a precious resource. It is usually much more expensive to find a new client than to keep the ones you have. Low turnover rate in your client base is a sign of a healthy, growing enterprise, and it is a metric that consultants and, hopefully, managers use to determine the well-being of the business. During your interview, if you show that you have what it takes to satisfy clients, then you increase the odds in your favor of securing a callback and an eventual offer.

The ability to work with clients is a learned skill. As mentioned, client retention is an important ingredient in firm profitability. It costs money to lose clients and replace them with new ones. And there is no guarantee the new client will replace any revenue lost from the absence of the old one. If you have critical client relationship skills, then you can make an enormous impact within your firm. Also, the ability to extract additional revenue dollars from an existing client, cross selling, is an important characteristic of great client managers.

Interview Insights

In some industries, professionals who deal with customers or clients are sometimes called "client/customer managers." The term then begs the question whether or not clients/customers can be "managed." Some firms have reacted by changing the name to "relationship manager." Others use the term "customer relations professional". Whatever the term used, professionals who deal with clients/customers must understand and protect the importance of those relationships to the long-term viability of the firm. To do otherwise could land you in the unemployment line.

Client Skills

If you do not already possess great client skills, then the following list should help you identify what they should be and help you develop your ongoing PAG offset strategies.

One skill is the ability to relate topics in a conversation to something you and your company do. That should sound familiar; it's like the connectivity skill you developed in your personal scripts work. This skill comes with practice and incorporates great listening, conversational skills, and creativity.

The following is a list of other client skills. If you have them, you should work hard at perfecting them. There are other skills, but these are fundamental to effective client interaction:

> ➤ Empathetic listening
>
> ➤ Honesty and integrity
>
> ➤ Proactivity
>
> ➤ Creativity and innovation
>
> ➤ Servant mentality
>
> ➤ Hard work and sweat equity
>
> ➤ Communication, presentation, and translation skills—written and verbal
>
> ➤ Wide knowledge bandwidth
>
> ➤ Native intelligence
>
> ➤ Understanding client's objectives and needs
>
> ➤ Judgment always trumps ego
>
> ➤ Let's consider each skill in more depth.

Empathetic Listening

To offer clients a product or service they truly need, you must be able to empathize with them. If you can put yourself into their shoes, see issues from their perspective, feel their pressures, and understand their requirements, then you can craft a solution that meets their needs. Tying empathy with effective listening skills is the key. Listening well is a learned art. It's the ability to focus only upon what is being said to you, not what you are going to say next. It also means tuning out distractions.

A good listening test is to ask your trusted agent or a friend to interrupt a conversation with you and have you repeat what he or she was saying as close to verbatim as possible.

Empathy is a basic emotional skill that can be developed if you practice it. Tests for emotional intelligence, a hot new area of study in leadership development, can help you understand your innate ability to achieve satisfactory levels of empathy. Basically, you need to trick your mind into "walking in that person's shoes."

At this stage, you are not looking at your own or your firm's issues. You are trying to get to the core of the dilemma or opportunity presented by the client. When combined with excellent listening ability, a client relationship manager can eventually get to the core issues confronting the client, and then hopefully satisfy his or her needs.

Honesty and Integrity

Truth is the bedrock of any true integrity-based relationship. Whether speaking of a marriage or a friendship or a client, breaches of honesty can ruin the relationship. You might seem to get away with an untruth at times, but in the end it will catch up to you. The client, a colleague, the market, the regulators, the compliance people in your firm, and your supervisor—someone will detect it and expose it.

So you should always be honest and truthful. This is not always easy, as business pressures build to the point where it is easy to look the other way, skirt the facts, tell half-truths, or obscure details. That is a loser's game. And in an interview, a hiring firm may want to test your integrity and may do this by:

> ➤ Presenting an ethics-based scenario for you to resolve

> ➤ Asking you to discuss an ethics dilemma you have encountered

> ➤ Checking references

> ➤ Taking a test (in some places, maybe a polygraph)

You can be the most truthful person in the world and still make mistakes. There is such a thing as an honest error, and if you make one, then it is best to enlarge the audience and tell your supervisor or your teammates. Little errors grow into big errors.

The media sharks love a good controversy, and the chain of events associated with a major crisis is a good place for them to start an investigation. On Monday morning, exploring those linkages often reveals that the catastrophe could have been avoided if someone had acted differently, spoken up, had the courage of his or her convictions, and/or been a whistleblower early on. What keeps people from acting? Many times it is simply a lack of basic integrity.

Clients generally will accept an honest error. It may not be pleasant, but it is much better to disclose it if you find it, than to have the client suspect you have obscured it for a dishonest reason. Honest errors usually result in second chances. Dishonest ones do not.

In fact, sometimes confessing an honest error can help seal a solid client relationship. There is no such thing as a little dishonesty, even when the error of omission or commission is small and seemingly insignificant. Clean it up quickly and move on. Interviewers are looking for people who will act responsibly.

Following are ways to think about an ethics problem:

> ➤ There's no such thing as "just a little bit wrong."

> ➤ Small problems become big ones if unattended.

> ➤ Black-and-white issues are easier than gray ones.

> ➤ A little sunlight solves a lot.

> ➤ Elevate it before it escalates you.

> ➤ Courage is never easy and requires personal sacrifice.

> ➤ Integrity can't be taken away, but it can be given up.

Proactivity

Proactive measures can mean additional revenue, forestall errors, and retain clients. Keep in mind that chances are if you aren't talking to your client, your competitor is.

You obviously can overdo this; you don't want to be a pest. An excellent relationship manager keeps in touch with a client's changing needs and can preempt disruptions in a relationship by reaching out to the client before issues develop. Few things disrupt a relationship more than a client feeling as though the only time his or her relationship officer gets in touch is when he or she is selling something.

By being proactive, you do what many others do not: you show clients that you are thinking about them, not just reacting to a client query or crisis. Proactivity comes in many forms, but a verbal conversation or visit is best. A call thanking a client for his or her business can positively surprise the client and create additional goodwill.

Creativity and Innovation

World-class relationship managers think constantly of ways to improve a client's circumstances. Creativity and its cousin innovation spark new business and further ensure the client believes you are acting with his or her best interests in mind.

Staid, run-of-the-mill ideas do not impress anyone. Do not be reckless, but offer thoughtful, risk-balanced ideas that can elevate your firm and your client's position. It may be as simple as a quicker, more personalized way of delivering information. Or it may be a unique method of mixing product to ensure a better outcome for the client. For instance, value chain analysis, a method of dissecting the economic value rendered throughout a product's life cycle, is a useful tool and can be applied to investigate ways of delivering a higher-quality service and product to your client.

Servant Mentality

Taking a servant approach to your client is not a bad model to emulate. Yes, you may be a high-priced manager, an engineer, a teacher, a politician, but if you are reading this, you are an interview candidate. Once you are on the job, however, you are the visible tip of the iceberg with an organization at your disposal to solve an issue.

For instance, your willingness to deliver a package in person, answer your own phone, or go the extra mile is impressive to busy clients. Obviously, you can't deliver a retail product to every customer in person, so you generally save such actions for important clients. But there are other ways you can elevate customer relationships to make them know you and the company value their business.

Adopting a servant's mindset creates a culture of service in an organization, and that is a good thing. It doesn't have to be complicated; sometimes simple things mean a lot. Adopting a four-ring rule in answering the phone is a good way to show how attentive and responsive you are to client inquiries. It also ensures that clients get to speak to a person first instead of going to voice mail.

There are always exceptions, but thinking of your business as serving clients keeps you attentive to their needs and makes them much happier, recurring buyers.

Hard Work and Sweat Equity

Success comes from hard work, especially when you are new to an organization. Few people succeed without putting in the hours. There is a sweat equity component to success, in client management, and in other endeavors. Working hard for your client pays dividends in the relationship. Clients like to believe that you are constantly thinking about them and them alone. If you are never in the office or always out of touch, clients might assume you are on the golf course.

Your hard work goes hand in hand with communication skills. Let your clients know that you are busy attending to their needs.

As a new hire, you will be expected to put in long hours. You have a lot to learn at a new firm, and long days show commitment and dedication. Besides, your clients probably know you are new to the firm, so you must work hard to overcome any reservations they may have.

Communication, Presentation, and Translation Skills

Communications skills are usually at the top of everyone's list—for good reason. They are enormously important yet so often lacking. And there seems to be a new antisocial phenomenon that is only now getting some attention in the business media. Increasingly, people seem to ignore basic communications protocols and courtesies. For example, how many of your phone calls have not been returned? Have you had to resend e-mails to get someone's attention? Have you ever had letters go unanswered? These days if you communicate effectively and in a timely manner, you will surprise people; many of your interview competitors ignore this basic skill. So, communicate responsibly and religiously.

Interview Insights

An executive once said, "I don't return phone calls unless someone calls back a fourth time. Then I know they're serious." Imagine how that person's clients must feel—or his employees? Do you think they believe they are important to him? Do you think there is a culture of attentiveness in that firm?

The ability to write well and to translate difficult concepts for clients is a lost art. One excellent relationship manager at a large New York firm had been an English major. He did not have an MBA and was not a "quant geek" steeped in advanced math and modeling techniques. He could, however, write really well. He was able to compose succinct letters that translated complex ideas into terms his clients understood. His business letters were concise and had a personal tone to them that communicated (here's that word again) empathy.

People often overlook presentation skills in business. Great communication skills go beyond the written form. The ability to present ideas in person also is critical if you want to be a great client manager.

Clients do not like long-winded speeches or boring slide shows. PowerPoint is terrific, but it has to tell a clear message. Your point needs to get to the client's agenda quickly and in a way that makes him or her act.

In some ways, the interview is like an advocacy briefing with PowerPoint without the slides. It must be hard-hitting, concise, interesting, and spur the audience to action.

Quotable Quotes

"No sale is really complete until the product is worn out, and the customer is completely satisfied."

L. L. Bean

Wide Knowledge Bandwidth

It is important in many positions to recognize that not all clients are alike, and they certainly have a wide array of interests. People who are great with clients understand how to relate to clients through a keen understanding of what makes people tick. A wide knowledge bandwidth means a professional life of continuous learning, and not just about your specific product area. It may be that studies in cross disciplines that are only marginally related to your expertise may get you closer to a client and help you solidify the relationship.

The global business world is increasingly complex. You should develop an understanding of other cultures, their languages and customs, as well some knowledge of cross-border transactions. These will serve you well with clients, and in an interview it will show you have a deeper understanding of issues than someone who is only regionally oriented.

The integration of world economies and geopolitics means that you should adopt a hybrid learning system that updates your knowledge in a wide variety of disciplines—music, art, languages, science, politics, business and economics, technology, and cultural trends. Develop a career-long professional reading program that spans a spectrum of topics—it will serve you well with clients. The reading list in this book is just a start.

Native Intelligence

A certain level of native intelligence is a prerequisite. However, the world is becoming more and more complicated, and the ability to understand sophisticated products and services demands a nurtured intellect.

In your interviews, your inquisitors may very well test you by presenting absurd questions to test your reasoning ability under pressure. For example, one may ask how you would determine the number of yellow umbrellas sold in Iowa in January? Or one may give you a quick serial-based math problem such as, "What is 100 minus 25 divided by 5, as a multiple of 5? (Is the answer 3 or 19?). Those darn order of operations rules! Try the following to nurture your intellect in anticipation of an interview:

➤ Play chess or bridge (great for strategists!)

➤ Learn math tricks (e.g., 25 × 25? Increase the 2 to 3 and multiply, equaling 6. Multiply 5 × 5 = 25. Answer 625. 35 × 35=1,225)

➤ Regularly do the *New York Times* crossword puzzle

➤ Play a mathematics-based logic puzzle such as Sudoku

These skills may help develop deductive reasoning skills that could help in interview case analyses, ethics dilemmas, or the client context.

Understanding A Client's Objectives and Needs

You can be all of the above, but if you do not understand what the client needs, all is for naught; eventually, you will lose the client. Understanding objectives and limitations, and practicing a system of copious note keeping can go a long way toward achieving this goal.

Asking clients to describe their risks, hopes, and worries allows you to determine several things:

> ➤ Sophistication of the client

> ➤ The client's understanding of your product or service offering

> ➤ The client's perception of what others have done that is either good or bad

> ➤ The limitations and constraints that will define the relationship

> ➤ Your ability to meet the client's expectations, or if you want to do so

It is a good idea to memorialize expectations, both yours and the client's, in a formal agreement, or at least in a written communiqué that outlines expectations, limits, behaviors, terms, and goals. Periodically refreshing this formal or informal contract is a very good idea. Forms given to a client to fill out can sometimes quicken the process, but a face-to-face meeting to discuss this topic is usually best—depending upon industry and type of service or product.

Judgment Always Trumps Ego

Finally, it is always a good idea to keep one's ego in check and not let it overwhelm good judgment. Humility is not a bad virtue even in the most mercenary and hubris-ridden industries. Too many careers are ruined by not putting good judgment ahead of one's ego. The world is littered with the business tombstones of people who thought they were above the rest of the pack.

How do you develop experience and good judgment? One way is by learning from veteran managers, developing a sense of humility, and reading and listening to stories of both good and bad managers. Imagine what you would do in a particular circumstance and scrupulously try to recognize the talents of others. It will help you realize there are other smart, successful people and that anyone can fail. It can happen on a grand scale or a smaller one. Make a commitment to keeping your ego healthy, but in check and tempered by judgment. Have an accountability partner who is close to you and who will tell you if this gets out of balance and trust his or her judgment.

Cross Selling to Clients

Marketing additional products to existing clients is a necessary part of good client management. Your firm is depending upon you to market the entire array of appropriate products to your clients or customers. How you accomplish this is somewhat dependent upon the depth and nature of the relationship you have with them.

You have to know what they are doing with the firm in total. In fact, other parts of the firm may also have intricate relationships with your clients, and you need to know the extent to which this situation exists. A data-capturing system that shows what products the firm has sold them, as well as what products they may be using with other suppliers, is crucial.

Cross selling is an excellent topic for interviews if you are asked, "How would you increase or deepen existing relationships from a revenue perspective?"

It certainly helps answer the million-dollar question.

Interview Vocab

Cross selling is the art of identifying the needs of the client and matching them with the products and services your firm has to offer. It is usually easier and cheaper to sell a product to an existing client than incur the expense of finding a new client.

Additionally, marketing to current clients can result in referrals to new clients and customers. Your best clients and customers are usually only too happy to refer their friends and other professional associations to your firm. One personal referral from a satisfied client is worth untold advertising dollars. In many cases, all you have to do is ask the question. Surprisingly, many new client managers find this difficult to do. Make your clients and customers happy, and they will help you acquire more clients and customers. And then the cycle can start anew.

Ask Clients for Feedback

There are many ways to keep relationships healthy and growing. Ask clients or customers what they would like to see in new services or products, or how your product compares to competitors'. This is a great way to satisfy your clients and yield additional business.

Focus Groups

Conducting focus groups with clients is also greatly beneficial. Listening to clients allows you to stay ahead of the competition. If you don't listen and adapt, your competition surely will. A learning organization uses its clients and customers as an asset to leverage its knowledge of how well the service platform is performing. Learning firms last!

Interview Vocab

Focus group is a marketing research term used to describe a gathering of current clients or constituents to survey their opinion on a range of topics important to a business, government, or other entity. Focus groups are used in politics to gauge public opinion or in business to determine purchase habits and desires.

Chapter Homework

1. Describe similarities between traits of good leadership and great client relationship management skills.

2. Review situations where you have seen both good and bad examples of how to treat clients and customers.

CHAPTER 21

Execution: Sales Skills as a Third Differentiator

In This Chapter

➤ Why selling is an important interview skill

➤ Attributes of great salespeople

➤ The perfect interview is a sales pitch

➤ Can you explain how to get a new client?

➤ A sample sales model

In this chapter, you will learn about sales skills. You will also discover that the interview is a sales pitch and the perfect interview is a big sell. You will also learn about one of the hardest things to do in business—get a new client. Like leadership and client management, knowledge and execution of sales skills can differentiate you from other candidates. By design, the tone of this chapter is a bit more academic. It illustrates a rigorous sales model that you can use during an interview to answer how you would conduct new business development activities. Wade through it and get comfortable describing it.

The Sales Process

Regardless of industry, companies grow by getting new clients and penetrating markets, and then maintaining service and cross-selling standards better than their competition.

The art and science of new client acquisition or new business development (NBD) is a skill that is often taught through self-instructional courses or, if more formally, through seminars from sales professionals who are selling a book or service. How do you sell a product from start to finish? Are you given sales leads, or do you need to source them on your own? When you get a lead, what do you say?

Interview Vocab

New business development is the beginning-to-end sales process. It's a method of sourcing, contacting, and converting prospects into customers or clients.

What follows is a brief introduction to a sales method once adopted by a Fortune 100 firm. The basic process underlying the method is based upon systems engineering concepts where a flow is developed and the interdependences between elements are calculated and monitored. Wow! That's a mouthful. But it's basically a system of investigating each step in the process of sourcing, contacting, and converting prospects into clients.

The calculus behind the acquisition of a new client and the maintenance of existing relationships is fundamentally the same. This kind of approach works regardless of whether you are a consultant, investment banker, retail merchandiser, marketing representative, publisher, or shoe salesman. Everyone involved in the sales process must have a method of finding prospects and converting them to clients who buy products.

How Can the Sales Process Help in an Interview?

As Figure 21A on the following page shows, the more discipline you apply to a sales system, the greater the opportunity for a sale, or as applied to interviewing, a new job possibility. Job prospecting is a numbers game, where the more lines you have in the water, the greater your chance of catching a fish. Your task, of course, also requires that you fish in the right pond. The PAG analysis can help uncover the types of jobs that may be the best fit for you.

In an interview you might encounter this question: "Tell me how you would create a market for our products in TufSell, USA?" Remember, you are really selling your skills when you answer this question.

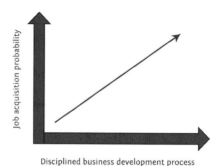

Disciplined business development process

Figure 21A
Source: Cavender Park Consulting, LLC © 2007

Objections to the Sales Process

Many do not have the fundamental discipline to carry out a systematic, organized sales process. For years, some sales people resisted the use of a customer relationship management (CRM) system to uncover, track, and then develop sales leads. You've seen them—they are the people with tons of sticky notes tacked to walls, papers everywhere, and probably a leftover cheeseburger in the front seat of their car.

For those who do adopt modern methods such as described in this chapter, you will usually find their names on honor rolls and membership rolls of champion sales clubs. If you learn and practice these disciplines, then your chances of achieving early sales wins go up dramatically.

Interview Vocab

CRM stands for customer (or client) relationship management system, which is a computer database management system used to store information about prospective or current customers (clients). It typically contains contact information, personal interests, interaction histories, and other pertinent data and can either stand alone or be integrated with other systems. You can make it as simple or complex as you'd like, but basically, CRM is used to automate the sales process and make marketing and customer relationships much more efficient and cost effective.

Your ability to describe a sales process during an interview could enhance your job prospects and, at the very least, prepare you for developing your own sales system if you need one at your new firm.

A Basic Model

The basic model is a two-part system: One part covers the NBD process; the other part describes a system to uphold existing client relationship standards (CRS). Based loosely upon a dynamic manufacturing model, this model incorporates systems design methods and work flow studies to enhance the ability of business development professionals and client relationship management personnel to grow the rate of acquisition of new clients and to maintain and cross sell to existing clients.

The Elements of the Model

Imagine an aircraft engine. You will notice that the front end of the engine is much larger than the back end. The design of the intake allows the engine to gulp large amounts of air, compress it, and then blow it up when mixed with jet fuel. The rapidly expanding gases from that explosion stream at high velocity out through a narrow rear exhaust, thus creating the high-energy propulsion necessary to fly the aircraft. A venturi, a short tube, is often used to measure pressures as the air flows front to back through the engine.

Interview Vocab

The Venturi effect occurs when fluids flow through a narrowing constriction in a pipe or conduit, causing a reduction in fluid pressure. The Venturi effect is named after Giovanni Venturi (1746–1822), an **Italian physicist** who discovered the effect. According to **fluid dynamics**, the fluid's velocity increases as it passes through the constriction, but its pressure decreases to compensate, thus preserving energy and mass. The drop in pressure offsets any gains in **kinetic energy**.

The front end of the business client acquisition's engine intake is also very large (see Figure 21B). It represents all of the possible new client segments that comprise your market. There may be a large number of possible buyers for your goods or services. The question is how to reach them in sufficient numbers to meaningfully grow your business.

What causes the funneling, or Venturi effect, evident in Figure 21B on the following page? The small black arrows show that externalities like the competition, the markets, government regulation, pricing, industry structural issues, product innovations and obsolescence, etc., continuously impact your ability to attract new clients and winnow the available universe of prospects.

Likewise, internal friction points like corporate bureaucracy, inefficiencies, lack of marketing prowess, brand, comparative skill levels, managerial turmoil, recruiting standards, etc., can also lead to a reduction in the number of prospects converted to client or customer status. The point is by eliminating or mitigating the effects of these reducing influences, you can increase the conversion rate to client or customer.

Ideally a Parallel Line

Ideally you have solved or offset all these reduction areas to the point that you have two parallel lines, and the conversion ratio is 100 percent. You will never get there, but the schematic is a good way of showing what you need to work on to increase your ability to gain new clients.

Value chain analysis, or understanding the effect each component in your system has upon the end product, provides a complementary framework that can increase your understanding of how and where your firm adds value to the client. Adequate value chain study can provide insight into those processes and products that move the channel lines from parallel to the venturi shape in Figure 21B.

Interview Vocab

Value chain analysis measures the value in activities performed on or around a product as it moves through a beginning-to-end production process. Done principally at the business unit level, the analysis hopes to show that the value of the inputs is less than the economic value of the final product. The difference is profit margin. Partitioning all of the elements of that product or process into discrete parts, and then determining the value that each component activity brings to the whole is an important component. Value chain analysis was first ascribed to the work of Professor Michael Porter of the Harvard Business School in the 1980s.

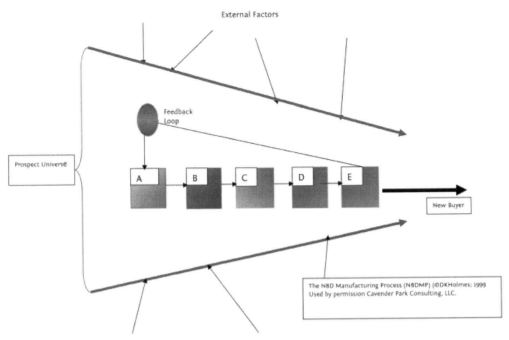

Figure 21B
The Manufacturing Process for New Business Development

Description of Phases in the Model

Within each of the five phases depicted on the diagram, a list of activities associated with that phase is developed. Specific tasks are assigned to specific people, functions, or units.

Interview Vocab

PERT, the acronym for program review and evaluation technique, is a programmatic scheduling device developed in the 1950s by consultants and U.S. Navy personnel under the auspices of the Department of Defense to develop the nation's Polaris nuclear submarine force. It is an operations management decision-making tool that schedules activities in such a way as to minimize delays and optimize resource allocation. It is often used to determine a critical path for a project from beginning to end. Current project scheduling software still utilizes the underlying logic in PERT.

Stockpiles of standardized marketing materials and responses are maintained using standard inventory control techniques for replenishment of material bins. Each of these tasks is given a complete no later than (CNLT) time, and electronic reporting mechanisms are used to signal follow-on units that a required task is completed or delayed.

Once notified, downstream entities can start subsequent activities or put them on hold. Similar to the program evaluation and review technique (PERT), analysis, this type of programmatic scheduling can ensure that all necessary steps dealing with a new prospect are completed on time and in phase. Lists or contracts with prescribed duties are made and given to each participating entity.

Each colored block in the venturi represents a phase of the business development process during which specific activities are required. A sequential process is necessary to ensure that all marketing bases are covered. In order for the NBDMP to have maximum effect, a disciplined daily program of business development activities needs to be scheduled and conducted.

Interview Vocab

Client segmentation is a marketing term used to describe the categorization of a market according to attribute-based criteria such as gender, age, and economic and marital status. It can be tied directly to marketing efforts such as by gathering data on the number of German sports car buyers by various income segments and geography. It also can be used to study current clients to determine buyer needs and purchasing habits for cross selling initiatives.

Initial Phase

Phase A is the discovery phase where, through client segmentation studies, you identify the size and nature of your target customer or client market. A needs and objectives analysis of potential clients or customers is conducted, focus groups are used to identify traits of buyers, sources of contacts are uncovered, affiliation groups with large pools of targets are identified, IT or client/contact relationship management (CRM) wrappers are put around the data to manage the prospect data. Overall prospecting strategy is developed, followed by tactical implementation plans. Revenue, contact, and conversion goals are set.

Second Phase

Phase B is the initial contact phase where first attempts to make contact with the prospect are made. Either large numbers contact campaigns or more targeted, directed campaigns are begun. If direct marketing is used, this is where initial mailings and phone inquiries are conducted. If targeted campaigns using referrals or other means are used, then initial events, conversations with sources, etc., can start. Standardized mailings and ads are used with the aim of creating economies of scale and scope where feasible. Advertising is coordinated with overall strategy, and must be used to complement other contact pathways (events, promotions and discounts, affiliations, etc.).

Third Phase

Phase C is the follow-up phase to the initial contact phase. By using a CRM wrapper, repository information about contact dates, mailings, meetings, unsuccessful activities, etc., is captured for later use and for any compliance or legal purposes. A good CRM system will provide tickler, or reminder, information for follow-on sales calls and activities. Copies of letters, types of events and mailings, and phone or electronic interactions are recorded within the CRM. Feedback to phases A and B is critical in making the entire system more efficient and productive. For example, if in the follow-up phase you discover that certain retail establishments are interested only in a specific type of merchandise, then you can use that criterion to further refine your universe of potential buyers in phase A.

Fourth Phase

Phase D is the sales phase when you start the hardcore work of providing data about your product or service to the buyer. You use comparative studies against the competition based upon your product or organization's performance. Reactions to prospect demands must be flexible, timely, and innovative. Here you must compete on time, and your system must be both reactive and proactive.

A dynamic internal process for reacting to prospect demands for customized solutions or a product is critical. Competing on time is a validated business concept, and it is here that you must provide quick-reaction high-quality, answers or products to meet the unique objectives or goals of your clients or prospects. If no customization is required, then delivery of standard goods or services must be quick and remain consistent with the quality level promised by your brand.

Fifth Phase

Phase E is the conversion and service phase when you convince the prospect to do business with you and to make the transition to customer or client as easy and painless as possible.

Reduced waiting times, premium service and checkout models, point of sale technologies, simplified account forms, easy-to-read statements, and e-commerce channels must all factor into making the prospect's decision an easy one.

By making it easy to become a client, you make it difficult for him or her to say no. Show as much as possible what the client experience will be like after conversion. Offers that include try-us-out options or reductions in price or fee for performance business models can also be used. Ongoing consulting or maintenance agreements can further heighten chances for a conversion. Show the prospect that his or her life or business and its employees will be made easier and better by doing business with you. The conversion process should be simple and easy to understand and require as little time as possible.

Standardize as much as possible, and where unusual circumstances require customization, show the new client that you will follow through with your promises. Realistic expectations about your service and product must be clearly delineated, or you run the risk of losing repeat sales.

As the new client enters into a relationship with you and your firm, a set of service management standards should be adopted and communicated to the client. It includes actions that the new customer can expect from you once a purchase is made. If it is a purely retail transaction, then one set of ongoing standards can be communicated. If a more premium, customized relationship is requested, then a detailed communication plan outlining how, when, and where the service will be rendered should be given to the client.

It is here that client interactions are scheduled, warranties are exercised, performance measurements are taken, repairs and maintenance occurs, etc. Feedback from the conversion process should loop back to phase A, as well as to any other phase in the cycle that might upgrade the process for the next prospect.

Summary of the NBD Manufacturing Process

NBDMP is a streamlined way of creating efficiencies when volume and throughput are critical to revenue generation. New client acquisition can be thought of as a manufacturing assembly line-based process that captures the efficiencies inherent in continuous replication systems. Much of what is accomplished in gaining a new client does not vary

Quotable Quotes

"When I was a young man I observed that nine out of ten things I did were failures. I didn't want to be a failure, so I did ten times more work."

George Bernard Shaw

with the number of prospects. Standardization should be built into your system as much as possible but with flexibility to adapt to customization demands upon request.

This manufacturing based NBD system will cut costs, reduce reaction times, uphold accountability standards, and grow revenue. Each NBD employee responsible for new client acquisition could be required to adopt these types of efficiency-based processes in order to ensure quality control and the maximum number of interactions with the marketplace.

Chapter Homework

1. Explain to a practice interviewer how you would get a new client or customer, then explain how you would market a new product, a hybrid automobile or HD television, for example.

2. If you have sales experience, use your recorder to explain the process you use. Listen to your recording and have a trusted agent critique it.

3. If you do not have sales experience, can you articulate an NBD process as applied to your prospective new job? Try using the framework presented in this chapter.

CHAPTER 22

Execution: Contracting to Be a Perfect New Hire

> ## In This Chapter
>
> ➤ Distinguishing yourself
> ➤ A contract, sort of
> ➤ Guidelines

In this chapter, you will consider an interesting way of being memorable during your perfect interview by contracting to be a perfect new employee by ascribing to a set of personal rules of conduct on the job.

Be Distinguished not Extinguished

Why not convince the interviewer that not only are you a great interview candidate, but that you would be a perfect new hire? After all, there is angst on the interviewer's side of the table, too. He or she may be under pressure to hire someone perfect or to make a better hiring decision this time around.

How can you reassure the interviewer that you will be what he or she hopes you will be? Make the interviewer's job easier by showing him or her what you will be like as a new hire: Make an informal contract with the interviewer!

By setting an informal agreement about your work behavior, you set a standard you are willing to live up to. It's not a contract per se, but a set of rules that you say will govern your behavior once on the job. Show the interviewer what you will become as a new hire. Say what you believe in and that leadership by example drives your work habits—even when you aren't the employee in charge.

As a new hire, many of you may not run an organization or business. You most likely will be a follower or at most a team leader. Any employee can, however, adopt leadership traits. Even those of you destined for the corner office with tons of leadership experience ought to sit and reflect on how you rate relative to the rules listed below.

Key Topic

You want to be distinguished as a great new hire, not extinguished in the interview. You accomplish this by developing within the interviewer's mind a comfort level about your first days on the job. Give them a glimpse of what it would be like to work with you as a colleague.

People who **exercise leadership, within appropriate boundaries, by showing initiative, creativity, accountability, and positive behavior regardless of title** have a powerful impact on a company. As a new hire people will be watching you. Why not commit to a set of rules that put you ahead of the pack from the start? They might make you memorable!

Guidelines to Work By

When first with a new company, you are under the gun. Many eyes are watching you: the clients, your peers, and your managers. Here are ways to make a positive impression in those critical first days on the job and to comprise your informal contract with the interviewer:

➤ Go to meetings with something to contribute, but contribute to add value, not words.

➤ Be five minutes early to every meeting.

➤ Go to work early and go home late—there's a lot to learn.

➤ Listen to the veterans. Stories told by experienced employees can enrich your own work product. Apply the lessons they have learned the hard way.

➤ If you don't know the answer, say so—don't fudge.

➤ Have an upbeat, respectful attitude.

➤ Return all phone calls the same day.

➤ Answer all e-mails addressed solely to you.

➤ Be a sponge and read everything.

➤ Mind your manners—practice simple business courtesy.

➤ If you make a mistake, confess it and inform your superiors.

➤ Have courage, be bold, persevere, and be right.

➤ Communicate and coordinate extensively.

➤ Ensure spelling and grammar are impeccable—in e-mails, too.

➤ Be cautious of e-mail; be professional, not a comedian. E-mails are like plutonium—they have extremely long half-lives.

➤ Earn respect, don't just demand it.

➤ Go the extra mile for peers, bosses, and clients.

➤ Be truthful.

Your prior experience is valuable and relevant, but only so far. You have to perform well in the early days on the job when everyone is watching. Don't bank on a grace period. Early impressions linger in the first stages of the interview, and they linger in the first stages on the job.

Summation

Whether you're naturally bold or naturally timid, there is a strong argument in some cases for showing the interviewer what you are made of. For some industries, you may have to show that you won't back down. Always keep it professional, though; don't lose your cool, but stand on your principles. In those instances, don't be a cardboard cutout afraid to speak up. In every case however, show the hiring firm it's buying the real you—your work ethic, your integrity, your diligence, your smarts, and your perseverance.

Use your personal scripts and chair flying to practice how and what you will deliver. The informal contract between you and the new firm should convince the interviewer that you will pan out after all. Practice your message until it is easy to perform. You might try something like this, nuanced with your own style:

"I realize we only have a few minutes together for you to judge my experience and qualifications against your needs. So, I want to tell you how I view my responsibilities to an organization, and what you can expect from me if I am selected as the new hire. [Then list four or five elements of your informal contract similar to those in the list above.] I have operated that way in the past and would do so at your firm, as well."

Saying something like that might add to your memorable quotient and allay interviewer angst syndrome.

Chapter Homework

1. Construct your informal contract of ninety-day rules. Practice how and when you will discuss this contract in an interview.

CHAPTER 23

 # Execution: Closing the Deal

In This Chapter

➤ How to make the sale

➤ How to close

➤ Negotiating the deal

In this chapter you consider how to close the deal in your favor, including negotiation techniques to get what you want.

Making the Sale

The final few moments of an interview are your opportunity to close the transaction, to make the sale. You have everyone's attention, and now the time for the grand soliloquy is at hand. You must summarize in a succinct, passionate way why the firm should hire you.

Closing the interview is where all of your practice hours much reach critical mass. Your closing should be a well-rehearsed, reasoned statement that encapsulates your desires, your motivation, your abilities, and—here it comes—your answer to the million-dollar question.

Interview Vocab

Closing is a term sales professionals use to refer to the ability to get someone to buy a product. In our context, *closing* means getting the interviewer to extend an offer or at least ask you to return for another round of interviews.

Great summations are hard to accomplish. It is easy to be long-winded, awkward, or arrogant. To get a sense of great summations, read excerpts from famous speeches, oral arguments, and testimonies. For example, try reading Clarence Darrow's closing arguments in the Leopold-Loeb case or Judge Robert Jackson's arguments at Nuremburg.

Other examples of stunningly memorable words are:

> ➤ American orator William Jennings Bryan's speeches

> ➤ Lincoln's address at Gettysburg

> ➤ English actor Kenneth Branagh's rendering in *Henry V* on the eve of the battle at Agincourt (the Band of Brother's speech)

> ➤ Actor Henry Fonda's soliloquies in the film *12 Angry Men*

These were closing statements delivered with passion, and they made a difference to the outcome.

Flamboyant Interviews are Flameouts

Don't misunderstand; do not use florid language or flamboyance, but do use a credible wow-factor ending that can put a tidy bow around the box you carefully built during the forty-five-minute interview discussion.

Here are some tips for a memorable closing narrative:

> ➤ Be simple, direct, and convicted. Let the interviewer hear your passion for the job and why you are the one to do it.

> ➤ If you want the job, ask for it! Playing coy can win a mate, but lose a job.

> ➤ Resonate! Great writers connect with their reader by appealing to universal truths. So, tell believable stories to illustrate your skills and how they connect to the job.

> ➤ Leave the interviewer wanting more by providing a solution to his or her problem.

> ➤ Close with three main points. These are what the interviewers may say to their colleagues about you—leave them something easy to remember.

In 1987, when President Ronald Reagan said, "Mr. Gorbachev, tear down this wall," he created a memorable line that resonated long after. That is what you want.

In preparation, write out a great closing statement. Remember, it is one of the personal scripts categories. Memorize it. It is what you would say if you found yourself in an elevator with the chairman of the board and he or she said, "Tell me why we should hire you." Chair fly it to death!

An Introduction to Negotiation

William Ury, of the Harvard Negotiation Project, cowrote a wonderful book entitled *Getting to Yes* in which he outlines a set of negotiating procedures that if followed ought to allow a person to get to an optimum result.

Interview Insights

In the early twentieth century, defense attorney Clarence Darrow's twelve-hour closing argument in the Leopold-Loeb case is a brilliant example of how to turn a weakness into strength. He opposed capital punishment and used this vehicle to advance his cause and thereby pull his clients off the hangman's platform.

Darrow turned the rich-kid status of his clients (a weakness in his case) to advantage by showing that environmental influences can affect behavior for good or for bad. He portrayed the boys as bystanders to the swirl of intoxicating influences that demonized their adolescent lives. He put the judge in an intractable predicament, and he sentenced the boys to life in prison.

The interview is a negotiation of sorts: you need a job and the interviewer knows it. The question up in the air is if there is a match between the firm's need and your set of skills. The optimum result is to get to a negotiated agreement in which each party at the table feels satisfied. You think there is a match, and you need to convince the interviewer.

Compensation Discussions

Discussing compensation can be touchy. Start too early and the interviewer believes you are more interested in the money than the job. Start too late and you have a lot invested before you find out if the job pays enough.

In general, you should first find if the job interests you and hold off on compensation discussions until later rounds of interviews. Preferably, let the interviewer bring up the subject. It is better to first stress the quality of the firm, the interesting aspects of the job, and to solidify the firm's understanding of who you are and what you bring to the table. Then you can negotiate from a stronger position.

For students, many job interviews are conducted on a campus and compensation is range-bound by the firms. But there is still room for negotiating some key points such as location, starting date, reporting lines, and project or team assignment. This may be especially true if you come from highly specialized schools or are a top graduate.

For those interviews that are not on campuses, there is more latitude. As a rule, sell yourself first, and then tell them the price. Create the demand first, and then the right price will come along after. If it doesn't, move on. Who knows, the firm may come back to you with a sweetener if it believes it is losing you to a competitor. Having a backup, alternate choice is a good place from which to bargain. That said, outlandish requests or trading one firm against another can breed resentment and in the long term could create turmoil.

Negotiation strategies can be supported by the laws of decision theory and can be quantified. For example, the financial amount at risk is the difference between your minimum acceptable offer (for example, $50,000 per year) and the firm's maximum acceptable offer ($75,000 per year, for example). If that gap is large, then negotiation could put more money in your pocket. If the range is narrow (for example, $2,000 instead of the $25,000 in the example), you have to ask if the possibility of irritating them is worth the small premium left on the table.

Quantifying the numbers is an act of research and should be in phase one of your timeline/ research plan. Then, calculate the firm's maximum acceptable offer point within a range and also calculate your minimum acceptable offer relative to opportunity costs elsewhere.

For example, the *Occupational Outlook Handbook* 2010–2011 edition shows that the median salary for an accountant (CPA) in the United States is roughly $59,500 with some making over $100,000. A candidate should determine what the salary range is for accountants of a particular type (oil and gas, financial services, audit) within the city or company of interest. The median might be $64,000 in your locale, for example. Based upon your baseline needs, you should put a band around that amount and determine, for example, that your minimum acceptable offer is $60,000. You should try to determine via informational interviews, salary surveys by local business organizations, newspaper articles, etc., what the salaries are for people with your background and experience who joined the firm or one like it. Find someone comparable. For example, you determine there is a comparable professional making $88,000 in a local firm of similar stature as your target firm. Add a 5 percent insurance premium and you have a band $32,400 wide ($92,400–$60,000) with which to bargain.

Knowing the numbers gives you added strength as you answer their question, "What will it take to get you on board?"

Some key points for consideration are:

➤ Trade off location and other benefits for more or less salary.

➤ Assume greater responsibility for more salary.

➤ Earn less for a longer employment contract.

➤ Be clear about how and when you will be paid and in what form (commission only, partial commission, etc.).

➤ Compute your bargaining range from comparables, your minimum acceptable offer, and the hiring firm's maximum offer.

The key is to start from a reasonable assessment of your value, and then leverage the demand as needed to bolster your position.

If you can attach revenue projections to your salary request by showing that you will be instrumental in finding, closing, or managing a revenue number, then you might be able to relate a percentage of that to a salary request—a form of informal commission or a fair share of the revenue pie.

A Mouthful of Negotiation

A respected senior executive once said, "Negotiation is a collaborative game played by greedy self-interested beneficiaries, supported by less than perfect knowledge, bounded by ever-changing internal and external constraints, resulting in an appalling lack of mutual satisfaction."

Say it isn't so!

OK, negotiated outcomes are usually much better than the cynical fellow above believes. First, remember that opening positions are rarely what the person or entity will really take; rather, they are stalking horses to test conviction, courage, and prior knowledge. There are a set of both formal and informal rules of behavior that can be used to test the other person's will to negotiate and what the terms of the negotiation might be.

Negotiation is like a basketball game viewed from the nosebleed section. From way up there, you can see all the players as though they are in one gigantic chess game. If you can displace yourself above the swirl of intense bargaining and see the positions of the players—their defensible and indefensible objectives—then you can bargain from knowledge, not ignorance.

There are definable lines beyond which the players will not cross, and it serves you well to have an understanding of where those lines might be. It is also imperative that you understand their underlying interests and motivations, not just the positions they state. Concentrating upon what drives their positions instead of just the position statements themselves allows you to place a wedge in their arguments, perhaps freeing them to consider your position. For example, why do they stick to $65,000 as a starting salary in the accountant example above? Is it because they are afraid of internal reactions by other accountants or have they not seen an impact analysis that ties your $80,000 request to new revenue you help generate?

The art of diplomacy can be a source of benefit to candidates. It continues the idea of the whole person, the memorable candidate. Engaging in an enlightened discussion about what is happening relative to the Korean peninsula and China and Japan's reaction may seem extraneous to some, but to an interviewer looking for a person to represent a global firm, it is a gold mine. Read about the diplomatic initiatives of great statesmen to see how they approached negotiation. That is why Henry Kissinger's books are on the recommended reading list.

Most negotiations reach a point where you are committed to a position, and if agreement cannot be reached around that point, then a deal may be dead—it is the bingo point. You must know when you can safely commit to a position, the location of the job versus your lifestyle desires, for example. How far you can push depends upon your strength of feeling and a sense of urgency and commitment conveyed by the prospective firm. In the beginning, you may want to articulate your must-haves early if there is a possibility that announcing them later might spoil the relationship.

Interview Vocab

A bingo point, is a point of no return. This is a point you cannot concede. It is a make-or-break issue for you. Once committed to a bingo point you cannot change your mind without doing damage to your overall position or well-being. You should decide these bingo points early and whether you want to disclose them. It is probably best to discuss these earlier rather than later since they are must-haves. At times, however, you gain additional leverage if you wait until the firm has bought in to you and is eager for you to sign on.

It is always good to hone in on the interests and issues faced by the hiring firm. If you understand those exceedingly well and can then map your strengths onto those interests, then you make the interviewer's or negotiator's decision to hire you much easier. How do you find out about the firm's interests? First, you ask. The interviewer may tell you outright or keep some of the powder dry for later. You can also ask competitors and inside employees. Questions like the following can help you bore in on an interviewer's interests:

➤ What concerns do you have about your business or people?

➤ Are there issues you face that make your competitors happy?

➤ What talents and skills do you think it will take from your people to make your targets this year and in the next five years?

➤ Can you specify your growth targets and associated strategies to get to them?

➤ Can you describe the quantitative measures of your growth targets?

➤ How do you value the importance of this job relative to others occupied by my peer group?

> ➤ Do you consider this job to have an impact on the bottom line of the business?

> ➤ Are you open to discussing how my personal business plan can impact your unit's target numbers?

Listen carefully when discussing the interviewer's challenges and needs. Are there disparities between what you hear and what you learned in your outside research, from analysts, for example? You might have leverage to use in your summation of your strengths vs their need.

How do you handle a jerk negotiator? Try these tactics:

Interview Insights

At some point you may meet the angry negotiator across a table. He tries to browbeat everyone and solve every issue by threatening to walk away from negotiation. This is the same bully you met on the playground in the sixth grade—sometimes you just need to call the jerk's bluff. In other words, put up or shut up, fellow. Like the bully, the angry negotiator may respect you for it and give you what you want. Every case is different, but don't let yourself be intimidated; stand firm on the facts and keep your cool.

> ➤ Body language is key. Look the negotiator squarely in the face and refuse to be intimidated.

> ➤ Reinforce the goal of mutually successful outcomes.

> ➤ Show why bully behavior is self-defeating: he or she walks, he or she loses (you). You walk; he or she again loses (you). The firm's competitor wins in either case.

> ➤ Argue from strength, and if you call the negotiator's bluff, be ready to fight by knowing the facts.

> ➤ Like nuclear deterrence, make the negotiator worry about your arsenal. Make him or her think, "Could the candidate help my competitor? Does the candidate have offers better than mine?"

> ➤ Convey this message: If pushed to fight, you fight to win big

Obviously the fighting references are metaphors for holding a position while arguing a point. At the end, the reality is that for most of us, the hiring firm holds the stronger position—it can hire or not. If you are stubborn about a point, you may lose. In all likelihood, with a bully interviewer or negotiator you have to ask even if you win the point, will you lose the match by working for a jerk?

Here are some points to keep in mind for interview negotiations:

➤ Know what you want as opposed to what you must have.

➤ Be clear about your objectives and the firm's early on.

➤ Know your bingo points.

➤ Know how to summarize the value captured by your strengths, and why they would enhance the new firm (in economic terms).

➤ Quantify all that you can, and use subjective arguments to shape the arguments in your favor.

➤ Calculate the firm's maximum acceptable offer point within a range; calculate your lowest acceptable offer relative to opportunity costs elsewhere

Negotiations can be either simple or complex. Try a few scenarios during your role playing. Much of the art of negotiation is experiential and learning from risk taking. Be ready to lose in practice, be ready to win in execution.

Chapter Homework

Quotable Quotes

"While the right to talk may be the beginning of freedom, the necessity of listening is what makes the right important."

Walter Lippmann

1. Decide on your bingo points.

2. Decide on the three or four main points to close your interview. Create a summation argument incorporating these points.

3. Record your summation and review it with someone you respect. Select someone other than a trusted agent and ask him or her to describe what you are trying to do after listening to the recording.

4. Set up a negotiation question or two during one of your mock interviews, for example, "We'll start you at $X in two weeks, with a week vacation after six months. What do you think?"

CHAPTER 24

Execution: What to Do When It's Not Working

In This Chapter

➤ How to handle objections

➤ Rejection is a fact of life

➤ Reaction to adversity

➤ Sample interviewer objections and comebacks

This chapter focuses on steps to take when the execution is not what you had hoped for or interviewers raise objections. I also offers suggested reactions to rejection.

Handling Objections

If the interviewer is raising objections to your suitability for the job, what do you do? It obviously depends upon the nature of the objections, but preemptive moves can help.

In your preparation efforts you discovered your weaker areas, so you can prepare a response ahead of time to possible interviewer objections based upon those areas of weakness.

The interviewer may have an objection and be reluctant to voice it. A well-framed proactive statement can defuse the objection before it festers. In this way, you control the timing. If done correctly, you might turn the objection into a positive point by stressing your offset strategies from the PAG.

Preparation is important for this reason: No objection should be a surprise. For example, if your lack of experience comes up, is that a surprise? How about age, job-hopping, GPA, performance, and other mismatches? You knew about all of these before the interview.

If the interviewer does raise an objection that catches you by surprise, then remain calm, for you have some things in your favor. You know yourself better than the interviewer does. He or she knows the job, but you know your skill set and experience. You must believe you can do the job. If so, then link the interviewer's objection to one of your positive attributes. Support your argument with facts about your background.

Here are some tips:

➤ Remain calm and pleasant.

➤ Remember a personal scripts storyboard about anticipated objections.

➤ Counter the objection through life and work examples.

➤ Connect your answer to the mission of the institution.

➤ Use positive, upbeat language; don't be defensive.

➤ Focus on aspects of the job you know you can do.

Here are some sample interviewer objections and suggested comebacks:

➤ Objection: You are a little short on experience.

Comeback: What I lack in experience, I make up in effort. I am a quick study, can get down the learning curve in a hurry, and will outwork people with more experience. In my last job, I was given responsibility earlier than my peers. I don't think time and experience necessarily equal competence. I will correct any misgivings you have very quickly if given the chance.

➤ Objection: Your résumé indicates you change jobs frequently.

Comeback: I never intended to leave any of the firms, but I was given opportunities to progress in my career, and I thought it was best for my family. For example, I was asked to lead a joint venture project with firm X and in so doing, it saw me in action. An offer ensued. Each departure was amicable. I assure you that I am looking for a long-term, mutually beneficial relationship with your company."

➤ Objection: Your salary requirements are too high for us.

Comeback: Let me stress that the opportunity to excel with a firm and progress in my career is my top priority. That said, I believe my impact upon your bottom line more than justifies my salary request. The $$$ amount is in line with what people in the industry with my track record make. Would a pro forma projection of my contribution make it easier for you to justify the number? For example, I usually contact X number of people per year, that results in Y number of new accounts with $$ on average per transaction. That yields…

➤ Objection: I wonder if you can cope with the travel burdens and demands of the work schedule. (Code speech for are you too old or too busy as a working mom or dad or unable to perform due to your disability?)

Comeback: Every job I have had was demanding in its own way. Travel is a fact of life in modern business. I enjoy it, thrive while doing it, and use it as a competitive tool. For example, not long ago I…

> ➤ Objection: Your résumé indicates your GPA wasn't among the top 10 percent of your class. We usually hire from the top of the class.

Comeback: What I would bring to your firm is initiative and an ability to work successfully under stress. Others may have a higher GPA, and I wish mine were higher, but I am proud that I have performed in my career at a high level. For example…

Or,

My grades are only part of the story. I have a number of talents ideally suited for this job that aren't captured in a GPA. For example, one week I donated ten hours at a local hospital, worked at my normal job, and took a particularly difficult history exam. Your firm's sales force is also pulled in many directions with many different products, correct? I can operate under that kind of stress just as I did in college.

Rejection is a Fact of Life

Ask prominent authors what they recall most about the early days of their writing careers and most of them will list the pain of experiencing rejection. Every day it seemed, the mailbox opened and another nicely worded rejection letter stared back at them. At times, interviewers share an author's pain. Everyone experiences rejection. Push on and get the next interview.

Reaction to Adversity

You've done all you could do and it just didn't work—this time. Now what?

First, a strong mental attitude going into the interview process is crucial. But if it just doesn't work out for you, then try doing what members of elite military forces such as the U.S. Army Green Berets and US Navy SEALS, do to overcome mental hardship in rugged, hostile environments. Here are some pointers:

> ➤ See the positive in everything. Replace each negative thought with a positive one no matter how small. Big victories sometimes come from a series of small ones strung together.

> ➤ Visualize success by thinking through a perfect operation (sound familiar?).

> ➤ Accept criticism and integrate it into the next activity.

➤ Focus on the next step and get it right, then the next step after that. You climb a mountain step by step.

➤ Overwhelm your fear by accepting fear as a natural emotion and choosing courage instead. It sounds impractical, but listen to the testimonies of Medal of Honor recipients and you will understand.

➤ Exercise regularly; it breeds a positive mental attitude.

By using these methods you can overcome the tendency to react negatively to rejection. Rejection only makes you better. Focus on your next interview. Integrate the lessons you learned. Overcome your fear of rejection. Imagine success and have confidence in your training.

Chapter Homework

1. List a set of possible objections to hiring you and compose responses as part of your personal scripts storyboard. Consider objections about age, experience, gender, and technical competence—any possible area that might raise your hurdle.

CHAPTER 25

Execution: Sample Interview Questions and Answers

> **In This Chapter**
>
> ➤ Questions on interviewers' minds
> ➤ Sample questions from E to Z

In this chapter you will find a number of questions that help you prepare for actual ones you might receive. In many cases, these questions were posed during interviews with students in MBA programs, career changers, and other professionals. Other questions are ones interviewers would dearly love to ask, but can't or won't. In this chapter you begin to think from an interviewer's perspective.

Questions Interviewers Would Like to Ask

Interviewers may want answers to questions they're not allowed to ask. Some questions are illegal, some are unethical, and some are personal and just none of their business.

Interviewers may wonder about your personal life and how it might affect your job performance. They may be inquisitive about why you left your last job. They may wonder if your age or health is a concern. They may challenge your experience. They may wonder about your skill level. They may wonder about your ability to work independently or in a team. They may question whether you can acquire new skills or a new client, or if you can develop a new process. They may doubt your ability to master the requirements of the new job. They may wonder if you lie, cheat, or steal.

An interviewer may, however, do an end run and ask a question in a roundabout way.

Interview Insights

It's hard enough to answer questions without having to fight the sleepy-eyed interviewer. Therefore, if you have the luxury of scheduling interview times, mid-morning is probably best. After lunch, you are apt to get that stupefied, bored look from an interviewer with a full tummy. That might throw you off your game. And, he or she might not appreciate the brilliance of your answer.

Do you address an interviewer's unasked question head on? If these issues are a question mark in their mind, it should also be apparent to you prior to the interview. If so, the answer is the same as in the previous chapter about voiced objections. Have a personal scripts answer ready for these issues and use it at the right time. For example, you might say, "You may be wondering about my ability to work well with others. Let me assure you that I believe teamwork is the best way to beat the competition, and I will do whatever it takes to support my teammates in that effort."

Questions that Interviewers Can't Ask

Consult the Department of Labor websites for updates, but as a rule interviewers should not ask questions about anything to do with civil rights or health. Privacy issues are personal issues and are not job related, therefore they should be off-limits. But what are you going to do if an interviewer asks such a question? Will you tell him or her that it's illegal to ask such a question and that you are going to sue? That's a surefire way to get a job there, right? The bar for proving an interviewer has committed an illegal act is quite high—you need substantive proof, not just your memory.

Here is a quote from the Department of Labor Hiring Compliance Assistance web page (www.dol.gov/compliance/index.htm):

"There are a number of federal laws that employers must follow when hiring employees. Generally speaking, these laws prohibit discrimination in employment decisions based on race, color, religion, sex, age, ethnic/national origin, disability, or veteran status. The U.S. Department of Labor (DOL) administers and enforces laws affecting the hiring of employees under the age of 18, veterans, and certain foreign workers. DOL is also responsible for laws that ensure that federal contractors and grantees provide equal employment opportunity to applicants and employees."

Likewise, state law also governs the actions of employers. Illegal activity on the part of employers may result in a dual charge situation. Check www.eeoc.gov for more information. Also, use the Internet to read about your rights under a number of important pieces of anti-discrimination legislation:

➤ The Civil Rights Act of 1964, Title VII

➤ Age Discrimination and Employment Act of 1967

➤ American with Disabilities Act of 1990, Amended 2009

Consequences of Asking

In many cases, it isn't the question per se, but the consequences that ensue. The firm would have to prove that bias had nothing to do with not hiring you for the job. The standard may be too onerous for most firms. So, those firms that have an HR department have most likely instructed interviewers to shy away from such questioning—it's not worth the risk of a lawsuit. If you are interviewing at a small firm, the risk may be higher.

Your Decision

The question you have to quickly ask yourself is whether or not you want to work at a company where the employees are so ignorant of the rules or flagrantly violate them. It may be wiser to move on and leave the crusading to someone else.

But, there you sit while this person is waiting for an answer to an age, health, gender, orientation, or disability question. You might look the interviewer calmly in the eye, and very pleasantly say, "I believe my experience is first-rate, and there isn't any impediment to being a top-notch employee at your firm. I look forward to competing for the position." Then let it go. If the interviewer pushes it, then move on.

Preparing for the Questions

Obviously, no one knows everything (although you probably know people who think they do). There will be questions you cannot answer. But, try as best you can to anticipate broad categories of questioning and then drill down into each. These then directly impact some of the content you develop in your personal scripts.

Try to look at the underlying reason why the question was asked. What is the interviewer trying to get at? Technical knowledge? How I react to stress? What kind of employee I will be? Can I answer the million-dollar question?

As you look at the sample questions that follow, try to come up with your own list that gets at the same underlying topic. The questions are geared toward those who are attempting to interview for a job with a U.S. company or in the United States. If that is not the case with you, then substitute similar questions with your target country or company in mind.

Words to Use and not Use

There is, however, some language that you should be reluctant to use in any interview when describing your background, activities, or personal traits. Exclude them from your personal scripts dialogue. They are:

➤ Curse words

➤ Can't, won't

➤ Feel, feeling

➤ Failed, failure to perform or anticipate

➤ Declined to accept

➤ Timid behavior

➤ Lack of interest

➤ Lost, isolated

➤ Confused, confusion

➤ Unexpected outcome

➤ Fatigue, tired

➤ Dissenting voice

➤ Under-perform

➤ Late, short of

➤ Underachiever

➤ Needed a vacation or time off

➤ Couldn't turn it around

➤ Lackluster or stymied effort

➤ Disorganized

➤ Lack of recognition or response

Instead, use positive language when discussing your achievements and experience. Try using:

➤ Accomplished, accomplishment

➤ Positive, predicted outcome

➤ Favorable rating

➤ On time

➤ Mutual interest

➤ Team building

➤ Highly confident

➤ Motivation, motivated

➤ Power, powerful

➤ Impact, believed

➤ Ahead of schedule

➤ Expense reducing

➤ Revenue enhancing

➤ Strength, strengthen

➤ Beat the odds and the competition

➤ Belief, believe

➤ On target

➤ Strategic, tactical

➤ Building, built

➤ Exceeded, exceeding benchmarks

Sample Interview Questions

Aside from a question being illegal, there really isn't a question an interviewer won't ask. Questions about age and health are the only two illegal federal categories; as mentioned earlier, questions about other subjects could be the basis for discrimination and bias lawsuits. Everything else is fair game. Use the sample questions given here as an indication of the type of questions an interviewer might pursue. There are three categories:

➤ Soft balls

➤ Down the fairway

➤ High speed

The first sample questions, soft balls, are questions that are highly likely and should pose little difficulty. The second sample questions, down the fairway, are ones that are more difficult and might require additional thought and preparation. Some should be expected. The final sample of questions, high speed, are ones that are the real discriminators and brainteasers. These are the ones that should help you exhibit the perfect job interview level of performance.

Some of the questions may not be relevant to your employment goals. Pick several questions from each category, and then craft similar questions germane to your situation to supplement them. Be tough on yourself.

Soft Balls

➤ Tell me why I should hire you as opposed to hiring someone else?

➤ Tell me about a situation where you failed and what you did about it.

➤ Tell me about a defining moment in your life.

➤ Who is your role model and what did he or she teach you?

➤ Describe your personality.

➤ Give me an example of a personality conflict you had with a colleague and how you resolved it.

➤ How would you react to the following: A project teammate says he discovers that the numbers on a spreadsheet he turned into your supervisor had a fundamental flaw in them? He does not intend to disclose this, hoping it won't really be discovered. What do you do?

➤ Tell me about the last book you read and why you liked or disliked it.

➤ Tell me about the last volunteer work that you did.

➤ Who would you invite to dinner and why?

➤ Would you rather hike to the top of Mount Hood, go to the Museum of Modern Art, or go to a professional boxing match? Why?

➤ Would you follow the advice of Warren Buffett or your best friend about buying a house? Who is Warren Buffet?

➤ What are your hobbies? Why those?

➤ Do you play chess? If not, why not?

➤ Who is your favorite celebrity and what is it about him or her that interests you?

➤ What is your favorite music? Why?

> Describe your last vacation and why you pursued that location or idea.

> What was your toughest course in school? The easiest? Why?

> If you had three options to follow, how would you select the best one for you? How would you advise your best friend?

> How do I know you would be a great hire? What can I expect from you in the first ninety days?

> Tell me a little about yourself (really open-ended).

> What are some of your interests (referring to your résumé)?

> Describe your ability to work with others.

> Describe your strengths and weaknesses.

> How would you describe yourself to others?

> Name the last six U.S. presidents.

> Which is not round: A baseball, a hockey puck, or a football?

> True or false: Mozart is to music as a cat is to a lion.

Down the Fairway

> What happened of consequence in 1865 in the United States?

> What happened in Europe of consequence in 1990?

> Who is the president of Russia?

> What countries are next door to Iraq?

> Does the United States support North or South Korea?

> What single incident provoked World War I?

> Name five classical composers.

> Is Antarctica north or south of the United States?

> Name five countries in Africa.

> Why is December 7th remembered?

> What is the periodic table? What is the symbol for gold?

> Describe your main area of competence. Pick an aspect and teach it to me.

> How do you get people to work with you?

> What is 5 degrees Celsius in Fahrenheit?

➤ Do you speak a foreign language? Why or why not? If so, please say …

➤ Tell me about a time you failed to accomplish something you were asked to do.

➤ Describe a project you worked on.

➤ Give me an example of a new idea you presented.

➤ How would you advise your best friend to decide on a new car?

➤ Give me directions to the airport from here. To a restaurant.

➤ What do you want to accomplish in this job?

➤ What other firms are you looking at?

➤ If you wanted to be in any other profession, what would that be and why?

High Speed

➤ Name a major economic issue facing the world economy. Do you have a view on what must be done?

➤ A company has a problem retaining its employees. What are some major issues you would investigate?

➤ What is the population of China? Of the world?

➤ What affects the airline industry and why?

➤ Describe the relationship between your industry and an aging population.

➤ If cost cutting is an issue at your new firm, what plausible strategies might work?

➤ What is the prime rate and what is its level today?

➤ What is the stock price of your chosen firm? What were its profits last quarter?

➤ What nations surround Iran? What states border California?

➤ What is the current rate of inflation and unemployment?

➤ How would you determine the total square feet of residential housing space in Phoenix?

➤ A company is losing market share, and a new CEO is taking over. He is not from within the industry. What issues should concern him and what would you advise him to do?

➤ What are the five competitive forces that shape the industry in which you hope to work?

➤ Solve for x if [250*1,100/550]-500/2x=1,000 (thirty seconds to respond to equation given on a note card. Hint: If you ate 4/8 of a pie, the part that was eaten)

➤ What causes a tornado? How would you predict its path?

➤ Name three brands you admire and the differentiating qualities that distinguish them from their rivals.

➤ Name the top four economies in the world and their approximate GDPs.

➤ What are three major cross-border issues?

➤ Name the countries that will most influence the U.S. economy over the next five and twenty-five years.

➤ What is microfinance?

➤ How would you get a new client?

➤ Name the number-one issue facing U.S. companies today and some plausible solutions.

➤ Five people are part of a team involved in developing a new product. You are the least experienced, but you feel you have the answer. How would you convince the team members to adopt your version?

➤ If you were to meet the CEO of your target company while riding down the elevator, what would you say?

➤ What is the U.S. unemployment rate and what does "full employment" mean?

➤ What do you hope to accomplish in this job?

➤ What is your career goal five years from now?

➤ What book have you read recently and what is its relevance to you and this job?

➤ Name the heads of three countries and the major economic issues facing each?

➤ If your product is overpriced relative to competition and your cost structure is also too high, what could be done?

➤ How do you determine if your product or service is good or not?

➤ What role does the federal budget deficit play in the nation's economy? What about the size of the national debt?

➤ Should Social Security be privatized through individual market-based accounts?

➤ Who is the president of France, and what is the size of the trade market between France and the United States?

➤ What is the subprime mortgage market, and why has it had such an enormous effect upon global stock markets?

➤ Where do you hope to be in your career ten years from now?

➤ In three sentences maximum, describe what you bring to the table.

➤ Where and what is the Strait of Hormuz?

➤ What is Sudoku? Ever played it?

➤ Would you rather read a philosophy text or a chemistry text and why?

➤ What is the difference between fusion and fission?

➤ Two of your coworkers are in a heated conversation. What would you do?

➤ If you are a teacher, how do you discipline an unruly student?

➤ If you are a lawyer, how would you grow the partnership?

➤ Bonus pools are down this year and salaries are flat. How would you break the news to your employees?

➤ If the roles were reversed, what criteria would you evaluate in order to hire someone for this job?

➤ If you were to describe your first two months on the job, what would it look like?

➤ Your compensation request is high. How can you justify your numbers?

➤ There is a person out in the hallway waiting for an interview whose credentials are better. Why should I hire you instead?

Selected Answers

To give you a flavor for what a good answer looks like, look at a few of the questions and answers.

➤ Question: Tell me why I should hire you as opposed to hiring someone else?

Answer: First, I am motivated to help this company continue to be successful. From school through my work and personal life, my experience shows a track record of success. I understand what it takes for a company to be profitable, and I am willing to commit my time and effort to achieving that end. I can't say anything about others' efforts, but I can say they won't outwork me.

➤ Question: Describe your strengths and weaknesses.

Answer: In preparing for this and other interviews, I have recently engaged in an appraisal process that analyzed my strong points and those areas where I need enhancement. In so doing, I reaffirmed my strong analytical skills, leadership talent, and ability to work across boundaries with cross-functional teams. I also discovered that I needed to enhance my cross-border understanding, particularly linguistically. So, I am currently learning French so as to be able to work with several key clients we have there. I find this type of self-analysis useful in upgrading my ability to contribute.

> ➤ Question: What happened of consequence in 1865 in the United States?

Answer: In April 1865, the American Civil War ended with the surrender of Confederate forces under General Robert E. Lee at the Appomattox County Courthouse in Virginia. I enjoy reading about the war because it shows what perseverance, sacrifice, and team effort are all about. It is inspirational that people could believe in their cause so fervently, regardless of side, that they would sacrifice their lives for it.

> ➤ Question: Tell me about a time you failed to accomplish something you were asked to do.

Answer: I've never failed at anything. Of course, I am kidding. Once, when I first got started in the business I went on a sales call and thought, "You're a bright fellow, great education. How hard could it be?" So, I went in unprepared and lost the sale. I learned firsthand early on that success comes after hard work and preparation, not luck. And that lesson stays with me today.

> ➤ Question: If cost cutting is an issue at your new firm, what plausible strategies might work?

Answer: In most organizations, inefficiencies and duplication in operations increase costs and make the firm less competitive. A thorough value chain analysis should be undertaken to determine where those costs are and how they influence the total cost of goods sold on an economic value-added basis. Perhaps there are better ways of accomplishing the same objective with less expense. A cost reduction task force might be a vehicle to accomplish this goal.

> ➤ Question: Solve for x if [250*1,100/550]-500/2x=1,000.

Answer: I like numbers, they keep the mind sharp. The answer is: -1/2. (Remember the order of operations acronym PEMDAS: parenthesis, exponents, multiplication, division, addition, subtraction.)

> ➤ Question: Name three brands you admire and the differentiating qualities that distinguish them from their rivals.

Answer: I admire Daimler Mercedes-Benz, Apple, and Boeing. First, I admire Mercedes-Benz for a pervasive commitment to quality, Apple for enduring innovation, and Boeing for the sophistication of its integration efforts. All three represent benchmark excellence—qualities to which I aspire.

> ➤ Question: If you were to meet the CEO of your target company while riding down the elevator, what would you say?

Answer: Candidate: Good afternoon, Ms. Johnson. I'm Mr. XYZ. I had the privilege of meeting with Ken R. today about the VP job in product improvement, and I was thoroughly impressed with the company and its people.

CEO: Oh, I am so glad to hear it.

Candidate: I believe my background at ABC Corp would complement your team. In fact, I mentioned a few thoughts about changes driving the industry right now, especially in product design. I would really enjoy working with your people.

CEO: Interesting. Did the team seem receptive?

Candidate: Yes, they did and hopefully we can re-engage at some point soon. That is, if Ken offers me the opportunity!

CEO: Well, we'll have to see about that. Very pleasant to meet you.

> ➤ Question: Where and what is the Strait of Hormuz?

Answer: A 29 nm-wide passageway separating the Persian Gulf on the east and the Gulf of Oman and the Arabian Sea on the west. To the north is Iran, and to the south are UAE and a small enclave owned by Oman. It is a strategically important waterway since much of Persian Gulf oil passes through it.

> ➤ Question: If the roles were reversed, what criteria would you evaluate in order to hire someone for this job?

Answer: First, I think analytical ability mixed with an appreciation for others' work. There is a tendency for some quantitative people to get pigeonholed, and I think you will need someone who can work well with other people. Second, I would want someone who is undeniably ethical and has the moral courage to do the right thing. Finally, I would want someone who keeps clients and the larger business picture in mind—after all, we need to make money in this firm!

Chapter Homework

1. Begin answering the questions above and formulate your own list of similar questions.

 **Execution: Case Analysis**

In This Chapter

> ➤ The purpose of case analysis
> ➤ How to handle cases
> ➤ A case opening

In this chapter you will learn how to approach case analysis, a tactic often used by companies to test a candidate's analytical abilities.

Case Studies in the Interview

Case analyses, or studies, are exercises in which a candidate is usually given a narrative where a character in an organization faces a set of underlying issues. The task facing the candidate is to analyze the issues at hand and develop a set of recommendations from which decisions can be made. In addition to traditional cases, firms sometimes use mini-cases or scenarios with role-playing.

The case study is often associated with American law and business schools, where the Socratic Method is utilized and where teachers and peers can openly deride students for erroneous answers.

Interview Vocab

The Socratic Method is a teaching method where students are presented a set of statements, oftentimes subtle and innocuous, from which they are to hypothesize, support, and articulate a set of recommendations. It was made famous in the 1970s movie *Paper Chase*, which was about students at Harvard Law School.

Interview Vocab

A case study is a problem facing a person or organization that is given to an interview candidate to determine analytical abilities and presentation skills. It can be either factual or fictitious.

The purpose of a case study is to determine if the job candidate has the requisite analytical skills to understand the facts of the case, investigate possible remedies, and then articulate recommendations.

How to Handle Cases

Cases are stories where there are characters, plots, conflicts, and usually dilemmas. If you are given a case, there are a number of things you can do at the start to get off on the right foot.

First, realize that the case has facts contained within it. It is upon these that you build a set of recommendations. Be careful that your advice is supported by the facts in the case. Characters, competitors, operational and organizational problems, technology issues, government oversight, product obsolescence, ethical or legal dilemmas, and other factors can cause issues, and you need to consider them all.

At the outset, read the material carefully. Take notes and record your general impressions and questions as you read through the case quickly. Then reread the case and make more detailed notes.

In many cases, the first two or three sentences contain subtle hints about the core issue facing the characters or business. Check for attachments or appendices that contain important numerical data. In some instances, superfluous data that has little or no relevance can be presented to lead you off track.

The case method is popular with consulting firms and investment banks and is increasingly presented to job candidates via the web. Some firms even have case method primers on their websites.

Case studies can be used in individual interviews, group interviews, or even online. However they are offered, case interviews can be intimidating if you are not ready for them. Elements of the following methods can also be used for mini-cases.

Tips for Handling Business Cases

Because of its broad applicability, adapt the scientific method where possible as a way of uncovering fundamental issues. This method is a proven way of approaching unusual phenomena, determining the validity of a scientist's initial observation, and extending the range of knowledge, hopefully, about the observed event. Some say it is a good way to minimize the effect of bias (disturbances caused by the observer or system, survivor bias, or preconceived impressions, etc.).

The scientific method starts with an inquiry:

> ➤ Ask a question
>
> ➤ Do background research
>
> ➤ Construct a hypothesis
>
> ➤ Test your hypothesis by conducting an experiment
>
> ➤ Analyze your data and draw a conclusion
>
> ➤ Communicate your results

In a case study context, after reading the narrative, consider an initial idea about the core issue. For example, does the main character really know what the major issue is? Is that the underlying problem or are there other issue drivers? Is the character part of the problem? What dilemma is he or she facing? Then, do your research by studying the facts as presented in the case. Make a few reasoned deductions. You might have to do a few calculations or use commonly accepted principles of logic (not your own version of what is logical, however).

The next step is to develop a possible reason or hypothesis about what is wrong, and test it against commonly accepted principles such as accounting, finance, science, production, and operations management; common sense; statements in the case; or the basic facts that are presented. Check the supporting data that might be embedded in a footnote or a table, then draw some conclusions and save your ideas as a possible recommendation.

Assumptions are Okay, But . . .

It is important to use only the facts in the case. Don't make up or bring in outside data. In some instances, however, it is acceptable and worthwhile to make valid assumptions that constrain your possible answers.

Some interview preparation experts recommend not using assumptions, but under specific circumstances, you can constrain a solution set through the use of defensible assumptions. Use caution, however, you cannot assume your way out of giving a thoughtful answer. You shouldn't go overboard on using assumptions, but if you decide they are needed, then make certain you state what they are and why they are legitimate. You will be asked to defend the validity of those assumptions, and if they are off base or unnecessary, you could be penalized.

A legitimate assumption could go something like this: "I assume that DOT data will support that the number of airline passenger miles is expected to grow at a statistically accurate rate per year, say 5 percent this year, and therefore the number of new ground utility servicing vehicles should grow at…" . If given this test in real life, an analyst would certainly want historic data on passenger miles, and armed with that, an accurate growth projection could be derived.

Having said this, there are usually sufficient facts given in the case to support an analysis without assuming very much.

Interview Insights

Hiring firms sometimes leave information out of a case in order to test a candidate's strength of conviction and whether the candidate would proceed in an erroneous direction without adequate information. In the real world, determining what information is needed is a problem—data sufficiency is crucial in deriving an optimum solution.

A Case Analysis Framework

How do you approach a case analysis? What do you look at and how can you be certain you are looking at the right problem?

First, investigate the situation across several key categories that affect an organization. The issues seem to generally develop around the same PPPPCFOMMG research framework described earlier in the book: people, product, platform, pricing, competition, financials, organizational, markets (structure and strategy), media, and government (legal). Look at the table below as a starting point for a case analysis. Remember: four Ps, a CFO, and a Mickey Mouse Government.

Category	Areas/Questions to Investigate
People (P)	Promotions, demotions, egos, jealousies, competence, experience, values, leadership, hidden agendas
Product (P)	Branding, pricing, positioning, sales force, distribution, technical data, production, rivals
Platform (P)	Vision, coherence, integration, articulation, evolving, acceptance

Pricing (P)	Price leader vs follower, margin analysis, discounts, promotions
Competition (C)	Intensity of competition, (reactions/actions), economic conditions, pricing power
Financial (F)	Coverage ratios, capital structure, cost of debt and equity, balance sheet changes, expenses, debt burden, cash flow, sales effectiveness
Organizational—Culture, Design (O)	Values-driven; integrated; transformative culture aligned with strategy; new hires integrated; flat, pyramidal, decision-making aligned with strategic interests, degree of bureaucracy, spans of control
Markets—Strategy and Structure (M)	Industry attractiveness, intensity of rivalries, distribution channels, short vs long-term strategic interests
Media (M)	Publicity, advertising spend and brand strategies, spokespersons aligned with strategy
Government/Legal/Ethical (G)	Dilemmas, conflicts, honesty and integrity, mores and standards, changes in government regulations or laws, compensation issues

Presenting Your Recommendations

When you present your analysis, be certain to have your notes handy. Give an opening summary of your findings, and then go back and give more detail about your assumptions, calculations, logic, etc., to support your arguments. Finally, give a quick overview concerning risks, implications, and next steps if your course of action were to be adopted. As you accomplish your PPPPCFOMMG analysis, make certain you discuss a backup plan in case your recommended action falls short.

Be professional and give the characters in the case some benefit of the doubt, and don't presume that you know all the answers. The case could be a disguised business issue facing the company, and the interviewer could be one of the characters. In other words, don't insult the people or strategy in the case by saying something like, "The idiots on the management team should have seen that one coming!" It's possible the idiot is sitting across the table from you.

Cases also come in parts. Some companies will give you a Case A and then follow up with a Case B, C, D with incremental updates and additional facts generated by the market, people, competitors, nature, etc. When you get a serial case situation, don't panic if your initial analysis of Case A is overcome by the subsequent case. Things happen in the real world. Just make sure your framework is in place, update it, and alter your core approach only after careful thought. Don't come across as a person without conviction in the face of trial, constantly blown off course by events.

Think of using bullet points in a presentation when you speak about your findings. In other words, be crisp and to the point.

The Case Setup

To give you a feel for what a case opening might look like, the following is fairly typical of the initial stage-setting paragraph or two of a business case with a fictitious company and fake references to figures, tables, and conversations. In an actual case, spreadsheets, quotations, figures, graphs, and all forms of data are usually given within the body of the case or listed as attachments or appendices. What would you do if you were in this man's shoes?

"John looked at the unread memo from the CEO Bill H. on his desk with apprehension. He thought he knew what was in it and then glanced at his telephone, waiting for the inevitable conversation.

As vice-president for Production at AB and Z Brands, John was expected to meet an ever-increasing monthly target for deliveries of his company's highly anticipated new product, a luxury women's fragrance, and for the third week in a row, unforeseen equipment problems and other factors had caused delays. He knew he was going to be blamed, but he thought the sales director and the vendors should be the ones skewered. He squirmed in his seat as he thought: *The guy changes his projections all the time, the digital autoloaders are lousy, and yet I'm the only one the old man is going to blame.*

John forgot the memo for a moment, and instead looked at the projected sales numbers he was given for the coming three months (Figure 1). He cross-checked those against his average production per run, idle times, and shift schedules (Figure 2), and his outlook had just begun to brighten when his phone rang. It was his line foreman Al B., and he was frantic.

AB and Z Brands, Ltd., was a manufacturer of luxury goods to the super-wealthy consumer. The private company, owned by a famous family with Italian heritage, produced generic products but also produced its own line of exclusive private label fragrances and leather goods. The world saw the company as an efficient purveyor of products to the beautiful jet set crowd. And although sales had been generally in line with expectations, there had been some alarming trends in the industry (Table 1), not the least of which was the arrival of trendy, on-site, micro-scent factories into AB and Z's client space.

And so on.

Chapter Homework

1. If you were the production manager in the case above, what could you imagine might be found in the sales figures that might give you an out? What about industry trends—what factors could affect the company there? What other elements of concern might you expect to find in a case of this type? What about the family's role? Are there any other personnel, production, or competitive issues to consider?

Quotable Quotes

"Take time to deliberate, but when the time for action arrives, stop thinking and go in."

Andrew Jackson

 Execution: Dress, Appearance, and Courtesies

In This Chapter

➤ The first moments

➤ First impressions are crucial

➤ Know what looks best on you

➤ Dinners and cocktail parties

➤ Suggestions

This chapter discusses how to execute a powerful impact in the critical first impression moments of an interview. The chapter offers suggestions on style, designers, and what accessories might be important. Further, mealtime and interview courtesies are also discussed.

The Basics of Appearance

First impressions linger. Opening statements and a memorable close are undeniably critical, but the first impression you make in the first moments of an interview undergirds them both. In fact, the first thirty seconds are arguably the most crucial and can determine the outcome of the interview.

So it is extremely crucial that your dress, appearance, and courtesies are additive and do not detract from

Quotable Quotes

"A fair exterior is a silent recommendation."

Publilius Syrus

your chances for success. There are colors of clothing, for instance, that are just inappropriate to a business setting: a lime green suit for women, or a pumpkin-colored jacket for men, for example.

This idea goes beyond clothing and extends to the overall impression you leave. Remember this: Fair or not, many interviewers believe they know in thirty seconds if an offer will be extended or not.

In this regard, do not neglect the power of good personal grooming. No matter what job you are trying to get, there is no excuse for wrinkled clothing, dirty or jagged nails, unkempt ratty hair, or discourteous behavior.

Good grooming includes the basics of cleanliness that your mama taught you: hair brushed and styled, teeth brushed, nails trimmed, shoes shined.

Interview clothing is an investment in your future; it will reap dividends. You don't need to buy the most expensive items, but do buy high-quality products. The difference shows. Inexpensive clothing usually wears out more quickly, looks cheap when you wear it, and can give the impression you are either more desperate than you are or don't care. Obviously, don't spend money you don't have, but the point is simple: Buy the best you can afford. It will pay for itself.

You should avoid large dangling earrings and body art such as body piercing and tattoos—these are best left for others at the beach. If you have them, keep them covered during the interview—your wild side can come out later.

If possible, avoid logos. There is a chance that someone might not like the topic, saying, or group. It might give the wrong impression—and you don't want to have to worry about that.

Interview Insights

A managing director in a global investment bank once interviewed a young lady for an important job in a major Midwestern city. Hours later, the interview room still reeked with the candidate's perfume. Unfortunately, all day long the perfume reminded the interviewer of the young woman's shallow answers and immodest dress. This is not the type of impression you want to make!

Self-Expression is Overrated

The golden rule of interview dress and appearance is to keep it simple, conservative, and easily overlooked. Your words and performance are the focus point, and your clothing should only play a supporting role.

In some jobs in some industries, the mistakes below may not be mistakes. If so, you may not need the suggestions offered next. For the rest of you, here are more notorious mistakes from the interview battlefield:

➤ Necktie is loose at the neck (absolutely destroys the look of the suit)

➤ Dress is too short

➤ Plunging neckline

➤ Scuffed shoes

➤ Wrinkles (on the suit!)

➤ Transparent blouse

➤ Clanking jewelry

➤ Nose, lip, eye, ear, or tongue piercings

➤ Bouffant, outlandish hairstyles and colors

➤ Shoes with holes

➤ Bitten nails, dirty hands

➤ High-water trousers, especially with white socks

Know Your Audience

Remember to dress for the occasion and the audience. Each company or industry has a prevailing standard. Obviously, industry standards vary in clothing, appearance, and conduct. For instance, in Silicon Valley or in parts of the advertising or media industries in LA and New York, suits may not be the norm—especially for follow-on interviews.

Without prior intelligence or direction, you should default to a suit for an on-campus or company visit. Don't be intimidated, ask the interview coordinator what to wear if you are uncertain—it's better to ask the question than be embarrassed at the interview.

Photos Tell All

Try to obtain pictures of people in the company to get a feel for the dress standard. If you can, drop by the exit door of the company around quitting time to get a feel for what the people look like.

For instance, if you want to work in the construction industry, you may want to rethink wearing an expensive coat and tie, especially if the meeting is to be held on a job site.

Try to look like you are one of them—wear what they wear, commensurate with your position in the company. The idea is to look like you already work there.

Clothing for the Office interview:

High-quality, freshly pressed clothing fosters the sense that you take pride in your work and will look good in front of clients—and that is a plus. Here are some tips:

> ➤ Leave the flowered shirts, sandals, and resort wear at home (unless you're specifically told to wear it)

> ➤ No glow-in-the-dark colors

> ➤ No overflowing pocket squares

> ➤ No provocative, alluring dresses

> ➤ No dangles and bangles—that means heavy jewelry

> ➤ Avoid anything that distracts from what you will say

> ➤ If you would wear it on a date, then leave it for the date

> ➤ Wear only a tiny, small, whiff, essence, hint of scent, or none at all

Interview Insights

Don't get comments like these. Get your trusted agent to look at your videotape and take his or her comments to heart.

"Ouch! His suit looked lumpy!"

"That striped shirt looked like a test pattern!"

"Her face looked like the moon it was so shiny with makeup!"

"Couldn't believe his hairy legs and white crew socks when he sat down!"

"I swore she had 2 carats in her nose!"

"Checks, stripes, plaids—the only thing he forgot were polka dots!"

"His tie was so short, I thought he was wearing a bolo tie!"

"I kept wondering how much her hair weighs."

Advice for Men

When choosing your interview clothes, keep iin mind that suits should be well cut and conform to your body type. Shirts should be crisp with a standard collar, but probably not with a spread or European point. Solid coloring in white or light blue is a conservative choice. The tie is the center point of your ensemble and should be 100 percent silk. Shoes should be freshly shined and broken in before the interview. Socks should be over the calf, so that a bare leg is avoided when sitting with crossed legs. Socks should also match the trouser.

You'll want to stay away from loud colors and ensure that your neckwear is tied with a Windsor or four-in-hand knot. Make sure it is tightly knotted around your collar at all times. For trendy industries where suits are still needed, try European designers that favor a tailored, slimming look or U.S. designers with an edgy look.

For business casual attire, avoid a slouchy look. Wear a belt, and although current styles allow men to wear shirts untucked, it is less risky to opt for a more polished appearance. Untucked shirting hides midriff bulge, but it can be taken as being too casual.

The What and Where for Men

The following designers and clothing cover a wide range of styles and prices. Prices are based on searches of popular Internet vendor sites (sale prices where possible). There are other fine providers, but the ones that follow consistently produce quality products:

➤ Suits: Hickey Freeman, Zegna, Canali, Oxford, Brooks Brothers, Joseph Abboud, Jack Victor, Tommy Hilfiger, Andrew Fezza, Calvin Klein. Colors: charcoal grey, midnight blue, navy. Choose solid or subtle pinstripe; avoid fabric with unusual patterns or shiny textures (price range: USD $300 to $1,500+)

➤ Shirts: Zegna, Piatelli, Canali, Hickey Freeman, Ike Behar, Brooks Brothers, Jhane Barnes, Joseph Abboud. Colors: solid white or oxford blue. It's best to avoid patterns. Standard pinpoint collar, barrel or French cuff is fine (price range: USD $80 to $400+)

➤ Shoes: Alden, Allen Edmonds, Ferragamo, Florsheim, Bass, Bostonian, Johnston and Murphy. Color: black (preferred), brown, or cordovan. Style: cap toe Oxford lace ups (preferred) or tasseled kiltie. French loafer if you're in a trendy industry (price range: USD $100 to $600+)

➤ Topcoat or outerwear: Hickey Freeman, Burberry, Armani, Kenneth Cole, Pronto Uomo. Colors: gray, camel, or midnight blue/black (price range: USD $150 to $1,500+)

➤ Belt: Coach, Prada, Allen Edmonds, Ferragamo, John Nordstrom, Boss, Brooks Brothers, Cole Haan. Color and style: Smaller buckle, black, brown or cordovan to match shoes (price range: USD $50 to $350+)

➤ Neckwear: Hermes, Ferragamo, Robert Talbot, JoS. A. Bank. Style: small print, solid, or regimental stripe. Colors: blues, reds, forest greens (price range: USD $60 $185+)

➤ Pocket square: Nordstroms, Saks, Amazon. Color and fabric: white cotton or linen, not silk (price range: USD $10 to $50)

➤ Pens: Waterman, Cross, Parker, Mont Blanc (price range: USD $70 to $350+)

➤ Cuff links: Brooks Brothers, Kenneth Cole. Style: sophisticated, but not heavily statement oriented (price range: USD $50 to $125+)

➤ Casual attire (includes shoes): Zegna, Boss, Jhane Barnes, Kenneth Cole, Brooks Brothers, Canali, Zanella, Corneliani, Armani, Prada, Cole Haan, Coach, Talbott, Nordstrom, Perry Ellis (ensemble price range: USD $400 to $1,200+)

Advice for Women

Clothing should exude confidence and professionalism by highlighting your best features and coloration. Wear subtle colors and flattering styles that do not detract from your presentation. For summer, choose light grays and tans. If you choose darker grays and blues, buy them in lighter fabrics that travel well. Red is a power color, so it should be chosen with care. Solids are best with light pinstripe, a second choice. Skirt length and blouses should be conservative. Expensive suits mean power and authority. Dark tweeds and interesting subtle patterns like houndstooth exude confidence. Skirts with classy, upscale jackets also show femininity and responsibility.

Dress as if you know where you are and where you are going. Clothing should have plain lines and classic cuts that draw attention to your face and underscores what you are saying, not what you are wearing. Lighten up on makeup. Elegance and sophistication are the rule. Light pinks, whites, grays, and blues are good choices for blouses.

Jewelry and other accessories should be understated and tasteful. Avoid large dangling earrings, and without question body piercing and tattoos are best left for others at the beach. Don't be foppish or runway cute.

Look at pictures of successful women in business—emulation is a good thing.

The What and Where for Women

A wide range of styles, prices, and brands are available for women:

➤ Designers/lines: Brooks Brothers, Armani, Ralph Lauren, Donna Karan, Jones of New York, Dianne von Furstenberg, Hickey Freeman, Nine West, Tahari, Kay Unger, Anne Taylor, Kate Spade, DKNYC, Trina Turk, Calvin Klein (price range: USD $150 to $1500 for suiting)

➤ Shoes: Cole Haan, Stuart Weitzman, Kate Spade, Nine West (price range: USD $80 to $400+)

➤ Scarves: Hermes, Loro Piana, Valentino, Alexander McQueen, Echo Design, Kenneth Cole (price range: USD $60 to $2,000+)

➤ Handbags: Coach, Marc Jacobs, Ferragamo, Michael by Michael Kors, Cole Haan (price range: USD $300 to $1,000+)

➤ Jewelry: David Yurman, John Hardy, Judith Ripka Style: subtle, simple earrings—pearls are fine; pinpoint, short drop or no drop (price range: USD $250 to $500+)

➤ Briefcases: Ghurka, Tumi, Kenneth Cole (price range: USD $135 to $500+)

➤ Pens: Waterman, Cross, Parker, Mont Blanc (price range: USD $70 to $350+)

➤ Necklaces, bracelets: Brooks Brothers, David Yurman, Alexis Bittar. Style: subtle (Price range: USD $185 to $1,000+)

➤ Casual attire (including accessories): Brooks Brothers, Akris, Armani, Gap, Ann Taylor, Dianne von Furstenburg, Tahari, Michael by Michael Kors, Theory, Urban Outfitters (USD $200 to $1,000+)

If you're not the kind who likes to go all over town looking for your wardrobe, here's a list of one-stop stores that offer a wide range of styles, prices, and consultants for men and women:

➤ Neiman Marcus

➤ Bergdorf Goodman

➤ Saks Fifth Avenue

➤ Brooks Brothers

➤ Paul Stuart

➤ Alden

➤ Ferragamo

➤ Macy's

➤ Nordstrom

> ➤ Bloomingdales

> ➤ Local boutiques (only if you know their quality)

> ➤ Dillards

> ➤ Lord and Taylor

Always get to your interview early to check your appearance. Consider carrying small spare items such as a brush or comb in your briefcase or purse.

Travel Hints

Your dress and appearance require special attention during business travel. Some tips on how to keep yourself looking fresh, pressed, and polished while on the road are as follows:

> ➤ American electrical appliances operate on 110/120 volts, whereas much of the rest of the planet uses 220/240 volts. If you have an interview in a foreign locale, buy a small travel appliance adapter, which can be found online and in some major department stores.

> ➤ Don't rely upon the airline to get your bags to the interview on time! Purchase a carry-on or hanging garment bag and use the overhead bin.

> ➤ Choose microfibers and wrinkle-resistant fabrics for casual or resort wear. For suits, choose Super 100 or Super 120 wool fabric. The S numbering system used by mills and suit makers refers to the quality of fabric. Generally, grades above 120 get too expensive for ordinary folk.

> ➤ Make sure your hotel has a business office you can use for faxes, computers, etc.

> ➤ Depending upon the grade of the hotel, the housekeeping or the concierge will take your suits, shirts, and blouses for a finishing press. Ask at check-in.

Quotable Quotes

"Clothes and manners do not make the man; but, when he is made, they greatly improve his appearance."

Henry Ward Beecher

Random Courtesies

During your interview, be assertive, but courteous. Acknowledge the interviewer is giving you valuable time. Do not trash former employers or employees. Be diplomatic but truthful.

Elevator etiquette varies with region and country. If you're waiting for an elevator, allow those in the elevator to exit first before you enter. If you're inside the elevator, step aside and allow women to exit from the rear of the elevator first, while holding the door for them.

In general, even in business settings men should open the door for women. It is not necessary, however, to hold a female colleague's chair for her when sitting down for a meal.

Use the interviewer's last name and Mr./Ms. (or foreign equivalent) unless the interviewer offers his or her first name. If you're interviewing in a foreign country, you will need to consult a guidebook or a handbook.

Useful Tips for Cocktail Parties

Depending upon your situation, you may be invited to a cocktail party or dinner as part of the interview process. Remember the American World War II slogan: "Loose lips sink ships." Perhaps, it should be "Loose lips sink jobs."

I have seen several candidates' chances scuttled by antics at a cocktail party. If there is wine or beer, and you feel under pressure to imbibe in an adult beverage, then nurse one for as long as you can. Be careful about drinking on an empty stomach. Clear sodas or carbonated waters with a twist are fashionable surrogates. So remember, if you flap your gums too much, you may bring that World War II slogan close to home.

Aside from drinking, some people do not know how to act at parties. Be careful not to reveal confidential information. Just don't engage in it. Don't dominate the conversation. Let your hosts speak to your questions. If you disagree on a point with your host, leave room for his or her point of view. It is okay to have strength of feeling and confidence in your view, and still acknowledge his or her expressed viewpoint.

Useful Tips for Dinners

Dining etiquette can be confusing. Keep in mind that your bread is on the left, just above your forks. Don't eat your neighbor's on your right! Everyone at the table will figure out you were the culprit. The bread plate is usually at the ten o'clock position. Dessert utensils are immediately to the top of the entrée plate. Glassware is customarily in-line to the top right of the entrée plate. The largest is the water goblet; next to it is the champagne flute; in front of those two, or the next two in line, are the wine and sherry glasses. If someone asks for the salt, include the pepper. If you need to excuse yourself during dinner, make your apologies, and then leave the napkin on the arm of the chair or on the seat—never put it on the table. Also, always serve food counterclockwise, to the right. The dessert spoon is horizontally placed just above your plate.

Start eating only after your host starts or after everyone else has been served. In some cases, the courses have been preselected. In others, you may have a choice. If so, pick items that are easy to cut, easy to chew, and easy to digest. If you have a choice between lobster and a chicken marsala, choose the chicken—it's much easier to handle.

Interview Insights

Don't set your own traps. Don't be like the young man who asked for steamed spinach (ouch!) to go along with his steak. You can guess what happened when he smiled—everyone at the table tried hard to stifle their giggles. That is, until after the dinner! The point is, don't order anything that can stick to teeth, drips or slides easily, or is hard to cut (imagine knocking over wine and water goblets on the table as you muscle through). Try the fish or lasagna.

Here are a few common sense tips about your conduct during an interview over a meal. Again, customs vary across countries, and you should consult a country-specific guidebook for information if you'll be interviewing overseas. For meals in the United States, the following will apply in most situations. Remember, those rules from childhood still apply.

➤ No talking with food in your mouth.

➤ When eating soup, use delicate spoon strokes away from your body.

➤ Use the salad fork, the smaller one on the outside left, for the salad.

➤ Remember, utensil position is arranged in order corresponding to the order of the entrées.

➤ Chew with your mouth closed.

➤ Eat at a moderate pace.

➤ Do not overload your plate—take moderate portions only.

➤ Use your napkin.

➤ Be respectful of the wait staff.

➤ Use the butter knife and salad fork only for those items.

➤ Your bread is on the left above your forks, perhaps with a small butter knife across the plate.

➤ Your forks are on the left, knives on the right (exception: occasionally a small shrimp fork is placed on the right).

When you're finished, place your knife and fork diagonally across the top of the plate to signal the wait staff that you are finished with the meal. Or if you prefer, you can place them on the plate at the five o'clock position pointing inward.

For most interview situations, your host will pay for the meal. If you are paying, arrange that with the headwaiter ahead of time. In any event, thank your interviewer or host for meeting over the meal.

Topics to Discuss at Dinner

The following are possible topics to discuss over dinner with your host and others, if it is a group interview. Keep your answers light-hearted, and avoid cultural humor. You will have a longer time with your hosts than you would over a normal office interview so pace yourself. You may be the center of attention, but keep your comments friendly and professional.

Likewise, it is best to avoid initiating discussions about religion, politics, social issues, or topics about a war. If a question is asked about a hot topic, then you can easily say it is a controversial topic, and leave it at that. If they press the point, state your belief diplomatically and politely. It is a good idea to say something like, "If the facts change, I am always open to other points of view." The point is that it is usually not a good idea to fall on your sword about a topic during an interview if that issue has nothing to do with the job.

Still, be ready to discuss:

➤ Sports events when in season (Wimbledon, Masters, Final Four, World Series, Stanley Cup, Super Bowl, World Cup, Ryder Cup, New York and Boston marathons)

➤ Pending elections

➤ Global news events

➤ Music

➤ Travel and vacation plans

➤ Recent holiday experiences

➤ Interesting books and movies

➤ Favorite things to do

➤ Favorite wines or places to visit

➤ Your family (don't haul out the family photo album)

➤ Hobbies

In Summary

Your purpose is to get hired, not be on the cover of GQ or Vogue as a trendsetter—unless you are in the fashion industry, of course. Your appearance is important and it takes effort to look good, but do it.

Your discussions during the interview are obviously critical. But don't blow it during a follow-on social outing. The general rule is to come off as a mature professional and a net positive to the company. Show that you are an interesting and well-informed person who can be a responsible, pleasant member of the team. Showcase how you would act in a similar setting with the firm's clients.

Chapter Homework

1. Take a photo wearing your interview clothing and get someone to critique it.

2. Dry run a meal at an upscale restaurant (if appropriate for your situation) to practice your etiquette.

PART FOUR

Ex-Military and International Candidates

CHAPTER 28

Special Section: For Separating Military Members

In This Chapter

➤ Special challenges

➤ The translation problem

➤ Your experience is real, but…

In this chapter you will find suggestions on how to address your unique needs in transitioning from military to civilian work life.

Thanks for the Memories

You are separating from the military with a deployment bag full of memories and accomplishments. You have a right to feel good for all you have done and the nation is proud of you.

Still, many of you will not have a job ready and waiting for you when you separate. In fact, you may only have a vague idea about what you want to do and are likely concerned about providing for your families on "the outside." Be assured that you have many valuable skills and experiences to offer private sector employers. It does take work, however, to translate the applicability of your skills and experiences into civilian life.

Quotable Quotes

"Everything comes to him who hustles while he waits."

Thomas A. Edison

Your Personal Challenge

Converting your military record into a dialogue that an interviewer understands is a task that will require special effort. There are five basic areas you should stress to confront the transition challenge:

➤ Overcome misperceptions

➤ Adopt a business-oriented mindset

➤ Reform your image and presentation

➤ Translate your experience

➤ Learn new skills

Misperceptions, Stereotypes, and Bias

Whether warranted or not, stereotypes occur, and many people in civilian life are not used to being around actual military folk. Many civilians know about the military only through characters from television or movies. To some, military people are inflexible, stubborn, by-the-book, chain-of-command automatons who only know one way to win: blunt trauma. You know that is bogus, but it only takes one action on your part to reinforce the stereotype, and it will be hard for you to recover.

It's generally not a good idea to wear your rank on your new business suit, even if you were a senior officer. That suggestion applies unless you are in the defense sector where rank still matters (higher retired rank means higher access in the Pentagon). In other words, don't tell your colleagues about your service unless they ask. Let them find out for themselves. And let your performance speak for itself without carrying the weight (good or bad) of your prior career.

In fact, some successful ex-military say several years passed before they volunteered their military experience to anyone. The ones who hire you will know, but let it lie there. Obviously, some civilian jobs require military experience, and then the rules change.

Installing a new civilianized personal code of conduct can mean real dollars—the difference between a run-of-the-mill offer and one that has more financial upside.

A Real-World Example

U.S. Navy SEALs are some of the world's most feared warriors. Highly trained in counter-terror and other special operations, these warriors perform superhuman tasks to accomplish their missions and will never give up.

A SEAL team leader once decided to leave the military and test his luck in private life. He possessed an undergraduate degree from the U.S. Naval Academy and was interested in a job with a major Wall Street bank. He was just graduating from a Top 5 business school when he began his interviews.

People soon heard an a former SEAL was interviewing, and their imaginations ran wild. Myths developed about his exploits. Feedback from one managing director said his background scared off some interviewers. Another managing director sent a note saying, "Not sure about his motivation." What?

If anything, Navy SEALs are about pushing through, getting the job done no matter what. They are among the most motivated people on the planet. So, what went wrong?

Regardless of whether the directors' statements were true (they weren't in this case), the young man failed to manage perceptions well. A ramrod straight posture, the steely-eyed look, and the ripped, muscular build all fed into peoples' bias. His issue was that he underestimated the power of stereotyping and how to deal with it.

Interview Insights

Read short stories by William Faulkner, Tim O'Brien, John Steinbeck, Philip Roth, T. C. Boyle, and Hemingway, and focus on character descriptions. Craft your own self-description. Your PAG should help. Surprise the interviewer with a positive story that devastates misperceptions.

Adopt a Business Mindset

You should read every business periodical you can get your hands on. Perhaps take a course at a community college or university. You need to change the way you think and speak. You need to create a level of comfort in the interviewers' minds that your perspective is not that different from others in the firm. One way of doing this is to speak in business language and look like you belong there.

First, use the vernacular common to the industry you want to enter. Stop using military jargon and acronyms (unless you will be a DOD contractor) and begin to train your brain to think civilian. No one in most civilian jobs will know what COMNAVFACENGCOM stands for. So, don't list it that way on your résumé or say it in public! You say you never would? It is done all the time by ex-military people without them realizing it.

Invest in civilian business attire purchased at an appropriate men's store (see chapter 26). Relax and cut out the Parade Rest posture when you are talking with colleagues at the water cooler. Also, drop the serious-as-a-heart-attack look many ex-military have. Given your background, it might scare certain people—like interviewers and customers.

Avoid telling war stories of your combat deployments in the military as support for an argument with a group of male and female colleagues during a meeting about the environment or the budget.

Interview Insights

Try this: Get a dictionary of business terms. Published under Barron's Business Guides, they come in all flavors such as tax, accounting, finance, computers, law, and marketing. The general nature of dictionaries of business terms is recommended because it covers so many topics—you will pick up terms from many fields of business. Start with the As and progress as far as you can to Z. You don't need to research or understand all of the terms. Pick a few on each page and understand those. Try to use these terms in everyday speech as you get ready to separate from active duty. Blend them into conversations. It will become more natural sounding to you as you do it over time.

Time to Un-Rambo

As a military member, you have terrific experiences not shared with many of your new civilian colleagues (notice civilian term *colleagues*, not *people in my unit*). Many in your new firm might feel insecure about their lack of a distinguished war record. Most will admire your accomplishments, but they will also be equally quick to look to your contributions to the company. You have to perform at the same level of high achievement in civilian life as you demonstrated in the service.

It is time to stand in front of a mirror and practice smiling. Yes, smiling. Adopt a pleasant demeanor, softer and less serious than your usual Rambo-like death stare.

Spend as much time as possible with civilian friends and family. It is easy to get locked behind the base/post perimeter and deal only with other square-jawed types and stay one yourself. So, get out more!

The Translation Problem

Simply put, many employers (even some inside the defense industry) just don't know what it is that you did—and many of you don't know how to tell them. Interviewers become confused by service differences, acronyms, the applicability of one-of-a-kind military skills, and their own insecurities.

It is up to you to articulate what you can do for an employer in terms he or she understands and in a way that does not support stereotypes. The employer's bias may be subconscious, well-meaning, but it still could derail your chances of landing a job. Why the bias? Because of the employer's lack of military experience.

Fewer and fewer citizens percentagewise serve in an all-volunteer force, and that ranger tab or submariners badge may intimidate some hiring managers—if they know enough to appreciate it at all.

You may have interviewed in the modern military, but the type of interviews you will need to endure in order to secure a first-rate civilian job are much different.

Make no mistake, in the real world the fungible commodity is hard-earned money. The importance of the the million-dollar question is particularly acute for you.

Learn New Skills

You are accustomed to rigorous training—and your preparation for civilian life needs the same sort of rigor. But, you need to adapt your training regimens.

In the interview context, the training mandate is no different from training to fly military aircraft, to jump out of planes, drive tanks and boats, lead scout platoons, or any other military mission. You simply must train, and train strenuously and properly, in order to maximize your opportunities.

You have to civilianize yourself. There is no question that military members offer a formidable set of skills to industry. Still, besides learning how to translate those skills for an interviewer, you should learn new ones, too.

There are plenty of courses you can take through distance learning via the Internet or at a local college or university. You are going from government to the private sector, which means going into some form or fashion of the business world of accounting, human relations departments, competitors, etc. If you want to learn a foreign language, wouldn't you take a course? So, learn new skills by enrolling in something. Get a designation or certification while you are still on active duty. That could be a real estate license, CPA license, or some other professional designation.

For example, logistics are a key part of deployments in the military. If you are in that field, then visit www.sole.org and learn about the certified professional logistician (CPL) designation. The CPL certification can be taken while on active duty, and you may be eligible for reimbursement by the VA for exam costs. This type of training can be a point of discussion in your interview and increase the comfort level of the interviewer that you are more alike than different.

Tips to Ease Transition

By law, there are numerous government agencies that are required to help you transition to private life. Even if you go into the defense industry, you will need to interview for positions. If you go into government, you will interview. Even if you go back to graduate school, especially a first-rate school, you will need to interview with an admissions officer. Here are some tips:

> ➤ Dress civilian-style according to chapter 26.

> ➤ Drop the white sidewalls or Ranger Mohawk.

> ➤ Learn the new language of talking like a civilian. Read business books and speak as a civilian incessantly.

> ➤ Buy a civilian briefcase, not a gray and plastic one from the base or post exchange.

> ➤ Be hardcore and aggressive, but don't intimidate.

> ➤ Loosen up the posture—drop the Parade Rest.

> ➤ Think broadly about alternatives and options.

> ➤ Stick to your principles.

> ➤ Adopt a friendly, warm-hearted disposition (even you hardcore combat types).

Mock Questions for Ex-Military Commandos and other Hardcore Types

You have to get through the following gauntlet of questions before you look at the ones listed in Appendix B. You have to relieve interviewers' apprehension and any misunderstanding about who and what you are and what you can do for them.

> ➤ Describe why your military experience is relevant to this job. (Some variant of this will be asked every time!)

> ➤ Military operations require lot of flexibility. How do you feel about working within strict company guidelines, for sales practices for instance?

> ➤ Describe how the concept of teamwork is different in business than it is in the military.

➤ Many of our employees do not have military experience. Would you be able to relate to and appreciate their backgrounds?

➤ Would you describe yourself as a person with strongly held viewpoints?

➤ Give me a sense of your analytical skills and how they would relate to a hypothetical business problem.

➤ How do you feel about working with people who have less "real-world" experience or within a diverse workforce with people of different opinions lifestyles, etc.?

➤ I notice your résumé has a lot of work experience that has little to do with what we do here at this company. Can you bridge the gap for me?

➤ You seem to have done a lot of very exciting, adrenaline-rush kinds of activities. What do you think about doing routine work tasks, day in and day out?

➤ You seem to be a macho military type. How do you feel about working with women? (Ouch, I hear the plaintiff's lawyers already. And, just how does that "type" act? Best to smile, and say something like: "Not a problem. The military has been a leading advocate for competence first, and some great women soldiers rode convoys in Iraq, and I'm proud we had them.")

➤ Your experience is very much appreciated, and I personally admire you for what you have accomplished. But frankly, I don't see any skills or experience that relate to what we do.

➤ How would you deal with a situation where you are working on a project with a team member and you notice the revenue numbers your colleague generated meets targets, but they are not supported by the underlying business facts?

In Summary

You have a lot to offer. Get a friend, cousin, or third-party businessperson to review your résumé for transition issues. Months before you separate, you should begin your personal civilianization project. Use your base or post transition office by all means, but remember people in that office do not work in the private sector.

Chapter Homework

1. Go to dinner with a friend and use only business language (each time you use a military term or acronym, charge yourself a fee).

2. Focus on a personal scripts or storyboards explaining your military experience in business-only language.

CHAPTER 29

Special Section for International Students

In This Chapter

➤ Choices and decisions

➤ Your special challenges

➤ Using your advantages

This chapter is intended for those people from a non-U.S. country wishing to interview for a position in a U.S. firm and work in the United States. In some cases, you may want to work for a U.S. company and return to a first- or third-party country. If so, then much of what follows will also apply to you.

Choices and Decisions to Make

If you are an international student studying in the United States, you will need to know about some of the special choices and challenges that confront you. The tips and techniques discussed in earlier chapters will work just fine for you—even if you choose to remain in your home country. There are numerous customs, however, that may cause you to emphasize some techniques at the expense of others.

Much of this chapter also applies to job candidates who want to go abroad to work. When you see *American, English language, or United States,* substitute the name of the country or language applicable to your situation. You will also have language, culture, social, and longevity issues to resolve.

First, do you remain in the United States after graduation and work for a company here, or do you repatriate to your home country or move on to a different country? If you repatriate, can you articulate a business case for why that makes sense? Those decisions will affect your marketability, your family, and your career in profound ways. Do you specialize in an area that is focused on your home country, or are you willing to work in other markets? These are questions that an interviewer will want to discuss.

Make certain you use your personal scripts to tie your answers to what you can do for the company—the choice shouldn't be solely personal. For instance, you may want to return to Hong Kong because of family connections with several businesses. Make sure you connect what these businesses do to the requirements of the job you want, thereby showing your reason to return to Hong Kong is good for the company. Surprisingly, many people just say, "It's my home and I would like to return for friends and family."

Special Challenges

There are a number of challenges to interviewing for international students that add additional height to your hurdle. They are:

➤ Language skills

➤ Cultural knowledge

➤ Work longevity

➤ Social network

Language Skills

First, language skills are obviously important to the interview because in a limited amount of time, you must impress the interviewer with your ability to communicate effectively in both business and social settings. You may have terrific listening and writing skills, but your oral communication ability may be limited. This is simply not acceptable in today's difficult work environment. In some industries, miscommunication at critical points in time can cost millions.

Your ability to effectively speak to colleagues and clients is critical for your long-range success. Simply passing the TOEFL English language test is not good enough.

Many foreign students do not have an opening set of statements that can get an interview off on the right start. A halting set of mispronounced responses is uncomfortable for you and for the interviewer. Rehearse your opening set of lines complete with hand gestures, smiles, and a reference to the attractiveness of the office, the company's recent announcements, etc.

If you are repatriating from the United States back to your home country, then your increased ability to use English will be considered a major job skill for promotions and advancement. English language facility will enhance your company's ability to compete.

Interview Insights

Very bright international students from Top 10 MBA programs ask tough questions. Sadly, often the difficulty is understanding what they are asking. Their pronunciation and word usage is often so bad, especially with a thick indigenous accent, that they are simply not employable by many companies where English is mandatory. Don't be like one of them. Here are some tips to help:

➤ Insist on only speaking English during school hours with friends—even over lunches.

➤ Continue personal study programs using advanced software programs such as Rosetta Stone.

➤ Enlist the aid of family and friends to speak English as much as possible.

➤ Shop in English-speaking establishments.

➤ Invoke a friendly fine system with friends where incorrect English usage results in a small fine that will fund a party later.

➤ Increase your business vocabulary and use of colloquialisms.

➤ Watch American television and films and parrot the language you hear.

➤ Learn to think in English.

Cultural Knowledge

You may not be able to become as fluent as a native speaker, but you should attempt to learn the basics of the language for social settings. Too many students coming to the United States remain immersed in their own cultures through friends and families. Relying on in-class associations is not enough.

Try to learn about various aspects of American culture such as sporting events, celebrities, politics, folklore, and traditions. These aspects of American life will help differentiate you from most foreign students in the United States competing to work for U.S. companies. The ability to relate to the interviewer and your American colleagues will help you get the job. Go to ball games, read the sports pages, and know whether it is baseball season or football season and who is playing in the big game. You would look like a complete outsider if you didn't know who was playing in the Super Bowl in early February and you had an interview the prior week! Americans love sports, remember that.

Cultural knowledge is an area in which you must show more than a casual awareness. There are a number of excellent texts about the different cultural aspects to doing business in a foreign country. Such knowledge can pay dividends in an interview as well as on the job.

Pick up a synopsis of American history and discuss it with an American classmate. We are an interesting country, and you might find it a fascinating subject to discuss over a cocktail party or during an interview.

Americans also love movies. Your ability to discuss something relevant in film will also help to dispel notions that you are an outsider who doesn't understand American life. Pick a film like *Casablanca* or *The Grapes of Wrath* or *Shenandoah* that uses a significant event in U.S. history as a backdrop (WW II, the Depression, the Civil War, respectively for the above). Your ability to tie these from a personal scripts storyboard to some larger issue further persuades an interviewer that you understand America.

The same is true in reverse, by the way, for U.S. students who wish to work for foreign companies abroad. I did this during my own Japanese language training before living in Japan for four years. It paid huge dividends.

Read the excellent book *Kiss, Bow, or Shake Hands* by Morrison and Conaway. It is an excellent book for any business executive looking to do business abroad or in the United States.

Work Longevity

U.S. immigration laws and the ability to live and work in the United States are complex. You should consult legal counsel and review the requirements of the visa process and other categories of work-specific visas as they pertain to you. Consult www.uscis.gov for more details.

Interview Vocab

From the U.S. Citizenship and Immigration Services website: "There are various types of nonimmigrant visas for temporary visitors to travel to the U.S., if you are not a U.S. citizen or U.S. lawful permanent resident. The purpose of your intended travel and other facts will determine what type of visa is required under U.S. immigration law. It's important to have information about the type of nonimmigrant visa you will need for travel, and the steps required to apply for the visa at a U.S. Embassy or Consulate abroad." There are many types of visas. The so-called "green card" is for those seeking permanent residency status. You may be able to petition for a green card through a job offer. Again, see the USCIS website and your legal counsel.

Your intentions matter to an employer as well as to the government. You should know what you want to do prior to the interview, and ask the prospective employer for assistance if needed. Human relations departments in most companies have experts that help with immigration and work permits.

Plan to discuss your desires with the company. Have an answer that supports your long-term career goals with the company. The major stumbling block isn't the ability to legally work in the United States, but the ability to convince an interviewer that your overall skills enhance the company's competitive position and may even fall into one of the specialty visa categories. Perhaps your international contacts could benefit the company that does business in your home market. Be ready to discuss how.

Social Networks

This is an aspect of life in America where your friends are a great resource. Attend social gatherings offered by your schools, firms, church, associations, etc. Attend class or section parties. Use opportunities to seek out local clubs catering to business executives from your home country. They can be invaluable sources of job information and counsel. Certainly use philanthropic endeavors as a way of enhancing your résumés and creating social networks. Use Twitter, LinkedIn, and Facebook as ways of extending your networks. I use them and have found them invaluable. This is a great way to enhance your business development skills and language skills concurrently.

Using Your Advantages

Do not underplay the competitive advantages afforded to you by your experiences gained in a foreign culture. In such a geopolitically connected business world, knowledge is power. You may in fact be part of a global team spread across many continents. Language, particularly, is an important asset. If you want to increase your competitiveness, learn a second or even third language and be ready to use it during the interview.

Experiences gained overseas should be connected to a business problem through your use of personal scripts scenarios. Have an example, for instance, that illustrates your understanding of the application of a concept, product, or policy in a foreign country because of your specific cross-cultural knowledge. This is especially true for emerging economies.

Chapter Homework

1. Write opening and closing personal scripts. Use a recording device and ask an English speaker to listen to your recitation.

2. Start reading a book covering a period of interest in American history (or some other nation if you are interviewing there).

PART FIVE

Integration and Follow-Up

CHAPTER 30

After the Interview

In This Chapter

➤ Leaving the scene

➤ How to secure a second round

➤ The offer you can't refuse

➤ The offer you can refuse

In this chapter you will learn what you do immediately following the interview and how to integrate the lessons you learned back into the dynamic interview model. It also includes information about securing a second, or follow-up, interview. And what do you do when the phone call or letter arrives informing you of the results, good or bad? What are the next steps you should take? What if the offer isn't what you expected?

Leaving the Scene

As you departed the interview, you made your great summation and hopefully feel great about your Oscar-winning performance. What do you do next?

Just as you are leaving, ensure that you have contact information for everyone you met. By all means, be certain you have contact information for your central contact person. Be sure that the firm has all of your current information as well.

Additionally, ask the last interviewer or your main contact what to expect in terms of a closing process. When will someone get back to you about the next steps? Do you understand the selection process? You don't want to call back about that, so make certain you get an answer before you leave.

Immediately After the Interview

The first thing to do immediately following the interview is record your thoughts about the interview and what you need to do better next time. What activities and behaviors will you roll back into your dynamic interview model to up your performance level for the next meeting? What additional preparation do you need to do, what additional research do you need? Here are some questions to ask yourself:

> ➤ Did I know enough about the company?

> ➤ Were there any surprise questions?

> ➤ How were my opening and closing remarks?

> ➤ What additional information did I learn about the position?

> ➤ Is the firm a place where I can work?

> ➤ What was said about company strategy, competitors, product, career, etc.?

> ➤ How was my delivery? Was I concise?

> ➤ What general comments do I have about my performance and the interviewers'?

Follow-Up Logistics, Correspondence, and Etiquette Rules

Immediately after you leave the interview, take your daily journal and record your thoughts. What did you do well and in what areas did you perform worse than you had hoped? As said previously, you will want to integrate those thoughts back into your preparatory and practice sessions for the next round of interviews.

There are a few logistics you need to take care of. Within twenty-four hours of the interview, while the details are still fresh for both you and the interviewers, write your thank-you letters or notes (see sample in Appendix D). The style is not as important as ensuring you get the notes out expeditiously. Take something from your journal or from your memory that describes a positive moment from the interview and mention that in the letter. It could be something the interviewer said or something about his or her professional life. Generally, stay away from sending gifts.

Regardless of outcome, you must send a note or letter thanking the firm or person(s) for spending time with you in the interview.

The correspondence should include several points:

> ➤ Acknowledge time spent with you

> ➤ Note particular items of interest

> ➤ State desire for a next step, if one is desired

> ➤ Formalize contact information

> ➤ Remind the interviewer of your three key points

The correspondence should be spotless, containing no grammatical or spelling mistakes. Be a stickler about perfection. If you just had the perfect interview, you must have the perfect letter.

You should send an acknowledgement of your interview to anyone who you met with who is part of the hiring decision. These are not lengthy tomes but short notes or letters that simply express your appreciation. This is different from the explanatory note I mentioned in an earlier chapter, which is used to clarify a point or correct an error you made during the actual interview. The recipient's name and address should be identical to that on the person's business card.

On occasion, an interviewer could misplace your business card, so it is a good idea to clip another to the top left- or right-hand corner of your letter.

Make It Worth the Paper It's Printed On

Any time you put something in front of a hiring firm it should be of the highest quality. That goes for your answers to questions as well as the quality of the paper you use to send thank-you notes. Your letter should be written on high-grade cotton paper with matching envelope. Visit Crane and Company (www.crane.com) for samples of premium paper products from high-quality business cards to letterhead.

The letter or note could come in many forms. Handwritten notes are still acceptable, but only if you have a legible script. It undercuts your purpose if you send a note that can't be understood—or worse, is misunderstood. It shouldn't be lengthy, but it should thank the interviewers for the meeting, summarize your thoughts relative to the opportunity, and make clear that you hope to see them again (assuming you do). I also recommend saying that you look forward to hearing from them—it puts the burden upon them to get back to you. Sadly, there are cases where interviewers leave candidates in limbo.

If you asked for a time frame within which a decision would be made, which is a good thing to do, then wait a reasonable period to make a follow-up phone call. Again, in most cases if you haven't heard from an interviewer, then the news is probably not what you want to hear. But the interviewing firm does owe you an answer one way or the other—that's just business etiquette 101.

Correcting an Error

If you made an error in the meeting and feel the need to correct it, then do so in the follow-up note. Don't assume the interviewer missed it and didn't notice your error. If you are attempting to correct a misstatement, try something like the following example about the economy: "During our discussion I mentioned 2.5 percent as an estimate for the U.S. GDP. I believe the correct consensus figure should be 2.6 percent—still anemic by most standards and far less than we need to stimulate job growth. I wanted to correct my misstatement as quickly as possible. Again, thank you for the opportunity to learn more about your firm."

What you have done once again is show the interviewer that you will not let a client operate with incorrect information. Although many clients demand that you be 100 percent correct all the time, the reality is that no one is. It is much better to correct an error than run the risk that the client finds out on his or her own that you were wrong. You gain credibility. Now you cannot be incorrect time after time, but an occasional slipup with a timely correction is usually just fine. In the interview context, it can help win over an interviewer—because it is so seldom done.

How to Get a Second Interview

The best way to get a second interview is to, of course, nail the first interview. Great performance speaks most loudly. Without it, your chances go way down.

There are a few things you can do to help your chances of getting to the second level if your first performance was lacking. Use voice mail, hand-delivered letters, and e-mail, whatever it takes to get your message to the interviewer or decision maker. There is a fine line between a successful follow-up and desperation, so don't cross over it. Be sure you don't abuse the interviewer's time or space, or your integrity. Here are a few ideas:

> ➤ Convey your earnest desire to work at the firm and to overcome any deficiencies.

> ➤ Send a note offering to work on a trial basis, if appropriate, or at a reduced salary or part-time or on alternate work schedules.

> ➤ In your thank-you note, remind the interviewer of what you bring to the table compared to the competition.

> ➤ Signal any changes in your personal circumstances that strengthen your position such as successful licensing, awards, or a change in career focus.

> ➤ Obtain or be willing to receive additional training.

> ➤ Send a memo with an attachment to the interviewer addressing one of the issues the interviewer discussed.

➤ Be willing to start immediately and wherever the firm wants you to start.

➤ Run through your informal contract to be a great employee.

➤ Offer to take a different job if that is best for the firm.

➤ After a week or two, determine if that the people who helped you get the original interview will check on your status and convey your suitability

The Second Round, or Follow-Up, Interview

All of the techniques espoused in this book will also apply to the second level of interviews. The main differences between the first and second interviews are that second level interviews have a rising set of expectations by the firm. The interviewers may begin to envision an offer and hope you take it. If so, you can begin to perform from a stronger position.

In fact, if you are meeting a group of people in the operational flow of the business, then that could be a sign they have an increasing level of interest in you. The HR person may shift from discussions about job requirements to company policies and benefits. Here are a few tips on second-round interviews:

➤ After the first round, you are expected to know more about the firm and its products and services

➤ You will most likely meet more of the seasoned, higher-level employees.

➤ The firm is getting more serious and will want to see more serious responses to questions.

➤ You should sense the firm's level of interest and ask about it.
The types of people you meet in this round may signal the firm's real interest level.

➤ Your questions need to evolve into discussions and not just be responses.

➤ Compensation may be discussed—be prepared for the firm to ask about requirements and expectations and know your numbers.

➤ Your strength of conviction should become more apparent.

➤ Expand your comments based upon what you learned or said during the first round of interviews.

➤ Probe more deeply into the challenges the company faces.

➤ Use more scenarios or examples of you operating within the company's context.

➤ At the end of the second round of interviews, ask when you can meet again to bring this to a close.

The Bright Side

Let's assume you get word that everyone at the firm is ecstatic about hiring you and want to extend an offer. What do you do then? First, you jump for joy while patting yourself on the back (silently)! All your hard work has paid off.

Seriously, you should thank the messenger robustly. Tell him or her that it is an honor and depending on your level of interest you may say that you would love to join the firm or that you are ecstatic at the idea of working at the firm.

In the first case, if you know you want the job, then take it. Realize of course, you may well not have talked about compensation and other benefits. If you have not already discussed benefits, then say something like, "Thank you for the opportunity. I sincerely hope to work with you. I would like to discuss the specifics of the job in terms of compensation, benefits, and responsibilities at your earliest convenience." That should evoke some sort of definitive response. Make certain both you and the firm are clear about items such as:

➤ Location

➤ Reporting lines

➤ Accountability

➤ Compensation structure

➤ Salary and bonus options (current, deferred, and future reviews)

➤ Goals and objectives

➤ Benefits (most importantly health and retirement but include education, discounts, etc.)

➤ Vacation time

➤ Advancement opportunities

➤ Training

➤ Start date and work times (if appropriate)

➤ Title (if appropriate)

It is always a good idea to make contact with a human resources professional within the firm to obtain an overview of the package of benefits and policies prior to making your decision about accepting the job.

In the second case, you aren't sure you want to accept the offer. Then you have a short period of time to contemplate your next move. Vacillating or waiting an excessive period of time annoys people. If you have done your homework relative to the industry and your other offers and possibilities, you should be able to make a decision expeditiously—up to a week or ten days is usually long enough. Beyond that, questions begin to arise as to your level of commitment. Some employers want to know immediately, so be ready.

Leaving a Message

If you need to return a call, you may be automatically directed to your contact's voice mail.

Interview Insights

Voice mail is a terrific mode of contact. However, you must be careful how you use it. Rambling, muffled, incoherent, disjointed messages do not enhance your image with a company. Leave no voice mail messages longer than one minute. You should leave a quick message and be professional doing it.

A good way to practice your voice mail technique is to record a message on a home recorder. Listen to it. Try it again leaving different types of messages. Do this until you can leave the following information in one minute or less:

> ➤ Name

> ➤ Appreciation comment and phone number

> ➤ Desire to meet again and interest in the job

> ➤ Contact information

> ➤ Sign off

Here is an example you can modify to your situation:

"Mr/Mrs. Jones, this is Joe/Nancy Smith. Thank you for the time you spent with me the other day to discuss possibly joining your company. I can be reached at [phone number] if you need further information. I enjoyed learning more about the opportunity and hope we can meet again to continue our dialogue. I remain extremely interested in the job and, again, I can be reached at [phone number]. I look forward to hearing from you and I hope you have a pleasant day."

Use a watch to time the length of your message. Do it from memory or read it from a card. Speak clearly and more slowly than normal. Leave your phone number twice—once at the beginning and once at the end of your message—to ensure the listener records it correctly.

No one—especially your busy interviewer—likes long, incoherent voice mail messages. So practice your messaging—it says say a lot about you.

The Underwhelming Offer

What if the offer is not what you expected? Refer to chapter 23, which describes negotiation strategies in the context of helping to close the sale during an interview. Those ideas can also be used to discuss other key points after an offer is extended.

Salary isn't the only potential stumbling block. Perhaps the offer includes a stipulation that you must relocate after one year to another city. How would you handle that? You could say, "I am sorry, but due to personal family circumstances relocation is out of the question" or you could concentrate on mutual interests. For example, you could say, "I am so excited about working at XYZ Company. I believe I can make a real impact on our business in Bigtown, where I have an existing network of contacts. I am less well-connected in Crummytown, and it would take longer to make the contribution we both believe I can offer. I hope that is a possibility." In the second case, you show enthusiasm and let the firm know that you have bought into the company already ("our business"). You also make a valid business point that influences the company's ability to grow. The statement is also professional and nonthreatening. The first case is too strident and unwavering. It forces the company's hand too quickly. My guess is that the firm will take the second statement more seriously and reconsider its position.

Try to be diplomatic and reasonable, and don't push your contact into a corner. There is probably a backup plan in place in case you turn down the job. Don't make it easy for the firm to go with plan B.

Interview Insights

You should know well your set of bingo points before you get to the offer stage. There are a number of common issues around location, start dates, titles, and such. As far as location is concerned, the answer depends upon your circumstance, obviously. But these days it seems more and more people consider location as nonnegotiable. Reconsidering this position may make you more competitive and offset other concerns the firm has. It is valuable to the firm to have people who consider the needs of the firm to be a priority over location.

The Offer You Turn Down

There may be bingo points that you absolutely cannot concede. Make certain to politely communicate your reasons both verbally and in writing. If the firm won't budge, then you have to make a decision: pass or accept? Your decision will be dependent upon how strongly you feel about the offer. If you turn it down, then do so with dignity and professionalism. Do not burn bridges—the firm may come back later after reconsidering its other options.

If you turn down the offer, then send another note of thanks expressing how wonderful the opportunity was and ask to be kept in mind if the firm's needs change.

World-Class Acceptance

Not only should you send a note following an interview, you should also send one upon accepting a job. In the note, reiterate how much you look forward to working with the firm and with the person you're addressing in the note. It's not gratuitous; it's pure business courtesy. It says a lot about how you will act going forward—again how you might treat a client. In some cases you will have a contract and others not. In any case, a short note of appreciation is always appropriate.

You should also plan to send a thank-you note to all those with whom you met; that is, if you know everyone's exact name and title. Otherwise, send the note just to the primary interviewer so as not to offend someone who didn't receive one. Also, consider sending a brief note of thanks to the primary interviewer's assistant or gatekeeper if that person helped arrange the meeting. Keep the assistant happy and appreciated, and future interactions will be much more pleasant.

Chapter Homework

1. Think of circumstances that would cause you to turn down an offer.

2. Determine how long you will wait for an answer, and decide on a plan to get a second interview.

CHAPTER 31

 **The Perfect Interview**

> ### In This Chapter
>
> ➤ Summary of key principles
>
> ➤ Encapsulation
>
> ➤ Nattering nabobs of negativism
>
> ➤ Life lessons

In this chapter you find a summary of what you have learned thus far plus a few observations about work life in a modern economy. You have investigated the dynamic interview model as a disciplined process that uses a set of principles and techniques to get you to the next level.

Guiding Principles

The Smart Guide to the Perfect Job Interview has given you a set of guiding principles and techniques governed by the iterative dynamic interview model: preparation, practice, execution, and integration. Some techniques are intuitive, some may seem creative, but all of them should help your efforts to obtain more offers of higher quality. During your quest for the perfect interview, you learned a few things:

> ➤ Discover and offset your shortcomings.
>
> ➤ Develop a set of personal scripts to build your dialogue.
>
> ➤ Use the research framework and explore types and sources of information.
>
> ➤ Practice using a simulation technique called chair flying.

> ➤ Think about executing an interview like an actor in a movie.

> ➤ Develop your opening and closing lines.

Encapsulation

The perfect pizza—is there any left in the box? To some degree the interview outcome is in the eye of the beholder. The perfect interview is one that allows you to move forward toward your ultimate target. If your goal is to get a job, then the interview that facilitates that is what we can call perfect. If the goal is simply to get another interview, then the interview that moves you to the next level is the perfect interview.

If you assimilate all you have learned in *The Smart Guide to the Perfect Job Interview*, you should be much more confident in your efforts to secure a job offer.

Requiem for Nattering Nabobs of Negativism

You know a smart aleck jerk or two, right? They are the know-it-alls who undermine your confidence or crush your opinions with a trite comment. This type of naysayer was once described by a former U.S. politician as the nattering nabob of negativism. Following is a list of positive responses you can use to counter comments made by the nattering nabobs of negativism.

> ➤ Nattering nabob of negativism: Remember your negatives!
> You: Develop offset strategies and remember your strengths.

> ➤ Nattering nabob of negativism: You aren't smart enough!
> You: Become well read and well rounded; initiate the whole person reading program.

> ➤ Nattering nabob of negativism: Networking is too hard!
> You: Leave no stone unturned.

> ➤ Nattering nabob of negativism: Settle for what you can get!
> You: Beat the competition—know who they are and stress your advantages.

> ➤ Nattering nabob of negativism: You look good enough!
> You: Dress like you have already arrived.

> ➤ Nattering nabob of negativism: Just Wing It!
> You: Use the dynamic interview training model.

> ➤ Nattering nabob of negativism: Stay back in the pack, it's less threatening!
> You: Act like a leader, even if you aren't in charge.

➤ Nattering nabob of negativism: You can't sell yourself—it's demeaning!
You: Sell yourself because you know the interview process is a sales process leading to a job.

➤ Nattering nabob of negativism: Getting an interview is too tough!
You: Personalize the new business development model.

➤ Nattering nabob of negativism: Oh No! Amazon Woman wants the job!
You: She has flaws you don't have; you're confident in your training.

➤ Nattering nabob of negativism: You don't have a story to tell!
You: Develop your personal scripts to tell your story—you are memorable!

➤ Nattering nabob of negativism: It'll never work!
You: Develop what-if scenarios.

➤ Nattering nabob of negativism: Practice is a waste!
You: Chair fly for extra awards miles.

➤ Nattering nabob of negativism: You don't need a schedule!
You: Use time phases to stay on track.

➤ Nattering nabob of negativism: Treat the interviewer like an interrogator!
You: Create a client-oriented context.

➤ Nattering nabob of negativism: Gatekeepers are scary!
You: Treat gatekeepers well and use them to your advantage—they hold the keys to the kingdom.

➤ Nattering nabob of negativism: Interviews are scary!
You: Know the types of interviews and interviewers so you won't be surprised.

➤ Nattering nabob of negativism: There's no golden nugget!
You: There is! You answer the million-dollar question.

The Perfect Job Interview Tool Kit

The list below summarizes most of the major issues and suggested solutions surrounding job interviews.

➤ Issue: How fast is your jet?
Solution: Engage a personal assessment.

➤ Issue: How good is the competition?
Solution: Implement prewar intelligence.

➤ Issue: How big is your hurdle?
Solution: Conduct PAG analysis.

➤ Issue: Do you have weaknesses?
Solution: Use offset strategies.

➤ Issue: Do you have trouble getting interviews?
Solution: Use NBD methods.

➤ Issue: Are you unorganized?
Solution: Use timelines and prepchek.

➤ Issue: Do you need an image remake?
Solution: Establish a personal brand.

➤ Issue: Do you know enough?
Solution: Do hard and soft research.

➤ Issue: Are you worried about harsh questioning?
Solution: Study the sample questions.

➤ Issue: Can you handle social and group interviews?
Solution: Review interview ROE.

➤ Issue: Do need better conversational skills?
Solution: Implement personal scripts.

➤ Issue: Can you sell?
Solution: Use integrated conversations.

➤ Issue: Are you a leader and client oriented?
Solution: Be a Green leader/use leadership skills outlined in the contextual leadership model from Chapters 19.

➤ Issue: Can you direct the outcome?
Solution: Close with three summary points.

➤ Issue: Do you need a great start?
Solution: Design your first ninety days.

➤ Issue: Are you memorable?
Solution: Answer the million-dollar question

From Atop Mt. Soapbox

For some of you who are unemployed or facing unemployment, these may be tough times. However, there is a light at the end of the tunnel, and it is not an oncoming train. The techniques offered in *The Smart Guide to the Perfect Job Interview* do not guarantee you will get a job, but they should make you much more competitive than you were before.

As you begin or change your career, remember that work can be a driving influence over your life, occupying an increasing amount of your time. Your objectives will drive your lifestyle, but work is not all there is to life. Here from atop a lofty mountain are a few final tips to remember:

➤ Be respectful and courteous to others.

➤ Maintain your physical and mental health by pursuing an approved fitness regime; watch your stress level and cardiac fitness.

➤ Commit to lifelong learning through a balanced reading program.

➤ Help your neighbors, teammates, and the less fortunate.

➤ Be a role model by being a responsible, involved citizen.

➤ Help create innovation.

➤ Support and protect children so they grow into responsible, healthy citizens—the next generation of able workers.

➤ Use your energy to do great things.

Following the above advice will make you someone that people will want to get to know— and to hire.

CHAPTER 32

Working For A Nonprofit Enterprise

> ## In This Chapter
>
> ➤ Why work for something that doesn't make money
>
> ➤ Gravity works everywhere
>
> ➤ Different mindsets
>
> ➤ Run it like you own it

In this chapter, you will learn about working for the not-for-profit enterprise (NFP). You will also discover there are more similarities to regular business organizations than generally realized. You will come to understand where differences in mission, people, and structure exist, and how the absence of a profit motive might affect you. Finally, you will see that sound judgment and practical business sense still prevail, and what skills are needed if you want to work in this area.

It's the philanthropy, not money, and that's all that matters

Well, that's not quite true. First, non-profits do make money. Upfront let's dispel the notion that they do not. They just don't pay taxes, by and large. There are many types of nonprofit institutions. If you desire to work there, then you must understand that while there are differences between an NFP and a "for profit" organization (tax liabilities for one), there are also many similarities. Let's first start with the basics.

Regardless of the type of not-for-profit organization it is, a focus placed by its workers simply upon their shared mission can lead to disastrous results. Many such mission-oriented firms, full of fine and well-meaning people, fail each year to achieve their desired results. Why? They forget one overarching principle that must apply to any organization. That is, that it must pay its bills. You can possess all of the righteous intent in the world, but if the enterprise cannot meet payroll, pay its vendors, produce its product, travel to where it is needed and the like, it will fall first into dysfunction then into failure. You must understand this if you decide to work for a nonprofit. A world class symphony may make beautiful music, but someone has to work hard to get the money for the musicians to travel, lodge, play, and bow. Someone has to raise that money, steward it carefully, dispense it appropriately, and account for it regularly. Otherwise, those notes grow silent.

Interview Vocab

A nonprofit organization: Nonprofit organizations don't pay income tax on the money they earn from fundraising activities or donations. The organization must further a religious, charitable, scientific, literary, educational, public safety, amateur sports or cruelty prevention purpose to qualify for tax-exempt status; it must also provide a public benefit. Examples of nonprofit organizations include churches, hospitals, and schools.

What is the difference between nonprofit status and tax-exempt status? According to the Internal Revenue Service (IRS), nonprofit status is a state law concept. Nonprofit status may make an organization eligible for certain benefits, such as state sales, property and income tax exemptions. Although most federal tax-exempt organizations are nonprofit organizations, organizing as a nonprofit organization at the state level does not automatically grant the organization exemption from federal income tax. To qualify as exempt from federal income tax, an organization must meet requirements set forth in the Internal Revenue Code.

So, how does a philanthropic mission change the running of an organization? That's a comprehensive question. Certainly, basic general management and leadership principles apply, but given the fact that there is a public or charitable purpose involved, the answer also becomes more complex.

People who work at charitable enterprises do so without the driving motivation to make a lot of money. If you are a donor to this organization, you want your donation to make the greatest possible impact upon the end user of the services provided by the enterprise – and that does not mean lining the pockets of the individuals working at the charity. Efficiency ratios, or the percentage of donor dollars used directly for the beneficiaries, are important factors when analyzing an organization with a philanthropic mission. There are some famous cases where few children, dogs, whales, musicians, artists, the homeless or hungry, or classrooms benefited, but executives at the charity flew around in big jets.

Still, I want to work there - so what do I do?

First, do your research as described in the earlier chapters. The techniques outlined in this book will work regardless of the profit nature of the enterprise. The major difference is to understand the motivations behind the people asking the questions during an interview. In their mind, the mission of the charity is everything and subordinate tasks can take a back seat. In other words, delivery of services to beneficiaries is the abiding principle, and all else falls into second place. This is really as it should be, but those back bench tasks often determine if the team continues to play on the field. So, there are opportunities for you if your skills support the areas that support the primary mission. We will go over some of those in the remainder of this chapter.

Interview Insights

GuideStar is a reporting agency on not-for-profit organizations. Millions of required IRS tax forms are available there. Tax forms? Yes, although a nonprofit, an organization must still file an IRS Form 990 outlining its finances. This is a watchdog function to ensure the public interest is well served. On GuideStar you can see assets, liabilities, composition of boards of directors, and other valuable information. Prior to an interview, this information is critical to an understanding of the purpose of the NFP.

If an interviewer asks about YOUR motivations, you must give them the heartfelt conviction that you BELIEVE in the mission. If you work for a widget company, your motivations tend to revolve around a specific technical capability or interest you possess, and not necessarily in the widget itself. That's not always the case, but generally it is. Working for a nonprofit on the other hand REQUIRES that you identify with the mission at hand. Otherwise, why would you be there to work for less money than you could get in the private sector? Therefore, your first task is to truly understand the elements of the mission and think hard about them. Where can you go to get the right information? Here are some hints:

➤

➤ Google the charity

➤ Discover who is involved with the organization

➤ Go to www.GuideStar.org and learn what documents are filed there

➤ Read news articles, books, blogs about the underlying topic driving the charity

What is important to know?

Key financial information is central to whether the charity can accomplish its underlying mission. For every dollar spent, how much is directly expended in support of the beneficiaries? How highly compensated are the key executives? The answer is to pay them enough to ensure the enterprise attracts top talent. It would be a shame to have an A+ cause derailed because top executives were C or D level management people. It is not always the case, but top talent can go anywhere. So does your prospective charity offer a grade-one manager enough to work there, but not tip the scales toward largesse? Here are some other things to look for:

➤ How many donors does the charity have?

➤ Are donations rising or falling?

➤ Are there one or two big donors, but few others to support the effort?

➤ How much is spent on getting new donors, versus spending the money on the mission?

➤ Are the key executives donors themselves?

➤ How long has the charity been around?

➤ Is there an accrediting agency in the charity's field of endeavor?

➤ What is the annual turnover amongst staff?

➤ Are staff trained or qualified for their jobs, or are they just paid/unpaid volunteers?

➤ Is the enterprise largely dependent upon the founder or other rock star leader? If so, what happens if that person leaves? Is there a succession plan in place?

There are many other questions, but the main point is that you need to ask hard hitting questions that uncover whether the enterprise is well managed or not. Often, because the mission is so transparent, simple business-related questions can filter big needs-based and heartwarming talk from the real talk that can determine the long run viability of an NFP (versus a for-profit company). For instance, ask a simple question about their "burn rate" of cash? Burn rate defines how much cash – which is the lifeblood of an NFP – the enterprise spends on average each day. This should give you the ability when combined with the Form

990 to make a reasonable guess at bank balances and how many months of operating funds they have. Or, just ask them!

Gravity works here, there, everywhere

While it is true that good management and leadership can be found in NFPs, there are many cases where zeal overwhelms competence. The art of leadership – listening, vision-making, storytelling, inspiration, frontline mentality – and all the things you learned earlier work in NFP gravity space just like in corporations working to meet shareholders' financial expectations. It is just as incumbent upon NFP management to provide first-rate insights and decision-making as it is for their non-NFP counterparts. If you can convince an interviewer that you have such talent, you can go a long way toward a successful outcome. In some cases, you may have the opposite problem, however.

The problem in some NFP organizations is that they suffer from the "not-invented-here" syndrome. They believe that unless you have NFP experience you cannot succeed. Nothing could be further from the truth. What difference does tax status make to a discussion with a chronically late employee, or deciding on one piece of productivity software or another? Just like gravity, good decision-making and leadership skills work or don't work in outer space just as well as in NFP space!! Show that you have these omnipresent skills and do it equally skillfully, and you may be able to impress an NFP interviewer. Be sensitive, however, to the interviewer's hidden/unhidden bias concerning skills that he/she does not believe easily translate into the nonprofit world. Some people who work at NFPs are career non-profiteers, and they may harbor resentments against someone who carries skills from the business world into their space. You will need to treat those biases just as you would any other with the techniques discussed in earlier chapters in this book.

Sample Skill Areas Needed:

> General management

> Donor acquisition and development

> Technology

> Database

> Accounting and Finance

> Event coordination

> Administrative

> Security

> ➤   Communications

> ➤   Video and Media

Many of the skills that are used in for-profit enterprises are also needed in tax-exempt organizations. General management techniques work here as well as anywhere. Time management, organization, communication – verbal and written – are all required. One of the skills most needed in any organization is leadership, and in small NFPs, that can often mean the difference between existence and going out of business.

One of the most critical needs is in the area of donor acquisition and relationship building. New donors, like clients, are the lifeblood of NFP enterprises. Acquiring a new donor uses many of the same skills exercised in businesses. However, another ingredient is often needed: alignment of prospects' values and philanthropic intent with the purpose of the organization.

Often it takes time to develop the degree of understanding and relationship necessary to convert from prospect to donor. Relationship building often means multiple visits, heart-to-heart discussions about life and personal goals, and often disappointments. Prospective donors in need of these kinds of relationships with the NFP require more time than a customary buyer relationship and are not likely to respond to hard sell techniques. Finding people whose interests and motivations are sufficiently in gear with those of the NFP is often a time-consuming and difficult process requiring a level of dedication and patience that often is not abided by a for-profit sales manager looking to book a sale.

Technology skills, especially those dealing with computational platforms and networking, are critical to both large and small NFP enterprises. Obviously, the larger the NFP the more sophisticated are the platforms and the demands of larger user communities. E-mail, presentation software, and internet access are critical to most enterprises, and the stability of these platforms can determine whether they complete their mission or not

The donor database is the lifeline for the NFP to its donors. Information concerning how to communicate with donors, the style and method of contact, the frequency of contact, and other preferred information are kept inside these databases. Donor dollars are often spread across many charitable enterprises, and competing with other tax exempt NFPs is often done through the efficient and timely use of its database. If the database is accurate and robust, then the ability of the NFP to reach its most precious resource – its existing donors - and continue to raise revenue will be enhanced. The opposite is also true. If addresses are inaccurate, salutations are inappropriate, or giving histories are incorrect, then donors quite naturally feel the enterprise is poorly managed. People do not want to give money to have it go to waste inside a poorly run NFP. Some databases that are commonly used are:

> ➤ Raiser's Edge by Blackbaud

> ➤ TrailBlazer

> ➤ DonorPro CRM

> ➤ NonProfitEasy

> ➤ Kindful

Knowledge and experience in these database management systems is a HOT area in the NFP world. An artful user of these systems can find themselves in short order being labeled as "Director, Database Administration", and in the NFP world they are among the highest salaried non-leadership professionals in the enterprise. Remember, the database is the lifeline to donors, and competing for a donor's dollar is tough, so any enterprise with a top-notch database pro is way ahead in the race.

Accounting and finance, along with human resources and general administration, are areas where jobs can be found. If you are familiar with Excel and financial modeling techniques, you can leverage the NFPs work and have a great impact upon its mission. Boards of trustees like to know that the NFPs financial resources are well accounted for and efficiently used. Financial ratios, forecasts, budgets, and other finance-related topics are palpable examples of skills that can help land a job. Too many NFPs simply do not employ these techniques stringently enough and suffer the consequences. Show an interviewer the effects of good modeling on cash management and you can find yourself in charge of it.

Likewise, human resource management is an often neglected area in NFPs. Government scrutiny of NFPs, however, is forcing many organizations to take greater care in dealing with their employees. State and federal regulations about unemployment taxes, FICA taxes, healthcare, performance appraisals, etc. are forcing many well-run NFPs to hire professionals to ensure the firm provides all of the required services and benefits prescribed under the law. In-house recruiting for new professionals is sometimes the best route to follow, and so if you have recruiting talent combined with general HR experience, you can often provide a highly leveraged resource to enterprises looking to consolidate workers' duties into fewer positions.

NFPs often hold events as a way of highlighting their need for donations. These public displays must walk a fine line between being a showcase and being too showy. Remember good stewardship is important to donors, and if you spend a dollar on an event it is their dollar that you spent – spend it wisely. Still, you must show that your organization knows what it is doing and often a shabbily run event indicates poor management of other areas. Event coordination is a good area to explore if you have experience doing it in the for-profit sector. A great event coordinator who can walk that fine line can be worth their weight in donation gold! The ability to keep track of a thousand details, booking the right venue, constructing the right program agenda, keeping things running on time, and making the donor experience worthwhile are all key strengths for a great NFP event coordinator.

In this day and age when political tensions can run high, especially those surrounding social issues, security is unfortunately a growth area for NFPs. People with skills and experience dealing with physical and cyber infrastructure and personal security issues are increasingly in demand. Prior military or law enforcement experience is a plus, as is any history of working in a global environment where cultural differences can exacerbate security concerns. Many NFPs operate in some of the world's most dangerous places, and personal security and pre-visit clearance work is especially important.

Finally, many NFPs need communications and media strategies with various media outlets to effectively underscore the importance of their work. People with skills in writing press releases, blogging, public relations, television and radio interviews, producing video content, and writing for websites and magazines are in high demand. This is especially true for those NFPs on the cutting edge of political trends in the world. NFPs without effective communications strategies are often left behind by the rspeed that news stories hit the public consciousness – and are often left to hear their stories told by others rather than shaping the message themselves. If you have these skills, and established relationships with media sources, you will find your interviews to be much more positive and rewarding.

The bottom line to working at an NFP is that it takes effort to prepare for an interview with this type of specialized enterprise. A clear understanding of the organization's mission and motivation is critical in determining whether there is a good fit for you. You will need something more than money to motivate you, and that something must come through in the interview with passion and zeal. Your story boarding talent as developed earlier in this book is a crucial means of acting out your ability to leverage your skills to the benefit of the NFP, and get that job that saves the whales!

The PrepChek Checklist

In This Appendix
➤ What are checklists?
➤ How to use the PrepChek checklist

This appendix will teach you the benefits of using a job interview checklist. The PrepChek checklist is designed to keep you on course as you approach an interview.

Checklists are Beneficial Tools

Checklists are used by hosts of industries, companies, and people. They are lists of activities that should be accomplished in either reaction to an event or in anticipation of one. Nuclear power operators, airline pilots, and many other professions use checklists. In fact, if you buy a new car and look at the owner's manual there is a lists of steps to start the car. Should an interview be any different?

Interview Insights

Always have an umbrella and a subway map if you travel to New York. Why? Because many job candidates travel to the Big Apple only to be left standing on a street corner riding out an unanticipated rainstorm. Then it is nearly impossible to get a cab because a gazillion New Yorkers want one, too. Candidates are left soaking on the curb without an umbrella and no idea where the subway is. If that happens to you, then you may arrive late at your interview looking every bit the part of a raggedy, less-than-sophisticated world traveler. That's not the perfect start to a perfect job interview scenario.

Other major world cities may suffer the same issue. Be prepared.

Checklists can be loaded onto your laptop for portability. Also, be sure to adapt the items to your conditions and experience.

Interview Insights

MB went for an interview in San Francisco. The host suggested lunch before beginning a tour of the office. *Enchiladas! That's great,* thought the candidate. He was hungry. As Mr. B stood from the table to leave the restaurant, he noticed his light blue (expensive) tie brushed against his plate. He was suddenly wearing a light blue tie with yellow and orange accents. He immediately thought about the replacement tie he hadn't brought—it had been on his preinterview checklist, but he thought bringing an extra tie was overkill. Well, as soon as MB got to the office, the host insisted on a grip-and-grin session with the CEO and others. MB is now an ardent believer in checklists.

PrepChek Checklist

Name:

Date of initial entry:

Begin time phases:

Scheduled Interviews

Date	Time	Location	Point of Contact/ Phone

Remarks and Follow-Up

Firm Name	Person	Phone	Action	Complete Yes or No	To Do By Date

Action Legend

➤ Follow-up letter: LTR

➤ Call back: CB

➤ Call person: CP

➤ Dead end: DE

➤ Schedule meeting: SM

Employment-Related Events

Date	Firm	Location	Reception Y/N	Host

Meetings with Career Center/Headhunter

Date/Person/Firm	Topic/Contact Info	Action Steps

Purchase Interview Materials

Item	Yes or No
Pen	
Attaché	
Books: business and non-business	
News services and alerts	
Research	
Magazine subscriptions online	

Smart Guide Personal Assessment Guide (PAG)

Date Started	Date Completed

Trusted Agents

Name	Relationship	Scheduled

List of Negative PAG Assessments

Weakness	Offset Strategy

Personal Scripts Initiation

- ➤ Charts showing topics germane to job in technical, personal, opening, closing, and connectivity categories
- ➤ Subtopics with details
- ➤ Learn connections between topics and subtopics
- ➤ Include three main selling points and contingencies

Date Started	Date Completed	Reviewed/Comments

List of Topics

Topic Name	Date Completed	Reviewed/Comments

List of Subtopics

Subtopic Name	Date Completed	Reviewed/Comments

Subtopic Name	Date Completed	Reviewed/Comments

Connectivity Charts

Subtopic Name	Connected to Subtopic name	Written Story Y/N Date Completed	Review Date/ Comments

Chair Flying: Three to Five Sessions Plus Dress Rehearsal

➤ A proven practice method

➤ Sit quietly and imagine the interview setting

➤ Think of scenarios, questions, responses, movements

➤ Visualize the environment and your reactions—see yourself and the interviewer

Date	Topic	Outcome

Feedback Session with Chair Flying Observer

Case Study Prep Tips

➤ Articulate assumptions.

➤ Throw out dead-end solutions.

➤ Defend your position politely.

➤ Ask for additional information.

Date	Case	Notes

Video of Interview Entry

Date	Reviewed Y/N Date	Observations

Feedback Session with Entry Observer

Date	Person	Observations

Additional Notes

Whole Person Reading Program

Title of Book	Date Started	Business or Nonbusiness	Application to Job

Weekly Schedule of Business/Industry Reading

Day of the Week	Periodical/Newspaper Title	Subject of Article	Application/ Observations
Monday			
Tuesday			
Wednesday			
Thursday			
Friday			
Saturday			
Sunday			

Clothing Guidance Session

	Date Purchased	**Date Completed**
Store	Fitting Date	Pick Up Date

Fitness Program Date Started

Day	**Exercise**	**Notes**
Monday		
Tuesday		
Wednesday		
Thursday		
Friday		
Saturday		
Sunday		

Interview Week: Check Items Yes or No

Activity	**Completed Yes/No**	**Date if Applicable**
Updates on company		
Finalize personal scripts		
Nail entrance and opening dialogue		
Nail three main points plus closing		
Review case study prep notes		
Full dress rehearsal		
Second rehearsal		
Visit interview area		

Clothing to dry cleaners		
Pick up dry cleaning (two days prior)		
Shoes shined		
Hair appointment scheduled		
Confirm interview time and location (day before interview)		
Check weather (day before)		
Discussions with peer group if applicable		

Day of Interview

Activity	Check Yes or No	Notes	Point of Contact/Plan
Weather update			
Taxi			
Update WSJ			
Update websites			
CNBC/Bloomberg/Fox Business/CNN			
Eat light meal or snack			
Check-in with career center for changes			
Interview on time			
Interviewer name			
Room number			
Group interview or format changes			
Feedback from others			

Last Minute Predeparture

Item	Check Yes or No
Attaché case (small purse inside for women)	

Item	Check Yes or No
Business cards and six to eight extra resumes	
Pen and writing tablet	
Cheat sheet on company	
Calculator	
Backup tie or scarf	
WSJ or business periodical	
Umbrella if needed	
Physical address of location	
Cash/credit cards	
Leave fifteen minutes earlier than planned	

Arrival Plan

➤ Freshen up

➤ Suit straightened

➤ Confirm timely start

➤ Locate interview area

➤ Review opening and introduction

➤ Review closing and three main points

Follow-Up

Action	Check Yes or No/Comments
Record notes from interview in daily journal	
Remedial steps	
Write down questions asked of you	
Write down answers to your questions	
Personal assessment of interview; lessons learned	
Write thank-you note	
Initiate plan for securing next round of interviews	
Other	

Mock Interview Practice

This appendix offers you several sample mock interviews with questions and answers, and some practice scenarios.

Sample Mock Interviews and Rules

Below you will find mock interviews conducted with a variety of candidate types. First, you will find an interview with a person for a chief executive officer (CEO) position. The questions are appropriate for the nature of the job and are set at a high level. Other mock candidates looking for paralegal, teaching, construction, and mid-level executive jobs follow. All are actual experiences in interviews with some fictional detail provided for filler. Comments in parenthesis after the candidate's answers point to a specific focus area.

For Chief Executive Officer (CEO)

Interviewer: This would be your first CEO position, so tell me why you think you are ready for this.

CEO Candidate: I believe I have the vision, leadership skills, tenacity, and experience. I also know how to assemble a great team. I am confident we can take the firm to the next level. (steering)

Interviewer: Would you expand on the strengths you believe you have and what a CEO needs to be successful?

CEO Candidate: First, a good CEO must have specific transparent qualities, and I believe I possess those. One is discernment, and by that I mean the ability to remain focused on the critical issues, while being bombarded by a wide spectrum of on-going responsibilities. Another is a sufficiently broad bandwidth of knowledge and experience to draw upon. No one knows all the answers, but a great CEO knows how to assemble talent—that's the human capital part—and then draw the best from them to leverage the firm's resources—that's the financial and operational capital part—to get the right solution, or at least to derive great options from which he or she can make a decision. And, then there is the leadership component. It is the engine that ultimately must drive a CEO's success. (closing and summary points; steering)

Interviewer: There is a tendency to assume the autocrat's role, i.e. "Now I am in charge." What do you think about that?

CEO Candidate: You should have a commanding and visionary presence, an inspirational personal style that communicates religiously. But you must also have "soft elbows" when necessary to make people feel appreciated. I don't advocate a tyrannical autocratic style, but one that fosters a culture of synergies, where people work collaboratively to craft the best possible solution given the circumstances. (body language; steering)

Interviewer: How about intersecting leadership style with building economic value?

CEO Candidate: Great question. You must have the ability to understand the key drivers of value across all business lines. For instance in my last assignment, my group developed a very creative new process that would have been terrific for my division, but I could see that it would cannibalize the firm's resources to such an extent that two other divisions would be impacted adversely. So I presented the project to my CEO with the recommendation that it be shelved until such time as resources were freed up. In fact, I think that decision is what caused him to recommend me for this CEO interview. He called it my forward "visioneering." (client context; steering; leading examples)

Interviewer: Interesting term. Can you explain how that works?

CEO Candidate: Business is conducted in a world of interdependencies, and my ability to understand how one area impacts another is key. My background shows the required breadth of experience and flexibility to adapt to changing market factors and to lead people and solve complex problems. Churchill provided a great recipe for a CEO when he said, "We shall go on to the end. . . we will meet them on the beaches. . .we will never surrender." In other words, a great CEO gets people to that level of commitment in order to beat the challenges that confront them. Forward thinking about strategies, opportunities, and the crafting of solutions—that's what it means. I believe I have what it takes. (client context; being memorable)

Interviewer: Speaking of leadership, what is the largest organization you have led? This company is larger than you've experienced according to your résumé.

CEO Candidate: The number of people you lead, by itself, doesn't indicate leadership effectiveness. You can get into as much trouble with 50 people as you can with 5,000. The real test is what you get those people to accomplish. No person actually leads 50,000 people anyway—other people who work for you lead those folks. The leader at the top leads other leaders who lead other people and so on. You have to provide clear and sustaining vision and presence for the people with whom you interact so they can carry the message.

So, while it's a big feather in a cap to say you lead a group of 50,000 people, the real test is what the people do two or three layers below you. Besides, what extra leadership talents are required that are not likewise used in a smaller organization? (quantifying; leading examples)

Interviewer: Don't larger organizations have more complicated problems?

CEO Candidate: Perhaps, but not necessarily so. Leading a 20-man insertion team behind enemy lines can be more complicated than leading 500 people in a sales organization. Context is important, so I urge you to look beyond the simplicity of numbers. Look at the 50 Japanese nuclear workers who tried to stop those leaks. There had to be a leader in there, and his job was very complicated. In fact, leading smaller enterprises can be more difficult because they have often have a devil of a time with payroll for instance, a problem not generally found as often in larger, deeper organizations. (connectivity; leading examples)

Interviewer: How about building a leadership team in an organization of this scale?

CEO Candidate: Although my leadership talents may have been honed in a smaller organization, they were built by dealing with complex problems across many different parts of the organization. I believe if you hire good people and lead them well, the organization wins. There may be scale differences in larger organizations related to time, culture, flexibility, and human factors, but basic leadership skills are portable across organizational size. I look for leaders who exhibit personal and moral courage, tenacity, a front-line in-the-trenches mentality, intelligence, and intellectual curiosity.

It is vitally important to avoid the pitfalls some new CEOs fall into such as an insular, only-by-the-numbers approach. And I would always try to remember that personal behaviors that don't correlate with the message undermine everything.

The bottom line is my track record shows that I thrive at overcoming challenges, and I am up to this one. (client context; summary; being memorable)

Interviewer: What about dealing with difficult people, say on your management team?

CEO Candidate: Sadly, there are always a few people who either don't get the picture, don't want to get the picture, or who couldn't care less. I recall dealing with one executive on my management team who was constantly on the negative side of any issue—he always seemed to dislike any new idea or program. His peers called him Donny Downer. Rather than let morale suffer, I took the fellow out for golf over a weekend and tried to get to know him better. By the third tee, I had had an earful. By the twelfth, he had offered an appraisal, all bad, on every new initiative over the previous six months. Finally, after he had spent his ammo, I asked him what he wanted to really accomplish out of life, out of his career. Did he think he had done all he wanted to do? Was he happy? He was stunned by the questions. After a bit, I realized the fellow was actually very creative and bright. Some of his thoughts were not just outside the box, but he didn't even recognize a box. So, I had HR move him over to a long-range R&D support group in new product development. He is thriving like gangbusters today, and so are we. (being memorable; relevant examples)

Interviewer: Good. Dealing with various constituencies is key to the CEO role. Describe your talents there and how you would work that for the company.

CEO Candidate: Every decision has an inside and an outside angle to it. Focus only on one and the other one will inevitably bite you or the organization. You have to communicate, communicate, and then communicate to all of the inside and outside stakeholder groups who have a share of the outcomes driven by your decisions. For instance, I always try to ensure employees at every level feel connected to the organization—share its values, help create its positive culture, and leverage each other's talents. Similarly, I want to ensure the firm's customers know we—as a totally committed organization—are dedicated to fulfilling the promises we have made to them about quality, service, price, and so forth. A decision that we make that affects employees adversely could very easily have a negative effect on customers and vice versa. No decision is independent any longer—everything is interdependent.(client context; body language opportunity; relevant examples; connectivity)

Interviewer: Can you give examples of groups you have worked with?

CEO Candidate: I have worked with community charity organizations, shareholders and investor groups, government regulators, media, and others. All of them have to be nurtured constantly. In fact, I carry a small pinwheel card in my wallet that outlines how a decision flows to each of these insider and outsider groups. And the heading is, "The Internal-External Rule." It has saved the day on many an occasion. (being memorable; examples)

Interviewer: One final question then. If you assume this position, what are some of the first steps you would take?

CEO Candidate: Obviously there are competitive factors I will look at, such as the financials, operations, people, and products. Meeting with the key members of the team, including the board, and other constituent groups would be important for getting a grip on the major issues. The board is enormously important. And I think you can't know where you are going until you know where you are. So the interface between the CFO and IT functions is crucial to making the right decisions. Ensuring that we are capturing the right data and setting up the right dashboard to see trends are important first steps. Understanding risk—where it exists, why and in what form—is undeniably important in avoiding surprises. Meeting clients is also an early must do. (summary; body language opportunity; examples; connectivity)

Interviewer: Very good. Anything you would like to add?

CEO Candidate: To wrap up my side of this discussion today, I ask you to recall what I consider to be the most valuable assets that I would bring to this role. First, I have a broad-based and deep understanding of the industry's structure, its competitive dynamics, supplier relationships, underlying trends, and externalities that affect the business. Second, I lead by empowering people to be the best they can be, by inspiring them to reach stretch targets, and giving them the resources and senior-level commitment to accomplish our objectives. Third, I communicate, coordinate, and collaborate with internal and external interest groups to ensure we are moving along the same path. I want to stress that if given the opportunity, it would be a great marriage between this corporation and me, and an honor to create our own version of the *Band of Brothers*. (summary points; being memorable; relevant examples; body language opportunity)

For a Paralegal Assistant

Interviewer: Good morning. Thank you for coming in to speak with us. First, can you tell me why this job interests you and what your career goals might be?

Candidate: Thank you for meeting with me. I have researched the firm, your mission statement, the practice areas in particular, and the biographies of the lawyers. I am very impressed with what I learned and find that my goals are aligned with the firm's objectives. (great opening; leading examples)

Interviewer: How so?

Candidate: I believe the practice is vibrant and would satisfy my interest in engaging in leading-edge work with attorneys who are aggressive and who take on challenging cases. I enjoy challenges. (steering)

Interviewer: Can you give me an example of a challenge you undertook both professionally and personally?

Candidate: At my last firm, I met with a difficult client who was very unhappy with the outcome of a preliminary mediation effort. The attorney of record was out of the country. I listened very carefully, took a lot of notes, and clarified a few points. My objective was to let the client know that I was empathetic to his arguments and that I would listen to his point of view. I didn't offer any legal advice but offered a summary of the attorney's proposed solution. I told him I would discuss his concerns in detail with the attorney upon his return and that we would make every effort to resolve the situation. I also was clear about a timeline for next steps. (steering; leading example)

Interviewer: Timelines? Can you describe your use of those?

Candidate: I find that timelines are a great way to keep things on track; they make me a better organizer. In fact, I use them to meet personal goals too. For instance, I wanted to run a marathon, and since I'm not a runner my friends thought I was crazy. But I did it by using a training timeline that started slowly and built momentum over time. I ran the local marathon in July—my first! It was great and has made me a better legal assistant as well. (body language opportunity; steering; connectivity)

Interviewer: Really, how has that happened?

Candidate: I find that being really fit means I can work the crazy hours that come with this profession in order to be first-rate. It keeps me sharp mentally and boosts my confidence. I feel if I can run 26 miles nonstop, then I can sure do the job better than I would otherwise. I am a striver and want to be a nonstop learner—and the environment in the firm seems to promote that. (connectivity)

Interviewer: Interesting. Let's say you are working with a coworker who is irritating. How would you handle that?

Candidate: I once worked for an attorney who did many things perfectly, but organizing well was not a strong suit. As a result, his assistants had to work on last-minute projects, usually late on a Friday. One of the assistants constantly complained and when things got tense, she would usually blame others when things got a bit off track. So I took her out for coffee and tried to discuss the working conditions and how we all had to pull together. She continued to complain so as a last resort I mentioned it to the attorney during a one-on-one meeting and suggested we both speak to the assistant about the issue. She modified her behavior somewhat, but after a few months she moved on. I was proud of our team for not getting overly emotional about the situation. I try very hard to be a calm voice in a storm. (being memorable; steering; leading examples; client context)

For a Mid-Career Executive

Interviewer: Please give me an example of a recent decision or proposed course of action that proved to be controversial in your organization.

Candidate: My team had run the numbers on the feasibility of closing down an aging plant. The EVP for operations cut his teeth on this particular facility and I think had an emotional investment in it. The analysis was clear-cut but unpopular within this fellow's group. During a board meeting I made my proposal and received quite a bit of flack, including from my own boss. But I knew my team and the recommendation was spot-on, so I persisted. Over time it has proven to be a great EVA (economic value added) decision, but it was a tough call. It points to my persistence to pursue a just cause——that is a key quality I believe in. Also, when it comes to ethical situations, which this example was not, adherence to this principle of persistence to a value system is critically important to an organization. (quantifying; connectivity; leading example)

Interviewer: Interesting. Can you give an example of that?

Candidate: Once I saw another executive take some documents out of the confidential area and put them in his briefcase prior to leaving for a business trip. He knew better than to do that; if those docs had been lost in transit, it could have been disastrous. I could have looked the other way, but I confronted him about it. He denied it at first but then agreed and was embarrassed. I think he appreciated the fact I helped him dodge a bullet. That's where organizational and personal value systems have to coincide. (connectivity; body language opportunity)

Interviewer: Tell me about a success story you admire and one you have achieved.

Candidate: I think what the wounded warriors group has accomplished for returning war vets and their families has been astounding. I think they overwhelm what most of us could ever accomplish.

In my own life, at my last firm I proposed a new way of shortening the time for new product reviews and approvals. It involved some expenditure for new technology up front, and a rearrangement of work flow, but the life cycle costs were dramatically reduced: it saved the firm about $8 million globally, and got the products out the door faster—about six months on average—and that meant earlier revenue. I first learned about the new process during my professional reading program, it was used in a different industry, but I thought it might just apply to ours and it did. (quantifying; connectivity; steering)

For a Construction Job

Interviewer: We need a site foreman at our new housing development. There are some strong personalities out there, so what do you consider your strong points?

Candidate: First, I know what the workers are supposed to do. I am very organized. I like to keep things on time and on cost. So I hold an end-of-day roundup with my lead guys, and we go over the day's activities, any issues and such. Then we brainstorm on solutions. Second, I get along with my guys. They know I insist on quality work, and don't take short cuts that are safety issues. In return, they are straight with me. I don't put up with pilferage or sloppy work on the job. They can work somewhere else if that's the case. (great opening; connectivity; steering)

Interviewer: Give me an example a problem you've fixed.

Candidate: Communication is the key, so I do a lot of it. We had a custom job, once, building a large single-family house, and the family kept changing specs so often that it was a real headache, especially for the subcontractors. They would install a fixture or something, and then the buyer would change it a week later. So I got with the developer, laid in some slippage schedules for modifications, and held meetings with the buyer at the beginning of each week to go over what they were thinking, progress, etc. I find identifying the problem early, communicating with everyone, and following up well will keep you out of trouble and save both you and the buyer money. (steering; leading example; body language opportunity; client context)

Interviewer: Why do people like to work with you?

Candidate: I am an honest guy who works hard. A dollar's pay for a dollar's work, know what I mean? People can trust me. Your reputation in this business is only as good as the work you do and your record of doing what you say you will do. Nobody can take your integrity; that's something you have to give up yourself. And I'm not going to do it. (being memorable)

Interviewer: How about your relationships with the subcontractors?

Candidate: They know I expect them to show up when they say they will. Most of my guys have been with me for a long time. I know what they do and the quality of their work. Sometimes I get someone I don't know, and I try to watch what he does a little more closely. I've done most of the jobs—electrical, plumbing, carpentry, etc.—myself over the years, and so I can tell pretty quickly if a guy knows what he's doing. Likewise, subcontractors know I know enough to tell if they are doing it right. It keeps things on an even keel. The thing is, you've got to be around—you can't phone it in. (being memorable; leading examples)

For a High School Math Teacher:

Interviewer: Describe a time when you had to be flexible.

Candidate: Once I was asked to substitute for the track coach who suddenly took ill. I am not a track person by any means and was out of my element. But I am a math teacher, so I recorded the athletes' times on my laptop, applied a statistical package to it, and was able to show the kids their mean times per event, projected times if they reduced their event times by 1–5 percent, things like that. The kids loved it, and they got interested in statistics too! (connectivity; body language)

Interviewer: Tell me about a situation where you set a goal and had to struggle to achieve it.

Candidate: We had a target of increasing our math averages in the upper school by 2 percent—a fairly heady goal for our department. We underestimated the amount of extra tutorial work that it took, but after some innovative scheduling and the use of technology such as animation software and PowerPoint, we were able to exceed our target. Of course, we were given an even higher mandate this year, but I think we can do it. I find technology can be a terrific method of presenting complex ideas in straightforward ways. (quantifying; connectivity)

Interviewer: How do you stay abreast of developments in that area?

Candidate: I engage in a personal continuing education program in addition to the state's requirements. I subscribe to various professional journals, use the Internet extensively, and look for new educational software to try. If the demand placed on students is high, then I should demand it of myself as well. (being memorable)

Interviewer: How do you handle discipline in your classroom?

Candidate: I believe you have to be consistent in your application of discipline, and very clear about what you expect. If you set out clear guidelines, are fair in the application of them, and are specific about consequences, then you have a much better learning environment for all students. For example, a student violated the no-talking, no-looking rule during a quiz. I took up his paper, reiterated that it meant a reduction in grade, and sent a note home with an explanation. If you apply consequences across the board, then you see results. But you must be consistently fair. (leading example; summary points; client context)

Practice Mock Interview Scenarios and Rules

Treat the practice mock interviews as you would an actual situation. Use your trusted agents to act as interviewer, observer, and recorder. Have them ask questions from the sample questions lists, then review your answers by watching the recording of the session. Following are some scenarios that can stage the scenes for your mock intreviews.

Scenario One

You are a recent high school graduate searching for your first job in retail sales in the consumer electronics department at a major chain. You may have had some summer job experience, but not in this line of work. You plan on working part-time toward your college degree. You have no other job offers. You want to start work in two months because you have a ski trip planned in Europe. You will accept daytime work only.

Scenario Two

You are an experienced executive, mid-forties to mid-fifties. You are interested in starting a new career in the oil and gas business. You have an MBA or other advanced degree but not in engineering. Having come from the medical equipment industry, you have no direct experience in the new industry. You are willing to take some salary reduction but do not want to start over completely. You are confident in your skills as a general manager. A friend works for the hiring company in its geophysics division.

Scenario Three

You are an experienced executive interested in upgrading by moving to a new company within your industry. You are willing to relocate domestically but do not want to go overseas because of family issues. The executive recruiter has indicated the new company would like you to consider a very lucrative opportunity in Singapore or Tokyo. The salary is 20 percent over your current package with significant increases planned in both responsibility and compensation in the coming years. You really want this job, but there is the family to think of.

Scenario Four

You are a recent college graduate in a technical field looking for your second job in the IT industry. You left your first job after only six months because of a conflict with your boss. Because you enjoy surfing, you do not want to move away from the Los Angeles/Huntington Beach area (the headquarters of the company is located there). Your GPA while adequate was not stellar. The firm is willing to talk with you, but you know there are stronger candidates who also want the headquarters job. Other company locations are in Boston, Atlanta, Melbourne, and Frankfurt.

Scenario Five

You are a college graduate with several years' experience in one industry (pick yours). You are interested in leaving your company to trade up to a better firm. You are looking for better benefits and more compensation. Someone from a small startup firm has contacted you and would like to speak with you about a vice president position, a significant upgrade in responsibility for you. You hear that the company may be having significant funding issues.

Scenario Six

You are separating from the military after twelve years on active duty. You plan to join the Reserves but are interviewing for a sales job with a large Fortune 500 company (take your experience and pick an industry most closely aligned with your military background). The company says you will go through a six-month training program and then be responsible for product sales in the U.S. Midwest. The company has experienced inadequate growth in that area for the past twenty-four months. You have another, more secure opportunity with a defense company near your current base that is offering 25 percent less compensation than the sales job. Your family wants you to take the Midwest job. You have doubts.

Scenario Seven

You are an experienced mid-fifties senior executive currently running the operations division for a major wholesale chemical company. A firm contacts you through a recruiter and would like to speak with you about a CEO position at a medium-sized agribusiness with large aspirations. You are vaguely familiar with the company and interested. You know it is thought to be very strong financially with a good product pipeline. It's smaller than your current firm, but you have always wanted to run your own company. The CFO has stated publically that he would like to take over. You also hear that a former CEO of a major chemical company is also in the running.

Scenario Eight

You are a nearly tenured professor of history at a large southeastern U.S. public university. You have been contacted about the president's job at a small northwestern private liberal arts college. The recruiter has outlined a number of challenges, including flatlined enrollment, a small sports budget, recent faculty departures, a narrow curriculum, and a somewhat cantankerous board of directors, although the external board members are mostly highly supportive business people. Still, you really aspire to be a university president.

Scenario Nine

You are a woman in her late thirties who has labored in construction, warehousing, airline baggage operations, and even in a body shop as an auto mechanic for three years. You see an advertisement for a position as a supervisor in the shipping and receiving department at a large discount store specializing in household appliances. The pay and benefits look great. The interviewer has an attitude—he thinks a woman can't do the job.

Scenario Ten

You are a recent college graduate with a secondary education degree in history. You are interviewing for a private school position. The only slot available is in middle school English. The school is terrific and you did take two courses in English literature in college.

The interviewer is an English teacher with fourteen years on the job. The alternative is a public school in a small town 25 miles away from your residence. Convince the private school interviewer that you can do the job.

Scenario Eleven

You have been selected for a third round of interviews for an associate position as management consultant. The hiring firm is a major global consulting company with offices in thirty-nine countries. Dual headquarters are in London and New York. This will be a group interview with one partner and two associates over dinner. The company is known

Interview Insights

After an investment banking group interview over dinner in New York, a candidate walked with an associate to the subway station. Assuming the interview was over, the candidate wondered aloud how he did, and then asked the associate if he thought the partner caught a mistake the candidate made in his analysis. The candidate was not asked back for a final round. Never assume the interview is over until you are alone and off the battlefield.

to favor people from Ivy League schools with hard technical skills and industry specialties, but generalists will be considered. Case analysis skills will be tested to determine analytical ability.

Personal Scripts

In This Appendix

➤ Personal scripts forms with example

Personal Scripts Chart Construction

Please use the templates below to record information for your personal job search. Recall that the personal scripts exercise is the repository for information that will comprise the narrative for your personal "movie." It forms the content of your dialogue. Use the example of the car salesman below as reference.

Position Description

Fill out the block below with your answer to the following question: I want to be a world-class _____ (The job you want). For example, I want to be a world-class luxury car salesperson in Los Angeles for AB Motorcars, Inc.

Position	Industry	Company	Location

Topics: List key knowledge areas, experience, opening and closing statements, emphasis areas, and any other key topic you think might be discussed in the interview either by you or the interviewer.

For example, topic A might be, "Knowledge of Ferrari, Maserati, and Bentley automobiles." Topic B might be, "Knowledge of incomes by zip code around Los Angeles."

Topic A
Topic B
Topic C
Topic D
Topic E
Topic F
Topic G
Topic H
Topic I
Topic J
Topic K

Subtopic Information

Next, begin filling in the substantive details related to each topic area. This is the actual technical content such as the facts, experiences, explanations, convictions, goals, and knowledge that will provide the richness to interview dialogue.

For example, subtopic A corresponding to topic A above might be, "Ferrari had x number of models with the following engine sizes. Performance indicators such as top-end speed, cornering features, acceleration, steering, etc."

Subtopic B corresponding to topic B above might be, "The median personal income for the four zip codes surrounding the dealership in LA is X$. The median home valuation in those zip codes is Y$."

Subtopic A

Subtopic B

Subtopic C

Subtopic D

Subtopic E

Subtopic F

Subtopic G

Subtopic H

Subtopic I

Subtopic J

Subtopic K

Personal Connectivity Charts

Fill out the grid below with your desired position in mind. For example, high-end luxury car salesperson in Los Angeles, California

Desired Position	Location

Write down examples and scenarios that illustrate the interdependencies between functional areas.

For example, in the AB Motocars, Inc., example, suppose one of your personal scripts charts outlines your career as an ex-driver of Formula 1 race cars and your certification as a Porsche demonstration driver on the track in Pforzheim, Germany. Your connectivity chart would list topic knowledge of Ferrari, Porsche, and Maserati. It would then list the connection between two subtopics: performance characteristics of the various automobiles and your personal testimony as a driver.

Write out what you will actually say in the interdependencies table.

Topic Area	Connected to Subtopics

Discussion of Interdependencies

Topic Area	Connected to Subtopics

Discussion of Interdependencies

Topic Area	**Connected to Subtopics**

Discussion of Interdependencies

Topic Area	**Connected to Subtopics**

Discussion of Interdependencies

Topic Area	**Connected to Subtopics**

Discussion of Interdependencies

Topic Area	**Connected to Subtopics**

Discussion of Interdependencies

Topic Area	**Connected to Subtopics**

Discussion of Interdependencies

Topic Area	**Connected to Subtopics**

Discussion of Interdependencies

Topic Area	Connected to Subtopics

Discussion of Interdependencies

Topic Area	Connected to Subtopics

Discussion of Interdependencies

Topic Area	Connected to Subtopics

Discussion of Interdependencies

Topic Area	Connected to Subtopics

Discussion of Interdependencies

Topic Area	Connected to Subtopics

Discussion of Interdependencies

Topic Area	Connected to Subtopics

Discussion of Interdependencies

Topic Area	Connected to Subtopics

Discussion of Interdependencies

Topic Area	Connected to Subtopics

Discussion of Interdependencies

Sample Letters and Reading List

In this appendix you will see sample cover letters and follow-up correspondence plus a suggested reading list.

Sample Letters

Crafting a great cover letter is an important part of presenting yourself as the perfect hire. The follow-up letter is a must do to show your level of etiquette and commitment.

Sample Cover Letter

John R. Busybee
1212 Laughing Lane
Monarch, New York 00000
Home telephone: (212) 555-0000
Mobile: (212) 555-0000
Facsimile: (212) 555-0000
E-mail: busybee@honey.com
Dateline

Ms. Angela R. Haute Couture
Managing Director

XYZ Company, Inc.
1111 Fancypants Avenue, Suite 125
New York, New York 00000

Dear Ms. Haute Couture:

I am writing to express my interest in working at XYZ Company as the store manager at your new location in White Plains, New York. The position as outlined in your announcement dated April 12, 2011, is an exciting opportunity and one for which I believe I am ideally suited.

As you see from the enclosed résumé, I have extensive experience in retail operations at both major outlet stores and smaller neighborhood specialty boutiques. Consequently, I understand the robust demands placed upon store managers, especially in new operating locations.

While at the RUReady Company, for instance, I initiated several new volume-based projects targeting staff at our newest retail stores and was responsible for year-over-year sales increases of 15 percent in those locations. I believe I could replicate that performance at the White Plains store during its first several years.

I look forward to meeting with you or your representatives to discuss this exciting opportunity and how I can contribute to your effort. I will call your assistant in the next few days to arrange a meeting, but in the interim please call me if I can provide additional information.

Sincerely,

Signature
JP/encl

Sample Follow-Up Letter

John R. Busybee
1212 Laughing Lane
Monarch, New York 00000
Home telephone: (212) 555-0000
Mobile: (212) 555-0000
Facsimile: (212) 555-0000
E-mail: busybee@honey.com
Dateline

Ms. Angela R. Haute Couture
Managing Director

XYZ Company, Inc.
1111 Fancypants Avenue, Suite 125
New York, New York 00000
Dear Ms. Haute Couture:

I enjoyed meeting with you over lunch at Le Pearl in Manhattan on May 14, 20xx. I appreciate the time you and your colleagues spent with me, and I enjoyed discussing strategies for the new White Plains retail store. Following our discussions, I am even more enthusiastic about the opportunity to work with you to make the new location a benchmark of excellence.

I am especially convinced that the application of your new sales incentive program will be instrumental in the store's success and could be an example for other locations to emulate. As I mentioned, my experience at RUReady taught me how to implement an incentive program without disrupting the existing sales force. In fact, following our meeting I completed a projected sales forecast based upon the figures you shared with me. I would enjoy discussing my ideas with you at your convenience.

I remain excited about the possibility of working with the team of professionals you have assembled at XYZ. It is inspirational to see such a disciplined group of people working together for a common goal. I believe my commitment to building a quality brand, my analytical judgment and ability to work well with others complements your efforts. I would be honored to join such a fine group if given the opportunity.

Once again, thank you for lunch and for considering me for the position. I look forward to hearing from you about a possible next meeting.

Sincerely,

Signature

Interesting Reading

Following is a selected list of books that can help further your knowledge and make you a more desirable hire.

Ambrose, Stephen, E. *Undaunted Courage*. New York: Touchstone Simon & Shuster, 1997.

Baumohl, Bernard. *The Secrets of Economic Indicators: Hidden Clues to Future Economic Trends and Investment Opportunities*, Second Edition. Upper Saddle River, New Jersey: Wharton School Publishing, 2008.

Chernow, Ron. *The House of Morgan: An American Banking Dynasty and the Rise of Modern Finance*. New York: Atlantic Monthly Press, 1990.

Day, George and David Reibstein. *Wharton on Dynamic Competitive Strategy*. New York: John Wiley & Sons, 1997.

Donald, David Herbert. *Lincoln*. New York: Simon & Shuster, 1995.

Ertel, Danny and Mark Gordon. *The Point of the Deal: How to Negotiate When Yes is Not Enough*. Boston: Harvard Business School Press, 2007.

Fisher, Roger and Alan Sharp. *Getting it Done: How to Lead When You're Not in Charge*. New York: Harper Business, 1998.

Gladwell, Malcolm. *Blink*. New York: Back Bay Books, Little Brown & Co., 2003.

Halberstam, David. *The Coldest Winter*. New York: Hyperion, 2007.

Harvard Business Review**.** *Harvard Business Review on Becoming a High-Performance Manager*. Boston: Harvard Business School Press, 2002.

Harvard Business Review. *Harvard Business Review on the Tests of a Leader*. Boston: Harvard Business School Press, 2007.

Helms, Nathaniel. *My Men Are My Heroes: The Brad Kasal Story*. Des Moines, Iowa: Meredith Books, 2007.

Jones, Judy and William Wilson. *An Incomplete Education: 3,684 Things You Should Have Learned but Probably Didn't*. New York: Ballentine Books, 2006.

Kao, John. *Jamming: The Art and Discipline of Business Creativity*. New York: Harper Business, 1996.

Kidder, David S and Noah D. Oppenheim. *The Intellectual Devotional: Revive Your Mind, Complete Your Education, and Roam Confidently with the Cultured Class*. New York: Rodale books/TID Volumes, 2006.

Kissinger, Henry. *Diplomacy*. New York: Touchstone Simon & Shuster, 1995.

Kotter, John P. and Dan Cohen. *The Heart of Change*. Boston, MA: Harvard Business School Press, 2002.

Lerner, Josh, Felda Hardymon, and Ann Leamon. *Venture Capital and Private Equity: A Casebook*. New York: John Wiley & Sons, 2005.

Levitt, Theodore. *The Marketing Imagination*. New York: Free Press, 1983.

Luttrell, Marcus. *Lone Survivor*. New York: Little, Brown, and Company, 2007.

Manguel, Polly. *501 Must Read Books*. London: Octopus Publishing Group, 2006.

Maxwell, John. *The 360° Leader: Developing Your Influence from Anywhere in the Organization*. Nashville, Tennessee: Nelson Books, 2005.

National Geographic Society. *The Knowledge Book: Everything You Need to Know to Get By in the 21st Century*. Washington, D.C.: National Geographic Society, 2007.

Porter, Michael E. *Competitive Advantage*. New York: Free Press/Macmillan, 1985.

Rasiel, Ethan and Paul N. Friga. *The McKinsey Mind: Understanding and Implementing the Problem-Solving Tools and Management Techniques of the World's Top Strategic Consulting Firm*. New York: McGraw-Hill, 2002.

Spade, Kate. *Manners*. New York: Simon & Shuster, 2004.

Tichy, Noel M. *The Leadership Engine: How Winning Companies Build Leaders at Every Level*. New York: Harper Business, 1997.

Ury, W. *Getting Past No*. New York: Bantam Books, 1991.

Useem, Michael. *The Leadership Moment: Nine True Stories of Triumph and Disaster and Their Lessons for Us All*. New York: Random House, 1998.

FINI

Disclaimers and Notes: The facts and circumstances used in the exercises, mock interviews, leadership cases, and personal scripts examples are for instructional purposes only. Likewise, the facts and persons named in the cases, exercises, and scenarios are fictitious and do not represent any specific person, personality, or company. Examples in Interview Insights are in some cases composites of people. Any resemblance to a single individual is entirely coincidental. Sample letters should not be used verbatim. No guarantees of employment or performance are offered by use of or reliance upon material in *The Smart Guide to the Perfect Job Interview*. All information is believed accurate at the time of publication but should be verified by users prior to use. No tax, accounting, or legal advice is offered in this book, nor should readers use comments contained herein to be the basis for any action in that regard.

ACKNOWLEDGEMENTS

I want to thank the loves of my life, Lisa and our two incredible daughters Lauren and Madison. I also want to thank my friends for life Joel Cohen and David Burrows, two of the nation's best on Wall Street, for their invaluable inputs and encouragement, and all of those in the armed forces with whom I served and taught me so much. I want to acknowledge my agent Mary Sue Seymour for finding this opportunity and all of those at Smart Guide Publications. I also must acknowledge the lessons I learned from all of those poor candidates who had the ill fortune to interview in front of me. Finally, I want to thank God for all the blessings bestowed upon me and my family.

INDEX

Made in the USA
Middletown, DE
25 January 2015